Negative Perception Theory

Award Winning Best Research 2020

Racial Equality in the U.S. Labor Market

Dr. D. Antoine Drain

TABLE OF CONTENTS

Title Information
Abstract
Dedication
Epigraph
Acknowledgements
Contents
List of Figures
    Black and white Americans differ widely in views on race and race relations
    A majority of U.S. adults say Trump has made race relations worse
    Most say it's now more common for people to express racist or racially insensitive views
    Blacks are far more likely than whites to say discrimination is a major obstacle for Black people
    Whites and Blacks differ widely in views of how Blacks are treated
    Over the past 20 years, the number of African Americans earning Master's degrees has more than tripled
    Overview of Agreement to participate in the Research Study
    Overview of Participants Gender
    Overview of Participants' Age Group
    Overview of Participants' Ethnic Background
    Overview of Participants' Country of Birth
    Overview of Participants' Religious Affiliation
    Overview of Participants' Highest Educational Attainment
    Overview of Participants' Country of Residence
    Overview of Participants' Marital Status
    Overview of Participants' Current Employment Status
    Overview of Participants' Fortune 500 Employment
    Overview of Participants' Job Categories
    Overview of Participants' Years Working for Company
    Comparative Sample of Whites & Blacks Working for Fortune 500
    Whites & Blacks Perception of Company Management and Diversity
    Whites & Blacks Perception of Company Acceptance of Differences
    Whites & Blacks Perception of Company Care and Concern

Whites & Blacks Perception of Company's Policies and Consistency
Whites & Blacks Perception of Company Policy Application
Which Company Policies were not Applied Consistently over 12 months?
Whites & Blacks Perception of Company Work Life Balance
Whites & Blacks Perception of Company Addressing Complaints
Whites & Blacks Perception of Company Taking Actions
Whites & Blacks Perception of Company Work Environments
Whites & Blacks Perception of Comfort Reporting Discrimination
Whites & Blacks Perception of Company Unlawful Harassment
Whites & Blacks Perception of Company Balance of Personal Needs
Whites & Blacks Perceptions of Individual Treatment with Respect
Correlational Results for Blacks' turnover and perceptions of their recognition within Fortune 500 organizations
Correlational results for Blacks' variable perceptions of their career ascension within Fortune 500 organizations
Correlational results for Blacks' variable perceptions of their job satisfaction with company effectiveness within Fortune 500 organizations
Whites, Blacks, Hispanics, Asians, and Other racial perceptions of teamwork and information sharing in Fortune 500 companies
Whites, Blacks, Hispanics, Asians, and Other racial perceptions of cooperation from other racial work groups in Fortune 500 companies
Whites, Blacks, Hispanics, Asians, and Other racial perceptions of people working well together as a team in Fortune 500 companies

List of Tables
  Correlation results between treatment and career ascension of African American professionals in Fortune 500 companies
  Correlation results between company effectiveness and job satisfaction for African American professionals in Fortune 500 companies
  Correlation results between respect of African American professionals and Perceptions of the Fortune 500 job itself
  Correlation results between employee recognition and retention of African American professionals in Fortune 500 companies
  Correlation results between racial equality and teamwork & cooperation for African Americans in Fortune 500 companies

Chapter 1: Introduction
  Racial Equality
  Annual Formal Performance Reviews
  Perceived Workplace Discrimination
  Effects of Race on Experience, Job Performance Evaluations & Outcomes
  Employment at Will
  Civil Rights Laws
  Title VII of the Civil Rights Act of 1964
  56 Years of Progress

- Statement of the Problem and Subproblems
- Purpose of the Study
- Research Questions & Hypotheses
- Definition of Terms
- Significance of the Study
- Overview of the Study

Chapter 2: Review of Literature
- Literature Review
- Historical Overview
- Theoretical Framework
- Organizational Leadership Theory and Models
  - What is Leadership?
    - Characteristics Attributed to Effective Leadership
    - Leadership Theories & Researcher's Experience
    - Charismatic / Transformative Leadership
    - Servant Leadership Theory
    - Personal-Situational Leadership Theory
    - Leadership Traits & Researcher's Experience
    - Interpersonal & Socioemotional Traits
    - Emotional Intelligence & Control
- Organizational Leadership Philosophy
  - Autocratic & Democratic Leadership Styles
  - Directive & Participative Leadership Styles
  - Consideration vs. Initiation
- Cultural Diversity, Ethics, and Fairness
  - Diversity Management / Conflict of Values
  - Diversity & Pluralism in Leadership
  - Justice
  - Discourse Ethics
- Board / Employee / Constituent Relations
  - Personal vs. Positional Power
  - Leaders Sharing Power
  - Ethics & Codes of Conduct
  - Interests of Stakeholders
  - Centralized & Decentralized Organizational Structure
  - Human Resource Management
- Visionary Leadership
  - Vision Statement
  - Corporate Values
- Personnel Evaluation
  - Performance Management - Task vs. Relations

- Performance Assessments & Appraisals
- Positive Development Culture
- Organizational Behavior or Culture Theories
  - Frederick Fiedler's Contingency Theory
  - Classical Organization Theory
  - Social Systems Theory
  - Open Systems Theory
- Organizational Leadership Theories
  - Trait Theory
  - Managerial Roles Theory
  - Early Situational Theories
  - Theory X and Theory Y
  - Path-Goal Theory
- Motivation and Needs Theories
  - Maslow's Hierarchy of Needs Theory
  - Alderfer's ERG Theory
  - McClelland's Needs for Achievement Theory
  - Frederick Herzberg's Two Factor Theory
  - William Glasser's Control Theory
  - Equity Theory of Motivation
  - Reinforcement Theory
  - Expectancy Theory of Motivation
  - Goal Setting Theory
- Upper Echelon Theory
- Disparate Impact Theory
- Rawls Theory of Justice
- Critical Race Theory
- Skin Tone Labor Market Segmentation
- Human Capital Theory
- Career Development Theory
- Structuration Theory
- Social Cognitive Career Theory
- Glass Ceiling Phenomena
- Career Ascension & Upward Mobility
- Diversity & Inclusion
- African American Mentorship
- African American Recognition and Retention Rates
- Image & Perception of African American Males
- Cultural Comfort of African American Males in the U.S. Labor Market
- Underrepresentation of African American Males in the U.S. Labor Market
- Disparate Treatment of African American Males in the U.S. Labor Market

    Managerial Progression of African American Males in the United States
    Conclusion
Chapter 3: Method of Research
    Introduction
    Research Design
    Research Setting and Participants
    Sample Size
    Data Collection Methods
    Data Analysis Methods
    Bias
    Methodological Assumptions
    Trustworthiness
    Subject Matter Experts (SMEs)
    Credibility
    Transferability
    Ethical Considerations
    Confidentiality
    Procedures
    Limitations
    Delimitations
    Summary
Chapter 4: Presentation and Interpretation of Data
    Restatement of the Purpose
    Research Questions
    Overview of Participants
    Findings for Each Research Hypothesis
        Hypothesis #1
        Hypothesis #2
        Hypothesis #3
        Hypothesis #4
        Hypothesis #5
        Hypothesis #6
    Findings for Each Research Question
        Question #1
        Question #2
    Theoretical Framework / Connection
    Summary
Chapter 5: Discussion, Conclusions, and Recommendations
    Introduction
    Summary of Findings
        Hypothesis #1

- Hypothesis #2
- Hypothesis #3
- Hypothesis #4
- Hypothesis #5
- Hypothesis #6
- Research Question #1
- Research Question #2
- Discussion
  - Implications of Findings
  - Succession Planning
  - Applications of Findings
  - Theoretical Framework - Negative Perception Theory
- Recommendations for Future Research
- Conclusion

References

Appendices
- Participant E-mail for Anonymous Online Survey
- Consent to Act as a Research Subject
- 2020 Fortune 500 Company Morale Survey
- Research Proposal Approval Form
- Request to Conduct Research Approval Letter

NEGATIVE PERCEPTION THEORY:

RACIAL EQUALITY IN THE U.S. LABOR MARKET

By

Dr. D'uAndre Antoine Drain, MSSM, LSSMBB

© Copyright by

Drain Corporation, LLC

All rights reserved

2020

ABSTRACT

Racial equality was one of the most critical issues facing African Americans (black people) in the 21st century. Particularly, in the United States labor market, black people, in overwhelming comparison to Caucasians (white people), said that they were treated unfairly in their places of employment. The purpose of this study was to understand the complexities of racial inequality and develop a theoretical model of the constructs that predict perceptions that employees of color had about their workplace arenas in the following areas: respect & treatment, company effectiveness, the job itself, and teamwork & cooperation. Specifically, the researcher explored the following quantitative research questions: (1) to what extent are lack of employee recognition, lack of career opportunities, job dissatisfaction, company ineffectiveness, and high job turnover correlated to employees' race in Fortune 500 companies?; and (2) how do differences in the racial composition of teams influence teamwork and cooperation in Fortune 500 companies?

A researcher-created questionnaire was utilized to collect study data. All study procedures took place using an online survey software – SurveyMonkey. The researcher used this online technology to facilitate an internet-based questionnaire and analyzed the collected data. The sample for this quantitative descriptive correctional study consisted of n= 502 with a return rate of 419 participants which is an acceptable return rate of 83.5%, utilizing a stratified random sampling selection process.

The hypothesis testing from this study discovered that

there was a statistically significant difference for all six hypotheses. In conjunction with statistically testing the six rejected null hypotheses, a detailed analysis was provided to analyze two specific research questions in this study. The number of data pairs for the research question were statistically significant (correlated) to African Americans' perceptive variables in Fortune 500 companies.

This study can contribute to organizational leadership by helping corporations better understand the relationship between the imposed unfair treatment, company ineffectiveness, and lack of respect & employee recognition of African American Fortune 500 professionals and the fewer opportunities for advancement, job dissatisfaction, negative perceptions of the job itself, and high turnover rates amongst blacks.

Table of Contents

DEDICATION

This body of work is dedicated to my African ancestry – paternal, Bamileke people living in Cameroon & maternal, Temne people living in Sierra Leone – and all African Americans that are currently pursuing the freedoms, equalities, and prosperities that encapsulate the American Dream and the subsequent attainment of leadership positions through hard work, determination, and initiative in these United States.

EPIGRAPH

Let America be America again.
Let it be the dream it used to be.
Let it be the pioneer on the plain
Seeking a home where he himself is free.
(America never was America to me.)

Let America be the dream the dreamers dreamed—
Let it be that great strong land of love
Where never kings connive nor tyrants scheme
That any man be crushed by one above.
(It never was America to me.)

O, let my land be a land where Liberty
Is crowned with no false patriotic wreath,
But opportunity is real, and life is free,
Equality is in the air we breathe.
(There's never been equality for me,
Nor freedom in this "homeland of the free.")

Say, who are you that mumbles in the dark?
And who are you that draws your veil across the stars?

I am the poor white, fooled and pushed apart,
I am the Negro bearing slavery's scars.

NEGATIVE PERCEPTION THEORY

I am the red man driven from the land,
I am the immigrant clutching the hope I seek—
And finding only the same old stupid plan
Of dog eat dog, of mighty crush the weak.

I am the young man, full of strength and hope,
Tangled in that ancient endless chain
Of profit, power, gain, of grab the land!
Of grab the gold! Of grab the ways of satisfying need!
Of work the men! Of take the pay!
Of owning everything for one's own greed!

I am the farmer, bondsman to the soil.
I am the worker sold to the machine.
I am the Negro, servant to you all.
I am the people, humble, hungry, mean—
Hungry yet today despite the dream.
Beaten yet today—O, Pioneers!
I am the man who never got ahead,
The poorest worker bartered through the years.

Yet I'm the one who dreamt our basic dream
In the Old World while still a serf of kings,
Who dreamt a dream so strong, so brave, so true,
That even yet its mighty daring sings
In every brick and stone, in every furrow turned
That's made America the land it has become.
O, I'm the man who sailed those early seas
In search of what I meant to be my home—
For I'm the one who left dark Ireland's shore,
And Poland's plain, and England's grassy lea,
And torn from Black Africa's strand I came
To build a "homeland of the free."

DR. D'UANDRE ANTOINE DRAIN

The free?

Who said the free? Not me?
Surely not me? The millions on relief today?
The millions shot down when we strike?
The millions who have nothing for our pay?
For all the dreams we've dreamed
And all the songs we've sung
And all the hopes we've held
And all the flags we've hung,
The millions who have nothing for our pay—
Except the dream that's almost dead today.

O, let America be America again—
The land that never has been yet—
And yet must be—the land where every man is free.
The land that's mine—the poor man's, Indian's, Negro's, ME—
Who made America,
Whose sweat and blood, whose faith and pain,
Whose hand at the foundry, whose plow in the rain,
Must bring back our mighty dream again.

Sure, call me any ugly name you choose—
The steel of freedom does not stain.
From those who live like leeches on the people's lives,
We must take back our land again,
America!

O, yes,
I say it plain,
America never was America to me,
And yet I swear this oath—
America will be!

Out of the rack and ruin of our gangster death,

The rape and rot of graft, and stealth, and lies,

We, the people, must redeem

The land, the mines, the plants, the rivers.

The mountains and the endless plain—

All, all the stretch of these great green states—

And make America again!

                -Langston Hughes, 1902-1967

ACKNOWLEDGE-MENTS

I would like to acknowledge my maternal grandmother, Laura Drain, for the love that she gave me, the life lessons that she taught me, and for her support through my adolescent years until marriage. Though she is gone from this physical world, I still feel her presence every day and I know that she is smiling down on me from the heavens above.

I extend a special thanks to my Mom, Lakita Drain-Tyler, for giving me life, strength, and the spirit of perseverance. Our life journey reminds me of the very popular "Mother to Son" poem written by Brother Langston Hughes in 1922. In that poem, the mother shared her thoughts of the world surrounding both her and her son and how best to overcome those obstacles by finding strength to push through life. The greatest gift that the mother gave to the son was an awareness of the many hardships in life and the need for courage to push forward. The mother personified the dignity, determination, and hope of a person facing problems and somehow conjured up the will to never give up. Like my mother, she spoke of tests, challenges, confusion, and struggles that she confronted, endured, and overcame. And, through her own life's example, she continued to instruct her son to face struggle with patience, resilience, and hope. Mom, as we progress through this short life, know that I will keep goin' and climbin' using you as my example!

To my wife, LaShannon, for two decades, you have listened to my dreams and ideals, supported my vision, and stood by my side when life was easy and when times were tough. As stated in the Holy Bible, "he who finds a wife finds what is good and receives favor from the Lord" (Proverbs 18:22 NIV). With you next to me, together, we have achieved far more than I could have ever imagined and the life that we built sustains me every day. I thank God for taking from my rib, making you, and bringing us together!

To my children and grandchildren, you are my greatest blessing, inspiration and reward. In the Book of Psalms, there is a Song of Ascents that was written by King Solomon, best known for his great wealth, writings, and most importantly his wisdom. In his writing, Solomon stated, "Behold, children are a heritage from the Lord, The fruit of the womb is a reward. Like arrows in the hand of a warrior, So are the children of one's youth. Happy is the man who has his quiver full of them" (Psalm 127:3-5 NKJV). King Solomon understood that a house is nothing without children blessing it as a home. Further, it was understood that the family was the basic unit and most important element of society; therefore, having children (the fruit of the womb) was the reward from God and happiness belonged to the man that had many of them. Since you are my arrows, I am honored to carefully: (1) shape and form you; (2) guide you with skill and strength; and (3) maintain you so that you may fly straight. Thank you for being my heart's delight and a source of my joy!

To the Supreme Basileus of the Universe, I give you praise and thanks for being my almighty Creator whose mercy, protection, and guidance have always been there and always sustained me. My Lord, you have put me in the right places at the right times and opened many doors to set me on the right path. You have given me more than I deserve!

TABLE OF CONTENTS

LIST OF FIGURES
LIST OF TABLES

CHAPTER I: INTRODUCTION
    Problem Background
        Racial Equality in the United States
        Annual Formal Performance Reviews
        Perceived Workplace Racial Discrimination
        Effects of Race on Experience, Evaluation & Outcomes
        Employment at Will
        Civil Rights Laws
        Title VII of the Civil Rights Act of 1964
        56 Years of Progress
    Statement of the Problem and Subproblems
    Purpose of the Study
    Research Questions & Hypothesis
    Definition of Terms
    Significance of the Study
    Overview of the Study

CHAPTER II: REVIEW OF LITERATURE
    Literature Review
    Historical Overview
    Theoretical Framework
    Organizational Leadership Theory and Models
    What is Leadership?
        Characteristics Attributed to Effective Leadership
        Leadership Theories & Researcher's Experience
        Charismatic/Transformative Leadership Theory
        Servant Leadership Theory
        Personal-Situational Leadership Theory
        Leadership Traits & Researcher's Experience
        Interpersonal & Socioemotional Traits
        Emotional Intelligence & Control

Organizational Leadership Philosophy
    Autocratic & Democratic Leadership Styles
    Directive & Participative Leadership Styles
    Consideration vs. Initiation
Cultural Diversity, Ethics, and Fairness
    Diversity Management / Conflict of Values
    Diversity & Pluralism in Leadership
    Justice
    Discourse Ethics
Board/Employee/Constituent Relations
    Personal vs. Positional Power
    Leaders Sharing Power
    Ethics & Codes of Conduct
    Interests of Stakeholders
    Centralized & Decentralized Organizational Structure
    Human Resource Management
Visionary Leadership
    Vision Statement
    Corporate Values
Personnel Evaluation
    Performance Management -Task vs. Relations
    Performance Assessments & Appraisals
    Positive Development Culture
Organization Behavior or Culture Theories
    Frederick Fiedler's Contingency Theory
    Classical Organization Theory
    Social Systems Theory
    Open Systems Theory
Organizational Leadership Theories
    Trait Theory
    Managerial Roles Theory
    Early Situational Theories
    Theory X and Theory Y
    Path-Goal Theory
Motivation and Needs Theories

   Maslow's Hierarchy of Needs Theory
   Alderfer's ERG Theory
   McClelland's Needs for Achievement Theory
   Frederick Herzberg's Two Factor Theory
   William Glasser's Control Theory
   Equity Theory of Motivation
   Reinforcement Theory
   Expectancy Theory of Motivation
   Goal Setting Theory
  Upper Echelon Theory
  Disparate Impact Theory
  Rawls Theory of Justice
  Critical Race Theory
  Skin Tone Labor Market Segmentation
  Human Capital Theory
  Career Development Theory
  Structuration Theory
  Social Cognitive Career Theory
  Glass Ceiling Phenomena
  Career Ascension & Upward Mobility
  Diversity & Inclusion
  African American Mentorship
  African American Recognition and Retention Rates
  Image & Perception of African American Males
  Cultural Comfort of African American Males in the U.S. Labor Market
  Underrepresentation of African American Males in the U.S. Labor Market
  Disparate Treatment of African American Males in the U.S. Labor Market
  Managerial Progression of African American Males in the United States
  Conclusion

CHAPTER III: METHOD OF RESEARCH
  Introduction

Research Design
Research Setting and Participants
Sample Size
Data Collection Method
Data Analysis Methods
Bias
Methodological Assumptions
Trustworthiness
Subject Matter Experts (SMEs)
Credibility
Transferability
Ethical Considerations
Confidentiality
Procedures
Limitations
Delimitations
Summary

CHAPTER IV: PRESENTATION AND INTERPRETATION OF DATA
Restatement of the Purpose
Research Questions
Overview of Participants
Findings for Each Hypotheses
    Hypothesis #1
    Hypothesis #2
    Hypothesis #3
    Hypothesis #4
    Hypothesis #5
    Hypothesis #6
Findings for Each Research Question
    Question #1
    Question #2
Theoretical Framework/Connection
Summary

CHAPTER V: SUMMARY, CONCLUSIONS, AND RECOMMENDATIONS
    Introduction
    Summary of Findings
    Discussion
        Implications for Practice
        Succession Planning
        Application of Findings
        Theoretical Framework – Negative Perception Theory
    Recommendations for Future Research
    Conclusion

REFERENCES
APPENDICES
    APPENDIX A: Participant E-mail for Anonymous Survey
    APPENDIX B: Consent to Act as a Research Subject
    APPENDIX C: 2020 Fortune 500 Company Morale Survey
    APPENDIX D: Research Proposal Approval Form
    APPENDIX E: Request to Conduct Research Approval Letter

LIST OF FIGURES

1.1 Black and White Americans differ widely in views on race relations

1.2 A majority of U.S. adults say Trump has made race relations worse

1.3 Most say it's now more common for people to express racist or racially insensitive views

1.4 Blacks are far more likely than Whites to say discrimination is a major obstacle for Black people

1.5 Whites and Blacks differ widely in views of how Blacks are treated

1.6 Over the past 20 years, then number of African Americans earning Master's degrees has more than tripled

4.1 Overview of Agreement to participate in the Research Study

4.2 Overview of Participants' Gender
4.3 Overview of Participants' Age Group
4.4 Overview of Participants' Ethnic Background
4.5 Overview of Participants' Country of Birth
4.6 Overview of Participants' Religious Affiliation
4.7 Overview of Participants' Highest Educational Attainment
4.8 Overview of Participants' Country of Residence
4.9 Overview of Participants' Marital Status
4.10 Overview of Participants' Current Employment Status

4.11   Overview of Participants' Fortune 500 Employment
4.12   Overview of Participants' Job Categories
4.13   Overview of Participants' Years Working for Company
4.14   Comparative Sample of Whites & Blacks Working for Fortune 500

4.15   Whites & Blacks Perception of Company Management and Diversity

4.16   Whites & Blacks Perception of Company Acceptance of Differences

4.17   Whites & Blacks Perception of Company Care and Concern

4.18   Whites & Blacks Perception of Company's Policies and Consistency

4.19   Whites & Blacks Perception of Company Policy Application

4.20   Which Company Policies were not Applied Consistently over 12 months?

4.21   Whites & Blacks Perception of Company Work Life Balance

4.22   Whites & Blacks Perception of Companies Addressing Complaints

4.23   Whites & Blacks Perception of Company Taking Actions
4.24   Whites & Blacks Perception of Company Work Environments

4.25   Whites & Blacks Perception of Comfort Reporting Discrimination

4.26 Whites & Blacks Perception of Company Unlawful Harassment

4.27 Whites & Blacks Perception of Company Balance of Personal Needs

4.28 Whites & Blacks Perceptions of Individual Treatment with Respect

4.29 Correlational results for Blacks' turnover and perceptions of their recognition within Fortune 500 organizations

4.30 Correlational results for Blacks' variable perceptions of their career ascension within Fortune 500 organizations

4.31 Correlational results for Blacks' variable perceptions of their job satisfaction with company effectiveness within Fortune 500 organizations

4.32 Whites, Blacks, Hispanics, Asians, and Other racial perceptions of teamwork and information sharing in Fortune 500 companies

4.33 Whites, Blacks, Hispanics, Asians, and Other racial perceptions of cooperation from other racial work groups in Fortune 500 companies

4.34 Whites, Blacks, Hispanics, Asians, and Other racial perceptions of people working well together as a team in Fortune 500 companies

LIST OF TABLES

4.1   Correlation results between treatment and career ascension of African American professionals in Fortune 500 companies

4.2   Correlation results between company effectiveness and job satisfaction for African American professionals in Fortune 500 companies

4.3   Correlation results between respect of African American professionals and Perceptions of the Fortune 500 job itself

4.4   Correlation results between employee recognition and retention of African American professionals in Fortune 500 companies

4.5   Correlation results between racial equality and teamwork & cooperation for African Americans in Fortune 500 companies

CHAPTER I: INTRODUCTION

Racial Equality

According to a Pew Research Center survey (2019) on race relations in the United States (U.S.) of America, the general public had negative views of the country's racial progress. Despite the historical significance of the 13th Amendment abolishing U.S. slavery in 1865, most adults contended that the legacy of subjugation continued to have a negative impact on the position of African Americans (Blacks) in American society today. In the Pew Research Center survey (2019), it was discovered that more than four-in-ten Americans believed that their country hasn't made enough progress towards achieving racial equality. Another startling fact was that more than half of the sampled population suggested that the 45th U.S. President, Donald Trump, had made race relations worse since taking office after the 44th President, Barack Obama. Further, according to the same Pew Research Center survey (2019), there was some disbelief, particularly among Blacks, that they will ever have equal rights with Caucasians (Whites).

While the 44th U.S. President was in office, a Pew Research survey (2016) was administered and it was discovered that three key differences existed in how Whites and Blacks perceived their current positions in life. First, with respect to racial equality, Blacks were more likely than Whites to say lower-quality academic schools (75% vs. 53%), racial discrimination issues (70% vs. 36%), and lack of professional jobs (66% vs. 45%) were major reasons that Blacks had a harder time getting ahead in comparison to their White counterparts. Second, 46% of Whites believed that the state of racial equality was generally good, 45% suggested that relations were generally bad, and 38% of all Whites believe that the country had made the changes needed to give Blacks equal rights with Whites. In contrast, 61% of Blacks from the same study contend that race relations were bad, 34% of Blacks believed that the state of racial equality was generally good, and only 8% of all Blacks believed that the country had made the changes needed to give Blacks equal rights. Lastly, according to Pew Research (2016) and Stepler (2016), Blacks and Whites were divided over the current state of race relations and the progress made on these relations during Barack Obama's presidency. See Figure 1.1.

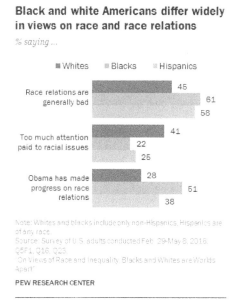

Figure 1.1: Black and White Americans differ widely in views on race relations

Since the 2016 Pew Research survey, the United States swore in the 45th President and, according to the latest survey, opinions on the state of U.S. race relations were found to be negative. Specifically, in the latest survey, it was said that approximately 58% of Americans felt that race relations in the U.S. were poor, and of those, few believed that they will get any better under the current administration (Pew Research, 2019). In fact, Horowitz, Brown, & Cox (2019) argued that "some 56% think the president has made race relations worse; just 15% say he has improved race relations and another 13% say he has tried but failed to make progress on this issue" (para.2). Additionally, two-thirds of Americans said that it had become a norm for people to assert racist opinions, feelings, and views since the 45th President took office. See Figure 1.2.

Figure 1.2: A majority of U.S. adults say Trump has made race relations worse

As previously stated, which had resulted in more Black adults having negative perceptions about the progression of U.S. race relations, it was the American opinion that the expression of racist views had become more common and acceptable since the 45th U.S. President took office. To put things in context, 65% of Americans including majorities across ethnic and racial groups said it had become more common for people to express racist or racially insensitive views since Donald Trump was elected president (Horowitz et. al., 2019). Since these racist covert/overt expressions had become commonplace, a substantial portion of the U.S. population (45%) felt that insensitivity had become more acceptable. See Figure 1.3.

NEGATIVE PERCEPTION THEORY

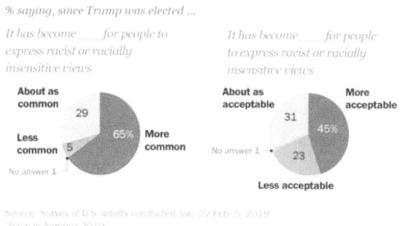

Figure 1.3: Most say it's now more common for people to express racist views

Since the Pew Research survey (2019) uncovered an increase in racial insensitive views in America, Black adults had simultaneously reported disproportionate views of how they had been treated in key areas of American life. For example, it is African Americans perception that they were treated less fairly than their White counterparts in hiring, pay, and promotion opportunities (Horowitz et. al., 2019). In this study, the researcher aimed to highlight the African American experiences and their negative perception of the: (1) 84% that said racial discrimination served as a major obstacle in their lives; (2) 76% that had less access to high-paying jobs (Figure 1.4); and (3) 82% that were subject to unfair workplace practices (Figure 1.5) which impacted their annual performance reviews, job opportunities, raises, bonuses, and retention. Additionally, the researcher interpreted employment and civil rights laws that were intended to address discriminatory issues in today's corporate workplace.

Blacks are far more likely than whites to say discrimination is a major obstacle for black people

Among those who say being black hurts people's ability to get ahead, % of whites and blacks saying each is a major reason why black people in our country may have a harder time getting ahead than white people

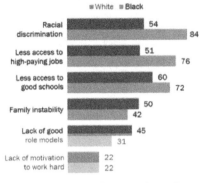

Note: Whites and blacks include those who report being only one race and are non-Hispanic.
Source: Survey of U.S. adults conducted Jan. 22-Feb. 5, 2019, "Race in America 2019".

PEW RESEARCH CENTER

Figure 1.4: Blacks are far more likely than Whites to say discrimination is a major obstacle for Black people

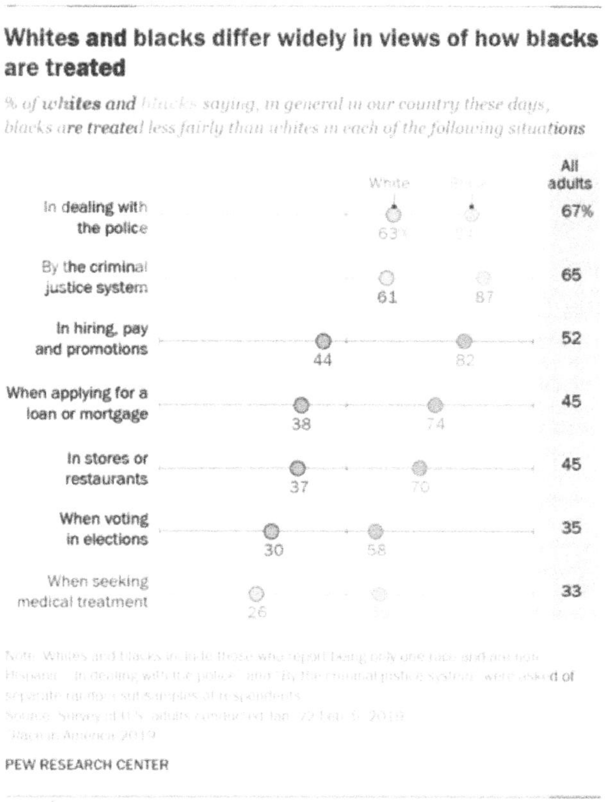

Whites and blacks differ widely in views of how blacks are treated

% of whites and blacks saying, in general in our country these days, blacks are treated less fairly than whites in each of the following situations

	White	Black	All adults
In dealing with the police	63		67%
By the criminal justice system	61	87	65
In hiring, pay and promotions	44	82	52
When applying for a loan or mortgage	38	74	45
In stores or restaurants	37	70	45
When voting in elections	30	58	35
When seeking medical treatment	26		33

PEW RESEARCH CENTER

Figure 1.5: Whites and Blacks differ widely in views of how Blacks are treated

Annual Performance Reviews

Formal performance evaluations were developed for ensuring that each employee's job performance was in line with the organization's expectations. These annual reviews were a means for managers to evaluate and share their respective subordinate's job status as it related to their targets, results, and competency. During these discussions, the lower ranked employee received detailed feedback to strengthen their capabilities as the supervisor encouraged changes in attitude, behavior, skillset and/or job knowledge. When performed correctly, these individual reviews were used as a system for supervisors to coach & counsel their team members while identifying countermeasures for any observable performance deficiencies. In a nutshell, these annual reviews provided systematic judgment criteria to support promotions, demotions, salary increases, transfers, and terminations. Presumedly, "if the EEOC (Equal Employment Opportunity Commission) were trying to show that a protected group had been disproportionately refused promotions, the lack of uniform performance appraisals could work in the agency's favor to show subjectivity and bias" (Casuga, 2016, p.4). And, "if an employer fails to maintain those records, it may prove difficult to defend against discrimination allegations using performance-related data" (Casuga, 2016, p.4). This fact, coupled with corporate America's black employees' perception that they were treated less favorably in their place of employment, had the potential to result in significant losses for an employer if the black employee proved disparate treatment.

Perceived Workplace Racial Discrimination

As the Pew Research Center (2019) had shown, 82% of blacks perceived that they were treated less fairly in the workplace due to their ethnicity. According to Triana, Jayasinghe, & Pieper (2015),

> *The history of discrimination against minority groups in the United States (Boswell, 1986; Chou & Feagin, 2010; Feagin & Sikes, 1994; Gonzalez, 2000; Jahoda, 1975; Spicer, 1969) could make them more likely to perceive discrimination (Kossek & Zonia, 1994). According to our results, minorities also respond somewhat more strongly to perceived discrimination. This implies that minor-*

ities pay close attention to diversity issues and discrimination in the workplace. It is not surprising that they would feel the most deterioration of job attitudes as a result of perceived racial discrimination" (p.505).

Due to an existence of racial discrimination and "the adverse consequences of poor job attitudes for organizational outcomes, it is important for employers to maintain a zero-tolerance discrimination policy and provide diversity training to help prevent discrimination and its associated effect on employees' job attitudes" (Triana, Jayasinghe, & Pieper, 2015, p.505). One possible reason that Black employees' performance reviews were less favorable than their White counterparts stemmed from the managerial approach of not sustaining good recordkeeping practices nor providing consistent, timely, fair and specific feedback to all employees.

Effects Of Race On Experience, Job Performance Evaluations, & Outcomes

Although the race effects of today were moderate in scale, the consistent trend of these differences cautioned businesses to be mindful in their attempts to guarantee equal opportunity. With respect to Black people in managerial positions, the race dissimilarity in perceived job independence and acceptance suggested that supervisors be thoughtful of the potential for disparate treatment of these minorities. In short,
it was recommended that the supervisors scrutinize their own behaviors toward protected groups for possible bias. According to Greenhaus, Parasuraman, & Wormley (1990), the number of African Americans occupying

> *Managerial positions in the United States has grown considerably in recent years. The percentage of managers who are members of minority groups increased from 3.6 percent of the national total in 1977 to 5.2 percent in 1982 (Qones, 1986), and in 1986 blacks represented 6 percent of all managers (Williams, 1987). Despite these recent gains, however, many observers have commented on the presence of an invisible barrier, or "glass ceiling," that prevents blacks (as well as members of other minority groups and women) from advancing beyond lower- or middle-management positions (Crotty & Timmons, 1974; Davis & Watson, 1982; Dickens & Dickens, 1982; DiTomaso, Thompson, & Blake, 1986; Jones, 1986; Morrison, White, & Van Velsor, 1987). Thus, although blacks have gained greater access to managerial jobs, there is still cause for concern that black managers may face "treatment discrimination" (p.64).*

With respect to the effects of race on experience, job performance evaluations, and outcomes, an inclusive work atmosphere encouraged equal employment opportunity and brought forth minimal race differences in occupational experiences and results.

Employment At Will

According to Sukys & Brown (2017), the United States followed the doctrine of employment at will, which stated that:

> *An employer can dismiss an employee at any time for any reason. Under this doctrine, the employer*

> *does not even have to give a reason for the firing. The rationale for the employment-at-will doctrine is that both the employer and the employee must be free to terminate the employment relationship at any time. This principle allows both parties to end an unsatisfactory relationship or take advantage of new opportunities. Unfortunately, the principle can be abused by unscrupulous employers (p.548-578).*

And, since the fact remains that some "individuals with unique abilities, special talents, or a highly specialized education often have the flexibility to negotiate their own employment contracts", many African Americans chose to become professional athletes, famous entertainers, artists, and writers due to the contractual exception that belongs to this category of professionals (Sukys & Brown, 2017, p.548-578). Since African American professionals were perceived to be treated unfairly during performance evaluations thus leading to fewer opportunities for transfer and promotion to top business executive positions, African Americans felt obligated to work twice as hard (as their white counterparts) to be recognized for their work efforts as they strived to avoid being terminated by an employer that was abusing the doctrine of employment at will.

Civil Rights Laws

Although civil rights were first recognized in the United States Constitution nearly after the Civil War, these rights had never been entirely enforced for Blacks in America. As recorded in U.S. history, it was not until after years of greatly publicized civil rights marches, demonstrations, and authoritative brutality that American political leaders decisively acted to enforce these rights for the African American people and other minorities. According to Sukys & Brown (2017), the decree that stated that:

> *An employer can discharge an employee at any time for any reason or for no reason is also limited by civil rights legislation, such as the Equal Pay Act and the various incarnations of the Civil Rights Act, as well as the Age Discrimination in Employment Act, the Uniformed Services Employment and Reemployment Rights Act, the Americans with Disabilities Act, and the Genetic Information Non-discrimination Act (p.548-578).*

Due to the Civil Rights Act and further legislation, an employer couldn't release an employee for no reason at all and, most importantly, that employer couldn't release an employee if the sole reason for the discharge hinged on the fact that the employee belonged to one or more of the protected classes. Having said this, to even the "playing field" (workplace), more African Americans were earning master's degrees while relying on the Civil Rights Act to secure their employment from wrongful discharge/unjust dismissal (The Journal of Blacks in Higher Education, 2006). See Figure 1.6.

Figure 1.6: Over the past 20 years, then number of African Americans earning Master's degrees has more than tripled

Title Vii Of The Civil Rights Act Of 1964

Since the creation of Title VII of the Civil Rights Act of 1964, racial discrimination of black professionals had historically been committed in one of two ways: 1) disparate treatment; and 2) disparate impact. In situations of disparate treatment, the employer intentionally discriminated against the employee/employees belonging to one of the protected classes. In comparison to disparate treatment, disparate impact was a subtler type of discrimination. According to Sukys & Brown (2017), discrimination "through disparate impact or adverse impact occurs when an employer has a policy that on the surface seems neutral but that has an unequal and unfair impact on the members of one or more of the protected classes" (p.548-578). In today's business environment, many employers engaged in disparate impact when performing the annual reviews of African Americans in corporate America which was in direct violation of the Civil Rights Act. According to Sukys & Brown (2017), the Civil Rights Act of 1964

> *Covers more than employment. It also outlaws discrimination in such things as housing, travel accommodations, and education. One of its primary features is the creation of the original five protected classes. Simply stated the act prohibits discrimination on the basis of race, color, creed, gender, and national origin. Employees who believe that they have been discriminated against can file complaints with the Equal Employment Opportunity Commission (EEOC) (p.563).*

Since its original infiltration in 1964, Congress had altered the Civil Rights Act numerous times. In 1991, Congress amended the Civil Rights Act as a major overhaul to toughen the disparate impact doctrine. According to Sukys & Brown (2017), the initial goal of the 1991 amendments

> *Was to strengthen the doctrine of disparate impact that had been weakened by the U.S. Supreme Court. The amendments make it clear that in disparate impact cases, the employer has the burden of proving that a business necessity exists for the alleged discriminatory practice that forms the basis of the complaint. The law also makes it clear that the employer must prove that the hiring or promotion qualification is directly related to the specific job in question rather than to general business needs. The party who files a complaint in a disparate impact case may also be victorious if he or she can show that the same business goal can be reached by using a nondiscriminatory employment practice (p.548-578).*

That said, the new 1991 Act made it evident that an employment practice such as presenting an unfair (biased) performance evaluation was illegal even if only a fraction of the practice was discriminatory.

Despite the perceived success of Title VII, some legal experts suggested that it was not a perfect system which meant that it did not completely eradicate discrimination, subtle or otherwise. In fact, Henson (2015) suggested that Congress's purpose for Title VII

> *Was the ending of the worst forms of discrimination and the preservation of the Doctrine. Since Title VII's purpose was not the eradication of all forms of employment discrimination, the Court,*

> *therefore cannot be at fault for reflecting Title VII's limited purpose in McDonnell Douglas II. There are no fixes for Title VII. It does the work it was designed to do under the Court's accurate stewardship. The Doctrine remains dominant. Since the Doctrine has always dominated Title VII, if there is a fix to be found, focusing on the Doctrine and its role in antidiscrimination law seems like a good place to start fixing antidiscrimination law (p.596).*

Since Title VII of the Civil Rights Act of 1964 did not eliminate all forms of discrimination in the workplace, the Equal Employment Opportunity Commission (EEOC) assumed the responsibility for establishing and achieving agreements, procedures and methods designed to escalate efforts, promote productivity, reduce conflict, struggle, duplication and disagreement among the functions, operations and jurisdictions of the various administrations/departments, agencies and divisions/branches of the federal government that were responsible for the implementation and enforcement of equal employment opportunity legislation, policies, and orders (U.S. Equal Employment Opportunity Commission, 2020).

56 Years Of Progress

Since the establishment of the Title VII of the Civil Rights Act of 1964, fifty-six years had come and gone signaling the passing of sufficient time to revolutionize the façade of the American workplace; however, the voyage in the direction of workplace equality for black professionals was far from over. In fact, due to ongoing issues in the business world, it was imperative that companies' "managers and supervisors understand the law. "Employers who are on top of these issues are doing yearly training with managers and employees" (Lytle, 2014, p.31). Human Resource departments in varying industries were encouraged to push for additional diversity and fairness in the workforce simply because it was in the best interest of the organization. Some asked why it was so important to strive for diversity in corporate America, but most of the U.S. population understood that "the purpose is so we can thrive as companies and as a country because we are taking advantage of this diversity of thought" (Lytle, 2014, p.31). And, as the Pew Research Center (2016) had demonstrated, the perception of how blacks were treated in the United States was an issue that could not be ignored.

Statement of the Problem and Subproblems

Racial equality was one of the most critical issues facing Blacks in the 21st century. Particularly, in the United States' labor market, Black people, in overwhelming comparison to White people, said that they were treated unfairly in their places of employment. And, for many African Americans, racial equality continued to be an intangible aspiration that resulted in distressing employee retention rates. Yet, black people persisted in their efforts for the attainment of career ascension (Williams, 2014), leadership development (Humphrey, 2007), mentorship (Ali, 2007), professional relationships (Carraway, 2008), and cultural comfort (Roberts-Clarke, 2004) in their workplaces.

Pew Research Center (2016) survey found that an overwhelming population of black people (88%) said that the U.S. must continue to make changes for Blacks to have equal rights with Whites, but 43% were doubtful that such changes will ever transpire. And, roughly 82% of Black adults said they were treated less fairly than whites in the workplace. Unfair treatment, company ineffectiveness, and a lack of respect & employee recognition had ultimately led to fewer opportunities for advancement, job dissatisfaction, negative perceptions of the job itself, and high turnover amongst Black Fortune 500 employees. Thus far there had been little, if any, formal appraisal of how Fortune 500 racial inequality had been addressed in the United States.

Purpose of the Study

The purpose of this study was to understand the complexities of the racial inequality of African American professionals in their Fortune 500 workplaces and develop a theoretical model of the constructs that predicted perceptions that employees of color had about their workplace arenas in the following areas: respect & treatment, company effectiveness, the job itself, and teamwork & cooperation.

In alarming numbers, Blacks in the United States had reported racial inequality in their workplaces. Despite the barriers placed upon them, black people persisted in their efforts for the attainment of career ascension, leadership development, mentorship, professional relationships, and cultural comfort in the workplace. In this study, the researcher interpreted employment and civil rights laws that were intended to help organizations address discriminatory issues in today's corporate workplace which impacted Blacks' annual performance reviews, job opportunities, raises, bonuses, and retention rates. In addition to highlighting these lived experiences, the research was designed to quantitatively establish relationship between the imposed unfair treatment, company ineffectiveness, and lack of respect & employee recognition of African American Fortune 500 professionals and the fewer opportunities for advancement, job dissatisfaction, negative perceptions of the job itself, and high turnover rates amongst blacks.

Research Questions & Hypotheses

The researcher's study of racial inequality was based on the extent to which African American professionals exhibit negative perceptions of their workplaces resulting in high turnover. Specifically, the researcher asked the following quantitative research questions:

■ To what extent are lack of employee recognition, lack of career opportunities, job dissatisfaction, company ineffectiveness, and high job turnover correlated to employees' race in Fortune 500 companies?

■ How do differences in the racial composition of teams influence teamwork and cooperation in Fortune 500 companies?

The research tested the following hypotheses:

- *Null Hypothesis 1*: African American professionals do not report more unfair treatment than Caucasian professionals in Fortune 500 companies.

- *Alternative Hypothesis 1*: African American professionals report more unfair treatment than Caucasian professionals in Fortune 500 companies.

- *Null Hypothesis 2*: There is no predictable correlation between unfair treatment and fewer opportunities for career ascension of African American professionals in Fortune 500 companies.

- *Alternative Hypothesis 2*: There is a predictable correlation between unfair treatment and fewer opportunities for career ascension of African

American professionals in Fortune 500 companies.

- *Null Hypothesis 3*: There is no predictable correlation between company ineffectiveness and job dissatisfaction for African American professionals in Fortune 500 companies.

- *Alternative Hypothesis 3*: There is a predictable correlation between company ineffectiveness and job dissatisfaction for African American professionals in Fortune 500 companies.

- *Null Hypothesis 4*: There is no predictable correlation between the lack of respect of African American professionals and negative perceptions of the Fortune 500 job itself.

- *Alternative Hypothesis 4*: There is a predictable correlation between the lack of respect of African American professionals and negative perceptions of the Fortune 500 job itself.

- *Null Hypothesis 5*: There is no predictable correlation between the lack of employee recognition and high turnover of African American professionals in Fortune 500 companies.

- *Alternative Hypothesis 5*: There is a predictable correlation between the lack of employee recognition and high turnover of African American professionals in Fortune 500 companies.

- *Null Hypothesis 6*:
There is no predictable correlation between racial inequality and teamwork & cooperation for

African Americans in Fortune 500 companies.
- *Alternative Hypothesis 6*:
There is a predictable correlation between racial inequality and teamwork & cooperation for African Americans in Fortune 500 companies.

Definition of Terms

- **Black people / Blacks / Black professionals** – refers to a term that is concise for African American Fortune 500 employees and counterpoint to White people / Whites.
- **Black Lives Matter (BLM)** – is a simple affirmative statement. Unfortunately, the need to assert, defend, or officially recognize this affirmation originates from the truth that this statement is not widely received as a truthful or real entitlement. Concomitantly, the opposing viewpoint is consistently present: "Black lives do not matter" (Gafney, 2017).
- **Career ascension** – is a term used for upward mobility or rising from a lower career level or degree to a higher position of authority, power, and responsibility on the corporate ladder (Williams, 2014).
- **Company Effectiveness** – refers to the organization's ability to engage and enable employees by way of positive performance on the following metrics: 1) clarity & direction; 2) confidence in leaders; 3) quality & customer focus; 4) respect & recognition; 5) compensation & benefits; 6) performance management; 7) authority & empowerment; 8) cooperation & structure; and 9) work & processes (Anumeha Chaturvedi, 2012).
- **Corporate America** – is a term used to describe

the world of self-interest corporations within the United States of America.
- **COVID-19** - Coronavirus (COVID-19) is an illness caused by a virus that can spread from person to person.
- **Cultural comfort** – is a term used to encompass the freedom of cultural speech & look, perceived acceptance of diverse cultures, and opportunities for observance of traditions and holidays (Roberts-Clarke, 2004).
- **Drain's Negative Perception Theory (NPT)** – African American Fortune 500 professional employees have negative perceptions of their organizations when they feel, recognize, and/or identify any racial composition of workplace teams, management, and/or the company that demonstrates a lack of the following variables: (1) team/group sharing information to achieve results; (2) management supporting diversity; (3) care & concern for employees; (4) fair & consistent application of company policies; (5) work/life balance; (6) company adequately addressing complaints of discrimination; (7) company taking preventative actions to prohibit discrimination/harassment; (8) work environment that is free from all forms of discrimination or harassment; (9) comfort reporting problems; (10) respect as an individual; (11) career development growth opportunities; (12) company effectiveness & motivation; (12) work/tooling/training provisions; (13) open & honest communication; and (14) job security.
- **Employee recognition** – is a term used for the interaction between a manager and employee where the leader rewards/recognizes/honors the subordinate for reaching a milestone, business objective, or company goal. According to Smith

(2016), the more that "people feel this authenticity within their teams, the more they will recognize it in the organization as a whole. Employee recognition increases employee retention which impacts an organization's performance" (p.168).

- *Equal Employment Opportunity Commission (EEOC)* – enforces laws prohibiting employment discrimination based on race, color, gender, religion, national origin, age, and disability in the Federal and private sectors (Equal Employment Opportunity Commission, 2009).
- *Fortune 500* – is a term used in the American workforce/labor market to reference America's 500 most desired employers with the largest annual revenues.
- *Glass ceiling* – is a metaphor for a barrier that prevents minorities and women from reaching the upper echelons of leadership positions within organizational frameworks (Witherspoon, 2009).
- *Hispanics / Latinos* – refers to a term that is concise for Latin American, Spanish speaking person living in America and counterpoint to Whites.
- *Job dissatisfaction* – is the unpleasant or negative emotional state resulting from an appraisal of one's job or job experiences (Locke, 1976).
- *Job Itself* – is a term that is used to describe the work that the employee is being compensated for and the encompassing recognition, opportunities to learn and grow/develop through training, authority, equipment & tools, job performance results & expectations, and leadership.
- *Lack of respect* – is a term representing the absence of acknowledgement, admiration, esteem, and/or regard for a person.
- *LinkedIn* – is the world's largest professional net-

work on the internet. LinkedIn is an American business and employment-oriented online service that operates via websites and mobile apps. Launched on May 5, 2003, it is mainly used for professional networking, including employers posting jobs and job seekers posting their CVs.

- *Minitab Software* – is statistics package developed at the Pennsylvania State University by researchers Barbara F. Ryan, Thomas A. Ryan, Jr., and Brian L. Joiner in 1972.
- *Minority groups / Minorities / Employees of color* – are terms that most commonly used in America to categorize to all ethnic groups apart from Whites (i.e., Blacks, Indians, Asians, etc.).
- *Negative perceptions* – is a term implying non-desirable interpretations/impressions of an entity.
- *Obama* – is a shortened name for the 44th President of the United States, Barack H. Obama, J.D.
- *Person of Color / People of Color (POC)* –
The term "person of color is today primarily used in the United States to describe any person who is not considered white, including in various points in US history, African Americans, Hispanic Americans, Asian Americans, Native Americans, Pacific Islander Americans, Middle Eastern Americans and others.
- *Retention/Turnover* – retention is a term that is used to articulate an organization's ability to sustain employees over a duration of time, turnover (employee turnover) represents the percentage of employees that leave the organization and the vacated position is filled with a new employee.
- *Self-efficacy* – is the "belief in one's abilities to systematize and execute the courses of action necessary to manage prospective situations" (Clarke-

Anderson, 2004, p.21).
- **SurveyMonkey** - is an online survey development cloud-based software as a service company. It was founded in 1999 by Ryan Finley and Chris Finley. The company provides surveys, and a suite of paid back-end programs.
- **Teamwork & cooperation** – involves a group of people working interdependently toward common goals/objectives with a sense of trust, open/honest communication, and collaboration.
- **Unfair/disparate treatment** – involves intentionally discriminating against the employee/employees belonging to one of the protected classes.
- **White people / Whites** – refers to a term that is concise for Caucasian Americans and counterpoint to Black people / Blacks.

Significance of the Study

In today's workplaces, there were a multitude of organizational cultures with varying values, assumptions, beliefs, and expectations (VABEs) that shaped the psychological and social environment within each respective business. Over the years, there have been many evaluative studies and surveys conducted throughout the world to better understand how these VABEs contributed to the validation of written and unwritten rules and cultural differences within each organizational culture. This culture was expressed in: 1) "the ways the organization conducts its business, treats its employees, customers, and the wider community"; 2) the extent to which freedom is allowed in decision making, developing new ideas, and personal expression"; 3) "how power and information flow through its hierarchy"; and 4) "how committed employees are towards collective objectives" ("What is organizational culture?", n.d.). The focal point of this study was to discover the lived experiences of current African American professionals regarding their perceptions of their Fortune 500 employer and its impact on the organization's retention rates. Furthermore, this research was instrumental in providing facts confirming Fortune 500 racial equality issues and the lack of career ascension, leadership development, mentorship, professional relationships, and cultural comfort of black professionals in the workplace.

Overview of the Study

As a descriptive correlational, quantitative research study, the research investigated racial equality in American Fortune 500 corporations. The research utilized a web-based, anonymous Likert-type survey questionnaire of sampled African American professionals. The stratified randomly sampled data was analyzed and using a statistical package for social science. To interpret the data, a Pearson Correlation Coefficient and sample t tests were completed to investigate relationship between unfair treatment, company ineffectiveness, and lack of respect & employee recognition of black professionals and the fewer opportunities for advancement, job dissatisfaction, negative perceptions of the Fortune 500 job itself, and retention rates amongst African Americans.

CHAPTER II: REVIEW OF LITERATURE

The review of relevant literature for this study began with identifying a problem that was relevant to the 21st century and the United States labor market. At the time of this research, in large numbers, black people said that they were treated unfairly within their respective organizations of employment. Following the identification of this racial equality problem and understanding the research approach to study this topic, the researcher narrowed the focus to six themes for uncovering previous noteworthy theories. Online databases such as ProQuest & EBSCOhost were used to discover prominent studies and this approach involved researching four topics of central importance to blacks' perceptions that employees of color had about their workplace arenas in the following areas: respect & treatment, company effectiveness, the job itself, and teamwork & cooperation.

Additionally, for many African American professionals employed in Fortune 500 companies, racial equality continued to be an elusive desire that most often led to blacks leaving their jobs at alarming rates. Despite these insurmountable barriers, black people persevered in their efforts for the realization of the American dream – career ascension, leadership development, mentorship, professional relationships, and cultural comfort in the workplace.

Since they were viewed as hard results and were easier to measure, most organizations focused entirely on their key financial metrics and completely avoided leveraging their internal/external cultural differences to build inclusion and drive innovations. According to Katz & Miller (2017), implementing "a change process that values inclusive mindsets and behaviors is one of the most effective paths for increasing productivity and innovation in today's organizations. The results speak for themselves" (p.61). That said, racial inequality was not simply a problem for black professionals it was a problem that impacted Fortune 500 organizations' competitive advantage.

As with all research design, literature reviews were conducted to share correlating literature that contained research questions, hypotheses, and findings from other related studies independent and dependent variables (Creswell, 2014). When done correctly, the researcher narrowed the focus of the present study to an ongoing discussion of all relatable literature to compare the results and/or fill in the gaps. According to Creswell (2014), in the researcher's quantitative research design, "the literature not only helps to substantiate the problem but it also suggests possible questions or hypotheses that need to be addressed. A separate literature review section is typically found in quantitative studies" (p. 48). Having said this, the researcher endeavored to uncover a multitude of studies regarding black professionals' lived experiences, exploit theoretical models to fully grasp the current theories, and bridge the gaps to develop a Negative Perception Theory that benefited Fortune 500's efforts to racial equality in the workplace.

Historical Overview

The researcher reviewed multiple studies concerning the lived workplace experiences of African American professionals, such as the work of Dotson (2008), and the findings that black professionals remain underrepresented in numerous professions. Dotson (2008) found that blacks sensed exclusion, racial intolerance, and unfair treatment in their workplaces that left them feeling devalued and disregarded. Additionally, Dotson (2008) suggested that many black professionals were: 1) idealist/warriors – "willingly endure, for now, matters of race as systemic within the engineering culture, while trailblazing inroads for greater inclusion"; 2) realist/conformists – "willingly acknowledge that race does matter but are not threatened by this notion, and are therefore amenable to the status quo engineering culture"; 3) opportunists/explorers – "reluctantly endure matters of race as systemic within the engineering culture, while searching for a more receptive work environment elsewhere"; and 4) disenfranchised/overlooked – "reluctantly acknowledge that race does matter, are threatened by this notion, and thus feel disregarded and devalued by most" (p.I). Additionally, the work of Gibbs (2008) found that black professionals experienced partiality, the effects of ethnic identity and preservation, and the effects of perception dissimilarity which formed barriers to career progression; therefore, mimicking conditions comparable to the glass ceiling effect.

Theoretical Framework

The researcher utilized numerous theoretical frameworks to guide this study such as: 1) organizational leadership theory and models; 2) organizational leadership philosophy;

3) cultural diversity, ethics, and fairness; 4) board/employee/constituent relations; 5) visionary leadership; 6) personnel evaluation; 7) four models of organization behavior or culture theories; 8) six models of organizational leadership theories; 9) nine models of motivation and needs theories; 10) upper echelon theory; 11) disparate impact theory; 12) Rawls' Theory of Justice; 13) cultural deficiency theory; 14) critical race theory; 15) labor market segmentation theory; 16) human capital theory; 17) career development theory; 18) structuration theory; and 19) social cognitive career theory. In addition, studies on glass ceiling, career ascension, mentorship, and cultural comfort served as logically structured frameworks outlining fundamental sources that presented barriers associated with racial inequality of African American professionals in Fortune 500 companies.

Organizational Leadership Theory and Models

Organizational leaders characteristically provided business objectives, motivation, operational supervision, and other managerial services to institutions. Additionally, while providing direction towards the realization of the institution's vision, effective Fortune 500 Chief Executive Officers (CEOs) assisted in prioritizing those business objectives for the organization. These CEOs influenced organizational leaders to understand their firm's mission statement, the process of human resource development, and the art of strategic planning. Each CEOs' specific characteristics, leadership style, and individual traits played an essential role in strategically aligning all actions with the firm's mission statement. That said, CEO leaders were responsible for establishing work environments where business transactions and interactions were open, trepidations and points of view were expressed freely, and mutual comprehension was the norm within the organization. With respect to organization's business success rates, each successful CEO's influence had to be progressive, individual and shared, and be both direct and implied to move the business forward with integrity, fairness, and morality/ethicality.

What Is Leadership?

Leadership was loosely defined as an individual concept for leading people or groups in the attainment of organizational goals while providing direction, information, and a vision for success ("What is a Leadership?", n.d.). According to Wilde & Messina (2019), leadership is "the application of influence in a manner that propels organizations forward. It has been the driving force for both human achievement and catastrophes" (p.27). In the United States' corporate private sector, Rost argued that there were roughly 221 definitions and 587 publications of leadership (as cited in Bass, 2008, p. 15). Having said this, the researcher contended that leadership ought to be examined from multiple perspectives to be applicable in the 21st century.

Most commonly, in today's business environment, CEO leadership was generally viewed as the interaction between the CEO and their respective subordinates with a concentration on the leader's behaviors and effects on the firm (Bass, 2008). According to McFarland & Childress, there were six themes of leadership that were most prevalent in the 21st century and they were:

(1) Leadership is no longer the exclusive domain of the top boss. (2) Leadership facilitates excellence in others. (3) Leadership is not the same as management. (4) Leadership has a sensitive, humanistic dimension. (5)

Leaders need to take a holistic approach, applying a variety of qualities, skills, and capabilities. (6) Leadership is the mastery of anticipating, initiating, and implementing change (as cited in Bass, 2008, p. 15).

That said, the researcher argued that effective leadership in the 21st century involved influencing organizational effectiveness, efficiencies, and productivity.

While fostering an environment of direct and indirect feedback, effective leaders strived to develop their mentoring, coaching, decision-making, and social skills to ensure the success for all personnel and resources. According to Bass (2008), leadership was the "ability to influence, motivate, and enable others to contribute to the effectiveness and success of the organizations of which they are members" (p. 23). Having said, the researcher contended that defining leadership in terms of achieving goals was notably useful because it afforded the application of the transformational leadership theory to better understand leader behaviors.

In summary, the CEO had to, at a minimum, demonstrate the basic skills of content proficiency, strategic instructional/managerial design, masterful communication of materials & information, tactical approach for exceeding evaluation requirements, and have a positive attitude. Additionally, the researcher believed "without determined leaders and effective leadership, no conversion project is likely to live up to what was hoped for it" (Mann, 2015, p.215). Regarding CEOs being essential to organizations, the researcher's governing thought was that all Fortune 500 leaders had to be wise, impartial coaches, possess high integrity, be fully trained to manage altering situations, and demonstrate the socioemotional cooperation needed for the organization to survive and thrive.

Characteristics Attributed To Effective Leadership

Effective Fortune 500 CEOs had characteristics, features, specific leadership styles, and role-specific actions that were essential for influencing followers towards the attainment of goals (Bass, 2008). As a current manager that characterized himself as a situational leader, a popular model of flexible leadership created by Paul Hersey and Ken Blanchard ("What is situational leadership", 2019), the researcher believed that it was important to build a long-lasting legacy of accomplishment for his institution and this had to begin with the establishment of an insightful system of beliefs & values, a mission statement, vision statement, and a cultural transformative strategy. To support the researcher's claim, Schein (2010) stated that "by obtaining self-insight, the organization is presumed to be more able to be effective" (p. 167). In the researcher's current organization, there existed an operating model that was developed by the Fortune 500 CEO to positively influence the success of his firm by training every employee on its features/characteristics. According to Krishnamoorthy (2015), this new cultural template

> *demands new ways of behaving. We even called our new cultural orientation "the GE Beliefs" to ensure that people changed their frame of thinking to the new way. The GE Beliefs are: Customers determine our success, stay lean to go fast, learn and adapt to win, empower and inspire each other, and deliver results in an uncertain world. They reflect a renewed emphasis on acceleration, agility, and customer focus. Interestingly, the GE Beliefs were crowdsourced from our employees for the first time — an attempt to drive a culture that the employees wanted to see (p. 4).*

Using the GE beliefs and various ongoing educational activities, the CEO developed a training and development plan to help each employee align their current performance with the expectations that were set forth within the company strategy.

From personal experience, the researcher developed an extensive list of characteristics required to successfully influence an organization towards meeting and/or achieving efficiency and productivity goals. For example, effective leaders were required to have: 1) cognitive capacities and skills; 2) social capacities and skills; 3) personality traits; 4) motivation; 5) expertise and knowledge; 6) and metacognitive skills. Additionally, the leader had to be cognizant enough to understand when to best utilize these skillsets for leader effectiveness. Through extensive research, the researcher observed similarities between his documented list of characteristics and the attributes of an effective leader that were articulated by Bass (2008).

Leadership Theories & Researcher's Experience

Today, in some organizational structures, there were many individuals serving in leadership roles and there were just as many leadership theories for them to choose from too. According to Ardichvili & Manderscheild, while "there are a great many leadership theories and styles being used by businesses, the Hersey–Blanchard Situational Leadership Model is one of the most commonly used in large businesses today" (as cited by Wright, 2017, p.27). From his personal experiences, the researcher identified with the situational leadership theory/model due to his belief in the non-existence of a "cookie cutter", "one-size fits all" approach to effective leadership on a global scale. Schermerhorn & Bachrach also supported the researcher's position by arguing that "as a consequence of adjusting one's leadership style to meet the followers' needs, the follower grows and becomes more capable of completing the tasks required. In this way, leaders can alter their leadership style to fit the follower's needs" (as cited by Wright, 2017, p.27). This situational theory directly opposed the trait theory due to theorists' arguments that "leadership is a matter of situational demands; that is, situational factors determine who will emerge as a leader. Particularly in the United States, situationalism was favored over the theory that leaders are born, not made" (Bass, 2008, p. 52). Having said all of this, the researcher did recognize the existence of three additional leadership theories – Charismatic-Leadership Theory, Servant Leadership, and Person-Situation Theory – since he had personally practiced these styles during his 21 years serving as a manufacturing leader.

Charismatic/Transformative Leadership Theory

The charismatic leadership theory described the transformative leader as being articulate, highly expressive, determined, self-confident, energetic, active, and emotionally appealing (Bass, 2008). Max Weber introduced this *charisma* concept "into the social sciences to describe leaders who are perceived as endowed with extraordinary abilities" (Bass, 2008, p.50). Often, it was said that followers greatly admired the charismatic leader as a hero/role model and they had implicit confidence in his/her ability to maintain positive influence over the workforce, organization, and society; however, for Bradford & Cohen, the CEO had to be "more than a hero of technical competence and organizing skills. He or she must become a developer of people and a builder of teams" (cited by Bass, 2008, p.51). That said, as a team-focused leader for his entire organization, the researcher closely identified with the descriptive characteristics of a charismatic/transformative leader and demonstrated his positive influence within his business and community.

Servant Leadership Theory

For many followers in the U.S. workforce, the servant leadership theory shared some of the same qualities – positive influence, foresight, reliability, and trustworthiness – as noted in the transformational leadership theory. This servant leadership theory was created by Robert Greenleaf and argued that "the needs of others must be the leaders' highest priority. Power has to be shared by empowering followers. Leaders should think of themselves as servants building relationships with their followers that help their followers to grow" (as cited by Bass, 2008, p. 51). This viewpoint was perfectly aligned with the researcher's personal experiences as a leader and member of the United Way board of directors.

Personal-Situational Leadership Theory

In human behavioral psychology, it was suggested that human behaviors were influenced by an interaction between people and characteristics of given situations; however, not much was known about the precise shape of the interaction (Blum, Rauthmann, Göllner, Lischetzke, & Schmitt, 2018). From this researcher's experience there was not only observed a strong connection between his leadership style and the before mentioned theories, but he also identified with the combined effects of those philosophies which were integrated within the person-situation theory. Introduced and

tested by
Blum, Rauthmann, Göllner, Lischetzke, & Schmitt (2018), a nonlinear interaction of person and situation (NIPS) model provided

> *A simple explanation for the different findings concerning the power of persons and situations. The answer to the question of which source of influence is stronger depends directly on what kind of sample is chosen. When working with groups of extreme participants (i.e. persons with either very high or very low personality trait levels but not when the whole range of personality is considered), the power of persons increases. This is especially true when observing behaviour in a sample of situations that do not differ much in their affordance levels. When extreme situations are sampled, the situation will overpower the influence of personality traits, particularly if, at the same time, the sample of individuals is restricted in its range of trait levels. This principle has been known for a long time (Golding, 1975), but this knowledge seems to have had little impact on P × S interaction research (p.301).*

This person situation theory suggested that "leadership must include the affective, intellectual, and action traits of the individual, as well as the specific conditions under which the individual operates" (Bass, 2008, p. 53). That said, the personal-situational leadership approach provided a balance for leaders to bring into focus each followers' unique work history, core competencies, and personal traits with the leader/CEO's job performance expectations.

Leadership Traits & Researcher's Experience

In the United States' private sector, leadership traits

had been generally defined as the personal characteristics and/or personality of a person that was serving in an authoritative capacity; however, according to Bass (2008), a trait "is a construct based on consistent individual differences between people. Personality is the organized pattern of distinctive traits of a specific person" (p.103). For example, cognitive intelligence, interpersonal confidence, and emotional intelligence & control were 3 traits of leadership that connected to the researcher's managerial experiences. As argued by Bass (2008), if a group "is to be effective, generally there should be a positive correlation between the intelligence of the leader and that of the members" (p.110). That said, the researcher argued that the cognitive/creative abilities of the CEO must be a predictor of that leader's effectiveness to manage and/or supervise the entire business.

Interpersonal & Socioemotional Traits

The researcher argued that an effective leader possessed the ability to think creatively but also exhibited interpersonal and socioemotional skillsets to clearly demonstrate the understanding of, care for, and consideration of his/her followers. According to Bass (2008), Riggio found seven basic socioemotional skills to be of consequence:

> *(1) emotional expressivity ("I have been told that I have 'expressive' eyes); (2) emotional sensitivity ("It is nearly impossible for people to hide their true feelings from me"); (3) emotional control ("I am very good at maintaining a calm exterior, even when upset"); (4) social expressivity ("I usually take the initiative and introduce myself to strangers"); (5) social sensitivity ("While I was growing up, my parents were always stressing the importance of good manners"); (6) social control ("I find*

it very easy to play different roles at different times"); and (7) social manipulation "If I really have to, I can 'use' other people to get what I want" (as cited by Bass, 2008, p.119).

Having said all of this, the researcher drew similarities between his personal experiences and the interpersonal traits of a leader that leveraged his/her followers' skillsets by manifesting a personalized and socialized motivation to lead his team.

Emotional Intelligence & Control

According to this researcher, effective Fortune 500 CEOs possessed emotional intelligence and control to which implied that the leader be insightful and demonstrate his/her ability to solve sensitive problems as they occurred. As reported by Bass (2008), this leadership trait

May be seen as an ability to solve emotional problems as a competency mixes observed abilities, traits, and socioemotional behaviors. The ability model points to success in (1) perceiving and identifying emotions in the thoughts of oneself and others; (2) using emotions to think creatively and make decisions; (3) understanding and interpreting meaning in emotions, being open to feelings, avoiding defensiveness, and reflectively monitoring emotions (p. 124).

Having said, the researcher drew similarities between his lived experiences and the traits of an emotionally intelligent leader by demonstrating his socioemotional abilities and traits, including self-consciousness; tactfully handling his own feelings and compulsions; positively influencing others; showing compassion; and building relationships with others through optimism, passion, and energy to achieve organizational business success.

Organizational Leadership Philosophy

To accomplish key performance indicators for their respective business operations, organizational leaders learned to equip themselves with various leadership styles to navigate their daily interactions with their functional, supporting groups. Once these groups met and/or exceeded their specific program and project goals, the CEO's invoked leadership style was deemed effective under certain business circumstances while others perceived the CEO's leadership style as being ineffective for relationship building and often was autocratic, directive, task-focused, and less desirable than alternative leadership styles. While providing direction towards the realization of the institution's goals, an effective Fortune 500 Chief Executive Officer (CEO) involved his/her team in the decision-making process prior to using his/her organizational authority to form an opinion regarding the appropriate course of action for the entire business entity. From this lens, each CEO retained the final decision-making authority; however, a participative CEO would efficiently develop the human resource skills and capabilities of his/her organizational leaders by involving them in the goal setting and problem-solving efforts to clearly understand the firm's strategic & tactical goals. Having said, each CEO's specific leadership style, whether autocratic or democratic, would play an essential role in strategically aligning all actions with the firm's business needs. Additionally, the CEO leader had the wherewithal to foster a cohesive and productive work environment that built trust, completed tasks, and produced healthy relationships among its members.

Autocratic & Democratic Leadership Styles

Most often, democratic leadership would roughly be defined as a process for a single group leader to lead individuals or groups in the attainment of organizational goals through involving everyone in determining which actions needed to be taken and how the individual contributors or groups would complete the tasks ("What is a Democratic Leadership?", n.d.). According to Ferguson (2011), a democratic leader "will facilitate the adoption of positive human relationships in an organization" (p.434). In the United States' private sector, Nelson argued that democratic leaders tend to solicit opinions, feedback, and shared information and some decision-making authority with his/her subordinates to leverage their skills (as cited in Bass, 2008, p. 441). According to Gill, five principles governed all democratic societies:

> *(1) personal responsibility, (2) empowering others to become leaders, (3) inclusiveness, (4) equality, and (5) full deliberation. Democratic leadership has internal conflicts and is often messy. It is not to be confused with laissez-faire leadership, in which the leader abstains, withdraws, or abdicates responsibility and shows none of the concern seen in the authoritarian or democratic cluster (as cited in Bass, 2008, p. 442).*

Having described the characteristics of a democracy, the researcher contended that autocratic leadership was an inverted state or condition of democratic leadership in the 21st century.

Commonly, in today's business environment, an autocratic CEO leadership style was viewed as an unlimited authoritative CEO relationship with his/her subordinates having no power or influence in the decision-making process within the firm. According to Smither, the "dark side of autocratic behavior is abusiveness, creating fear and distrust, using arbitrary and unconditional punishment, ignoring subordinates' information and inputs to decisions, and relying exclusively on one's own judgment" (as cited in Bass, 2008, p.440). And, Bass (2008) contended that autocratic leadership would "contribute more to a group's dissatisfaction and lack of cohesiveness than to productivity" (p. 138). This viewpoint implied that autocratic leadership produced a lack of satisfaction among the group's members; however, in the right context and/or in extreme circumstances, "despite the aversion to autocratic leadership, when organizations need to be turned around quickly, autocratic and directive leadership is needed. Sometimes unpopular decisions are required along with legitimate and reasonable goals and fair and respectful treatment of subordinates" (Bass, 2008, p.445). That said, the researcher argued that autocratic leadership in the 21st century involved the practice of CEOs exercising absolute authority of power and control over their organization's roles, supportive values, tolerances, and all individual relational orientations.

When comparing autocratic and democratic leadership styles, researchers suggested that differences in power existed among the two styles with autocratic leaders using more force/coercion to persuade subordinates to complete tasks (Bass, 2008). According to Bass (2008), the autocratic-authoritarian leader "encompasses being arbitrary, controlling, power-oriented, coercive, punitive, and closed-minded" (p.439). When reviewing the relationship between autocratic-authoritative leadership styles of coaches and their athletes, the researcher observed that these coaches were disliked by their team; however, this dislike eventually evolved into reverence, admiration, and devotion when the team met their performance goals (Bass, 2008). With respect to Fortune 500 corporations in the United States, the toughest bosses were labeled as callous/ruthless with subordinates "who tell them less than the truth. They are intensely persistent, imperious, unwilling to entertain ideas that don't fit with their own. They get the job done, but the cost to themselves and others may be high" (as cited in Bass, 2008, p.440). Having said this, the researcher asserted that the behaviors associated with a Fortune 500 CEO's democratic leadership style produced greater satisfaction throughout the business; however, if a sense of urgency was needed from the business stakeholders, productivity would be greatly magnified by an autocratic leadership style in the short term.

Directive & Participative Leadership Styles

To efficiently complete a work requirement with high quality expectations, organizational leaders often used a directive leadership style to provide detailed instruction for subordinates to follow (Solomon & Steyn, 2017). As these fundamental work instructions were communicated by the Fortune 500 CEO to his/her subordinates, these interactions were considered vitally important for stimulating the behaviors and actions of all employees towards the attainment of goals (Bass, 2008). Further, Bass (2008) suggested that directive leadership implied that leaders "play the active role in problem solving and decision making, and expect followers to be guided by their decisions" (p.460). From Berlew & Hellers' observation, directive leadership had been split into two patterns of leader behavior: 1) "the leader makes the decisions for the followers often without an explanation and without consulting or informing them until he directs them to carry out his decisions"; and 2) "other directive leaders play a more active role and try to persuade their followers to accept them. They gain acceptance of their proposals by using reason and logic" (as cited in Bass, 2008, p.460). Through directive leadership, Fortune 500 CEO leaders assigned goals, established instruction and command, and carried out reprimand for unmet business targets ("What is a Directive Leadership?", n.d.).

Since directive leadership involved the leader making all decisions and directing the subordinate's behaviors, the differing participative leadership style maintained that the subordinates and their leader served as equal and active participants in the overall decision-making process ("What is a Participative Leadership?", n.d.). For instance, Miao et al. stated that, unlike autocratic decision makers, a participative leader "modestly encourages the involvement of employees in both decision-making and problem-solving" and this participation was likely to be of great value for the company and employees alike (as cited in Lythreatis, Mostafa & Wang, 2019, p.637). And, according to Bass (2008), participative leaders used "group processes to promote follower inclusion, ownership, involvement, consensus, mutual help, cooperative orientation, and free and informed choice. These leaders try to avoid unilateral control, hidden agendas, and inhibition of expression of feelings and relevant information" (p.461). Through the establishment of a mutually inclusive communication system, the researcher believed that participative leaders purposefully engaged with their followers to foster ownership in the planning & decision-making process and actively achieved buy-in from the workforce.

When comparing directive and participative leadership styles, the differences lay in how the Fortune 500 CEO leader made his/her decisions with or without input from the followers. According to Muszyk & Reimann, directive leaders "do not ask their followers to get involved in making decisions. They direct followers' activities and give permission to their followers to carry out duties as the leaders see fit to do" (as cited in Bass, 2008, p.460). And, the traditional judgement was that participative leadership was more satisfying, effective, and favored over directive leadership (Bass, 2008). According to Stewart & Gregersen (1997), a potential reason for this preference stemmed from the fact that the "leader equalizes power and shares the final decision making with the subordinates. Consensus is sought. Participative leadership aims to involve followers in decision processes—in generating alternatives, planning, and evaluation. Such involvement is expected to enhance satisfaction and performance" (as cited in Bass, 2008, p. 460). With that said, the researcher believed that the participative leadership style implied a true partnership of equals with a greater level of autonomy for the followers.

Consideration Vs. Initiation

Today, in some organizational structures, there were subordinates expressing concern that their leaders were not actively showing concern nor appreciation for their contribution to the firm's local and/or global success. According to Bass (2008), a considerate leader actively showed appreciation for a job well done, closely monitored employee morale & job satisfaction, preserved and reinforced employee confidence by "treating them as equals, makes special efforts to help subordinates feel at ease, is easy to approach, puts subordinates' suggestions into operation, and obtains subordinates' approval on important matters before going ahead" (p.539). From his personal experiences, the researcher identified with the descriptive factors of consideration due to his belief in the humanistic need for individual care & concern to be experienced by followers. Atwater also supported the researcher's position by arguing that "considerate leaders provide support that is oriented toward relationships, friendship, mutual trust, and interpersonal warmth. Participation and the maintenance of the group accompany such support" (as cited in Bass, 2008, p. 539). When consideration for followers was demonstrated, the Fortune 500 CEO leader was actively treating the followers with respect, considering their feelings, ideas and suggestions, and explained the reasoning for new and/or modified initiatives.

In the initiation of structure, the Fortune 500 CEO leader triggered action in the business, established and arranged the workforce, and decided the manners in which the task/work ought to be done. According to Bass (2008), initiation "includes such leadership behavior as insisting on maintaining standards and meeting deadlines and deciding in detail what will be done and how it should be done. Clear channels of communication and clear patterns of work organization are established" (p.540). This leader activity was deemed more important when the group did not already have a strong structure in place. For example, if there was no structure, the orientation was to the task and the leader "acts directively without consulting the group. Particularly relevant are defining and structuring the leader's own role and the roles of subordinates in attaining goals" (Bass, 2008, p. 540). Having said all of this, the researcher observed that initiation and consideration were important during business transactions between the leader and follower.

Cultural Diversity, Ethics, and Fairness

In the United States, much research had been conducted to study the issues of diversity and the multifaceted values that were being brought into each organization through individuals from the local communities, society, and the world. This mixed workforce brought a variety of abilities, knowledge, experiences, strengths, and weaknesses to each

organization's culture. Managing a firm's diversity of cultural and social backgrounds, while educating the employees about respect and inclusion, was a business practice that must be supported by the business Chief Executive Officer (CEO) through the various levels of the Fortune 500 organization. To properly assess the current needs of each respective organization and appraise its acceptance of diversity and inclusion, it
was essential that the leader and his/her human resource team developed a systemic method for evaluating the behaviors that were unique to the social and psychological work environment. Equipped with the appraisal of the organization's primary & secondary values, the CEO created developmental processes and strategic/tactical approaches to meet the specific transformational objectives and requirements for his/her firm to successfully compete in a diverse world of political, social, and physical differences.

Diversity Management / Conflict Of Values

Diversity management was a common business practice that supported the personal characteristics of each employee and supported the variation of distinctive lifestyles within the defined group. In effectively managed diverse organizations, it
was common to observe activities that focused on educating stakeholders about diversity topics and provided support for the acknowledgment of and approval for various religious, political, social, and physical differences that existed within the business ("What is Diversity Management?", n.d.). According to Bass (2008), "managing diversity needs to be part of an organization's reward structure" (p. 945). That said, the researcher believed that Fortune 500 CEOs were capable of achieving significant performance gains and positively impacting the firm's culture by simply employing and effectively managing the diversity within its organizational struc-

tures; however, for an organization to benefit from diversity, mutual understanding and true unification had to be well-established and openly supported by its leadership team.

From the perspective of the organizational leader and follower, effective diversity management yields profit for the organization and required much effort by the leadership team. For example, Bass (2008) argued that the leader needs to

> *Bring the followers together in a common work culture to fit the work done and the character and capacities of the stakeholders to the benefit of all concerned. Leaders create a set of group values that supersede organizationally inappropriate ones and replace them with values all can accept and work under (p. 949).*

This required leaders to create unity out of diversity, breakdown barriers and remove obstacles – such as power struggles, opinions, perceptions of empathy & tokenism, and inertia – and focus on similarities instead of differences. In support of this viewpoint, Rebore (2013) argued that "as conflict arises in concrete situations, a practical and reasoned resolution is required" (p. 231). That said, while individuals were pursuing the 'good life' for themselves at work and/or school, any reasonable settlements from the arisen conflict of values had to be in line with organizational goals and managed by the organizational leader. Lastly, all supervisors had to be willing to accept that values were conditional, incommensurable, and incompatible across multinational worksites.

Diversity & Pluralism In Leadership

In the United States' corporate culture, due to its heterogeneity in political, social, and physical attributes, diversity was loosely defined as a characteristic of a blended workforce that offered an extensive range of technical knowledge, experience, abilities, strengths, and weaknesses to businesses ("What is Diversity?", n.d.). According to Slay, it was vital that organizations pursued diversity for three distinct reasons: "(1) diverse insights and skills are potentially valuable resources; (2) diversity enables organizations to gain legitimacy and access to diverse markets, and (3) fairness and avoidance of discrimination are moral imperatives" (as cited in Bass, 2008, p. 943). Further, Bass (2008) argued that diversity offered significant gains for corporations, U.S. Department of Labor awards, and "showed greater increases in stock prices after the award than they had experienced before" (p. 943). That said, the researcher believed that organizational diversity had its' competitive gains as well as costs to which were generally associated with the emotional and intellectual divisiveness that diversity brought among leaders and followers alike.

In the same way that procuring organizational diversity brought benefits into the organization, diversity and pluralism naturally introduced worry and concern for social justice within the workplace. According to Rebore (2013), the "rights and responsibilities of people as individuals and as members of various groups bring into play certain tensions that are often manifested through intolerance and discrimination" (p. 210). As an aftereffect of immigration and multiculturalism in the United States, many public and private-sector workplaces were experiencing human rights issues such as racism and discrimination based on disability, age, illness, gender, and religion. Rebore (2013) argued that

Within the profession of educational leadership, the

greatest current issue is how principals, superintendents, and other administrators will be able to exercise effective leadership within a milieu of tremendous diversity. These professionals are responsible for providing educational leadership not only to diverse groups of students and parents but also to diverse groups of teachers and staff members (p. 210).

In response to the issues surrounding cross-culturalism, it was the researcher's belief that corporate and educational leaders had to recruit diverse staff members into their respective organizational structures to create developmental processes, procedures, policies, and strategic approaches to meet the specific transformational diversity & inclusion expectations of the student, teacher, employee, leader, government, and the institution.

Justice

In U.S. business environments, justice was broadly defined as impartiality in the protection of human rights and punishments for those individuals that had committed harmful acts and/or mistreatments on other persons ("What is Justice?", n.d.). According to Rebore (2013),

Justice regulates how people live their lives as members of a given community. The substance of justice is entitlement, the rights to which individuals and groups of people have a claim. Distributive justice refers to the responsibilities of society to the individual, legal justice refers to the responsibilities of each person to society, and commutative justice refers to the responsibilities that exist between individuals (p. 232).

In the researcher's opinion, while all legal systems aimed to uphold this ideal through fair and proper administration of the law of the land, it was possible to have unjust laws; therefore, all institutions had to consider John Rawls' theory of justice that: (1) each person should have equal rights and liberties that were accessible to all people; and (2) all economic and social inequalities must help the least-advantaged person to achieve equal opportunities to obtain business responsibilities and positions as everyone else (Rebore, 2013).

Discourse Ethics

As it pertained to moral and interpersonal development, philosophers had come to favor the perspective that leaders should focus their efforts towards mediation instead of arbitration when significant matters and complications arose in the workplace. According to Rebore (2013),

> *The ordinary communication that takes place in everyday life touches on the most significant issues and problems facing contemporary humanity. Yet there is a lack of insight into how this communication can effectively address and find a way to deal with the complexities of life. Habermas perceives the overarching problem to be isolation; an isolation of the tenets set forth by science, technology, the arts, and morality. The philosophizing of those who have the ability to demand attention tends to infuse culture with the hope of arbitrating a consensus, whereas Habermas believes that philosophers should assume the role of mediator rather than arbitrator. Arbitration seeks to give an answer, whereas mediation seeks understanding in order to facilitate. This is a profound distinction because it provides a framework within which people can communicate in a non-defensive manner (p. 227).*

In the researcher's opinion, Habermas' views of discourse ethics could productively lead to an answer that was fair and advantageous to all stakeholders; however, if it was not applied to questions that could be addressed through impartial judgment, the leader would not generate dialogue nor unforced convictions from the participants of the mediation to resolve the diversity issues.

Board/Employee/Constituent Relations

In corporate America, the Chief Executive Officer (CEO) position was one of the most sought-after titles by senior leaders; however, due to limited exposure to lower level followers, appeared to be one of the least understood managerial roles in most Fortune 500 organizations. Many organizational subordinates assumed that CEOs possessed the authority to do anything that they desired, were all powerful, and were marvelously proficient at all organizational tasks; however, contrary to popular belief, the job requirements of a CEO involved meeting the needs of the Board of Directors, customers, employees, investors, communities, and the law. With respect to positional power, a small fraction of Fortune 500 CEO's responsibilities could be delegated to share control, but all remaining aspects of the job had to be done by the CEO alone. In this position of power, the CEO leader modeled the Fortune 500 organization's culture through his/her values, behaviors, and compliance with regulatory requirements. As a newly hired leader from outside the organization, this researcher was ultimately responsible for the: (1) establishment and guidance of the entire workforce; (2) development of strategies that would promote and support the safety and security of the stakeholders and the assets of the firm in an ethical and legal manner; (4) recognizing and communicating the value of collaborating with families and community members in response to diverse community interests and needs;

and (5) mobilizing community resources.

Personal Vs. Positional Power

In the traditional sense, when a person was perceived as possessing the authority to make things happen and/or prevent things from happening, at their discretion, the leader was believed to possess a power to influence other's duties within the community, governmental establishments, and/or global organizational businesses ("What is Power?", n.d.). According to Emerson (1964),

> *Power is the force that can be applied to work. It is the rate at which energy can be absorbed. Social power is the ability to take actions and to initiate interactions. It is a force underlying social exchanges in which the dependent person in the exchange relationship has less power and the person with more power is able to obtain compliance with his or her wishes. Compliance implies acceptance of the more powerful person's influence. It can be assent given enthusiastically or reluctantly. The compliant person depends on the more powerful person for desired outcomes that cannot be obtained from other sources (as cited in Bass, 2008, p.263).*

Therefore, a CEO's power was expressed in his/her capacity to both impose and enforce guidelines, principles, rules, and boundaries on a group and to specify what was expected of followers to achieve rewards and/or refrain from punitive actions from the leader.

In the United States, individuals were said to possess personal power if they possessed an internal source, from within themselves, of influence over others rather than being vested by the position he/she held in the organization ("What is Personal Power?", n.d.). According to Bass, those "with personal power can grant affection, consideration, sympathy, and recognition, and can secure relationships and attachments to others" (as cited in Bass, 2008, p.266). Within the realm of personal power, it was suggested that two types of correlating power existed – expert & referent power. From the researcher's observations, expert power depended largely upon the characteristics of the Fortune 500 CEO and the knowledge he/she personally possessed, and referent power was based on being liked or identified with in the personal relationship (Bass, 2008).

If a leader possessed power that had been bestowed upon them by their position of authority, it was said that the influencer simply held positional power by occupying a position, office, or station ("What is Position Power?", n.d.). According to Krech & Crutchfield (1948), the leader's rank that was "associated with one's position gives one power to influence those who are lower in status. Custom, tradition, rules, and regulations assign power to incumbents of positions. Some superiors can be the "purveyors of rewards and punishments" to their subordinates" (as cited in Bass, 2008, p. 267). It was also suggested that reward power, coercive power, and legitimate power were all organizationally derived from positional power (Bass, 2008).

As previously stated, an individual's power could derive from within the leader and from the position that was held. Power could assist leaders with managing and influencing others towards meeting objectives and, unfortunately, could corrupt both leaders and their followers. With respect to positional power, a small fraction of CEO's responsibilities could be delegated to share control, but all remaining aspects of the job must be done by the CEO alone. In this position of power, the CEO leader models the organization's culture through his/her values, behaviors, and compliance with regulatory requirements.

Leaders Sharing Power

In autonomous workplaces with foundational pillars of trust and mutual respect, leaders often shared their positional power with the subordinates to foster a positive culture in their work environment. According to Bass (2008), "in a trusting workplace, sharing power is seen positively and is unlimited" (p. 270). When leaders shared power, an inclusive culture was discovered and developed to collectively handle problems which arose from interactions among its members, and between them and their environment. In the researcher's opinion, the leader had the overall ability to influence the culture and determine what was acceptable or unacceptable, important or unimportant, right or wrong, workable or unworkable; however, when the followers were included in the decision making process, a sense of power was learned and shared and this empowered the community, organization, Board of Directors, and political members to explicitly share knowledge, norms, and values, as well as attitudes, behavior, dress, and language ("What is Culture?", n.d.).

The distribution of power established a platform for potential leaders to influence their fellow citizens in the local community. According to Bass (2008), community & political power

> *Shows itself and its effects in how it is distributed in communities, in formal organizations, and in smaller groups. In small communities, citizens may have the power to directly participate in decisions, such as at town meetings. In cities, they may have the power to participate indirectly through attendance at civic meet-*

ings, consultation with officials, and keeping themselves informed. They may reveal their power in elections, formal petitions, protests, initiatives, and referenda (p. 295).

In the researcher's opinion, it was very important to share community power to give individuals a strong voice to enact strategic change that directly impacted their homes, schools, and churches in a democratic, political process. Further, the leader recognized and communicated the value of collaboration with community members in response to diverse community interests and needs.

In formal organizations across the United States, power revealed itself in each firm's formal authoritative system of power and the shared system of ideology of the members. To this extent, the organization's system of authority contained the way "legitimate power is distributed and enacted in goals, rewards, sanctions, and the division of labor. It is based on the legitimate power of the different roles and positions, and the status and authority of the position holders" (Bass, 2008, p.297). And, according to Alexander (1984),

Management may resist sharing power, not only from a fear of losing its prerogatives but also because of a disinclination to learn new leadership styles involved in consensus building. Unions may not only fear a loss of power but may remain suspicious of the management's motives. And employees may be satisfied with their current inefficiencies in getting the work done (as cited in Bass, 2008, p. 312).

Despite the opposing views of shared leadership in organizations, the researcher believed that much was to be gained, in the development of the followers and procurement of practical benefits, by the leader sharing power in the planning and decision-making with organizational followers.

Ultimately, leaders were responsible for the establishment and guidance of all communal, political, and/or organizational members' performance and it was in their best interest to share power to increase the chance of organizational success. According to Bass (2008),

> *Sharing power under normal conditions has many benefits. Opportunities to consider a proposed change facilitate the acceptance of the change by members who will be affected by it. Participation in planning and decision making regarding the change induces a still higher degree of acceptance. As a consequence, power-sharing programs and restructuring, both voluntary and legally mandated, have become common. Their acceptance depends on the nature of the problems and decisions to be reached, as well as on whether the power sharing is voluntary or legally mandated, direct or through representatives (p. 318).*

Typically, the total power of a diverse group strongly influenced the compliance of all standards, regulations, rules, and laws as well as the members' attitudes and behaviors (Bass, 2008).

Ethics & Codes Of Conduct

In accordance with organizational values and ethical standards, a code of ethics was a written set of ground rules that were issued by an organization to its followers and leaders to help them regulate their actions ("What is a Code of Ethics?", n.d.). The term 'code of conduct' was simply an alternative phrase for the 'code of ethics' or 'code of practice' ("What is Code of Conduct?", n.d.). According to Bass (2008), the New York Stock Exchange "began requiring all listed firms to provide a code of ethics. An ethical code is the norm for larger organizations. But scandals occur in firms despite their written codes of ethical conduct" (p. 209). And, Darley (2001) argued that "a corporation's code of ethics ought to be consistent with its incentive system, which should avoid shortcuts at the expense of the reputation and long-term survival of the corporation" (as cited in Bass, 2008, p. 212). In the researcher's organization, the codes of ethics and conduct provided multiple examples of conflicts of interest to positively influence the leader and follower to align their actions with the codes. Further, the codes assisted the leader in the overall development of strategies that would promote and support the safety and security of the stakeholders and the assets of the firm in an ethical and legal manner.

Interests Of Stakeholders

A stakeholder was mostly defined as an individual, group or organization that had interest or concern in a business/organization ("What is a Stakeholder?", n.d.). In the U.S. market, stakeholders could affect or be affected by the business' activities, operations, objectives and policies. In this context, although not equal partners, stakeholders were typically identified as directors, creditors, employees, owners (shareholders), government (and its agencies), unions, suppliers, and the local community to name a few. Additionally, a firm's customers possessed the right to fair trading practices; however, customers were not eligible to the same perks as the firm's employees.

External stakeholders were very attentive to situations that may have a negative or positive impact on their interests. For example, when an organization had to cut costs to satisfy investors and the Fortune 500 CEO planned a round of layoffs, this negatively affected the local community of workers and therefore the local economy. Additionally, when a company such as Apple developed a new product, stakeholders that owned shares in that business were positively affected by the: (1) release of the new device; (2) surge in profits; and (3) increase in stock prices. According to R.S. Peterson (2001), transformational leaders' "moral values take into account the costs and benefits to all stakeholders, the application of distributive justice, and universal moral principles" (as cited in Bass, 2008, p. 218). That said, the job requirements of a Fortune 500 CEO involved meeting the needs of external stakeholders such as customers, union/non-union employees, investors, and the community-at-large.

Centralized & Decentralized Organizational Structure

In today's business world, some enterprises had multiple business units strategically placed in different geographical locations while other firms participated in a more centralized approach to realize savings. There were factors that influenced which stance a business took in its organization. According to Monczka, et al (2011), several factors

> *Determine the degree of centralization or decentralization that an organization considers when implementing its supply structure. These interaction factors must be considered in total because decisions should not focus on just one factor. Oftentimes one of the more dominating factors will move the organization to a more hybrid form of organization. These factors include: 1) the firm's overall business strategy; 2) the similarity of purchases; 3) total purchase dollar expenditures; and 4) the overall philosophy of management (p. 231).*

In the researcher's opinion, his organizational structure was a balance between centralized and decentralized control across the globe. The main advantage of having a centralized purchasing structure involved the organization's ability to further promote the unification of similar buying requirements and standardizing the buying processes at the different facilities.

Human Resource Management

Effective Fortune 500 CEOs were essential to organizational success and this benefited the firm, employees, and society at large (Wilde & Messina, 2019). Additionally, Wilde & Messina (2019) contended that positive leaders worked with human assets to "bring about new ways of thinking, acting, and learning. It involves everyone, thrives on diversity, and is process oriented. It knows that the organization is stronger and makes better decisions when many ideas are generated and considered" (p. 28). Through effective communication, CEO leaders established business policies and priorities, addressed reoccurring humanistic and psychological issues, and presented robust solutions for further developing the firm's operational systems and processes.

From his managerial platform, the researcher maintained that open communication regarding the Fortune 500 CEO's direction, organization's financials, and employees' morale all helped the leader to establish a culture of trust within his business. For instance, Palestini (2011) stated that management must establish a culture that nurtures "honest upward communication as a way of counteracting employees' tendencies to hide potentially damaging information. Such a culture encourages employee participation in decision making, rewards openness, and limits inflexible policies and arbitrary procedures. It also promotes creativity and innovation" (p. 91). And, according to Shein (2010),

> *We have to define leadership because there are now so many definitions running around both in the academic and applied literature, there are so many prescriptions of what a leader should be in terms of basic competencies and what a leader should do in terms of increasing the effectiveness of organizations (p.17).*

Through the establishment of a mutually inclusive communication process, the researcher believed that the Fortune 500 CEO could positively influence his firm's ability to sustain itself over time.

In summary, the Fortune 500 CEO had to, at a minimum, demonstrate the basic skills of content proficiency, strategic instructional/managerial design, masterful communication of materials & information, tactical approach for exceeding evaluation requirements, and have a positive attitude. Additionally, the researcher believed "without determined leaders and effective leadership, no conversion project is likely to live up to what was hoped for it" (Mann, 2015, p.215). Regarding CEOs being essential to organizations, the researcher's governing thought was that all Fortune 500 leaders must be wise, impartial coaches, possess high integrity, be fully trained to manage altering situations, and demonstrate the socioemotional cooperation needed for the organization to survive and thrive.

Visionary Leadership

With respect to the social and psychological environment of businesses, an organizational vision and culture evolved from the values and behaviors of the company's CEO leader and followers. The organizational culture included values, assumptions, beliefs, and expectations (VABEs) that held it together, and was expressed in its ideas, inner business practices, corporate interactions with the outside world, and future projections (Clawson, 2012). Each respective culture was based on shared beliefs, attitudes, rituals, habits, and written/unwritten standards that had been developed and maintained over time and were thought to be valid. According to Wan (1999), corporations possess the power to turn diversity into a "comparative advantage by maintaining a highly diverse organization to link their business to their diverse customer base. Such firms can better understand, attract, and handle the needs of customers outside the mainstream" (as cited in Bass, 2008, p. 944). That said, the researcher contended that visionary leaders of successful organizations valued cultural diversity, trained the leaders to effectively manage diverse teams' primary & secondary values, and provided periodic feedback about performance expectations to drive the organizational culture in the right direction.

As organizational and educational leaders both strived to effectively manage humans and their behavior, it was vital for the Fortune 500 CEO and/or Superintendent to understand that values could naturally occur in humans and/or be caused by humans themselves. For instance, primary values were generally universal and were associated with human health/well-being and disease (naturally occurring) as secondary values vary with cultures, historical periods, societies, and persons' views of what constituted the 'good life' (caused by humans). According to Rebore (2013), there existed a "multiplicity of genuine values, which differ from culture to culture and from generation to generation. These values must be considered from a perspective that appreciates diversity" (p. 231). Further, in the researcher's perspective, primary values (e.g., nutrition) could be interpreted differently by human leaders therefore were not absolute and were subject to secondary values (e.g., cultural method of food preparation, servings, and consumption). Having said, an organizational and/or educational leader's ability to effectively manage diversity within his/her institution was driven by that leader's primary and secondary values; therefore, when significant changes occurred in the organizational population, the leader must re-evaluate the organization's policies & procedures to ensure that all individual rights and responsibilities, even those that differed from the leader's values, were recognized and respected by all.

Vision Statement

In the United States, most organizations developed a visionary declaration of objectives to guide the business entity and its employees towards the attainment of mid-term and/or long-term success ("What is a Vision Statement?", n.d.). According to Bass (2008), the core of a vision for the business was "its mission, but it adds meaning and purpose for the activities, arouses emotions, and is inspirational and intellectually stimulating" and it should declare an optimistic "view of the future. It should express complex ideas in simple words and be a clear and credible statement of the future" (p.630). Furthermore, the vision should reveal an illustration of what could be attained, why it was advantageous for the stakeholders, and how it could be accomplished by the organization. Once the vision statement was developed and communicated to all stakeholders, the leader focused all organizational efforts on the overall objectives, purpose, and mission of the business to coordinate employee performance expectations.

As a current member of management, the researcher had a global vision to lead the way to the future of mobility, enrich lives around the world with the safest and most responsible ways of moving people. Through a commitment to quality, constant innovation and respect for the planet, the researcher and his team aimed to exceed expectations and be rewarded with a smile. From this vision, the researcher's organization met challenging goals by engaging the talent and passion of people, who believed there was always a better way to perform the work. This was the vision for positioning his business as a company capable of sustainable growth. And, that growth would continue to be the result of delivering great products/services while contributing to the vitality of all host communities and host nations.

Corporate Values

From the perspective of Mahatma Gandhi that we (humans) should role model the change that we would like to see in the world, the researcher aimed to create corporate values at every level of the organization that demonstrated his acceptance of effective leader standards. Specifically, in leader standards, the researcher expected to use his managerial role to drive improvements in goal attainment and effectiveness while modeling personal behavior to set the example for all organizational stakeholders. That said, the researcher expected that all team members, at every level, use the following values in their daily work and interactions:

- HEALTH & SAFETY: To establish health and safety as a priority, all employees must: (1) accept personal responsibility for their individual well-being as well as the safety of others; (2) create, uphold and administer policies and practices; and (3) arrange, work and sustain processes, resources and commodities to prevent illness, injury, and undesirable events.
- CUSTOMER VALUE PRIORITIZATION: To gain customers' admiration and devotion, all em-

ployees must: (1) wholeheartedly believe in the ideology that the next business operation/process is an internal customer that deserves to receive high quality products and services; (2) expect/forecast, adapt to and meet the needs of all external customers; and (3) deliver first rate, world-class products and excellent assistance/services.

- MUTUAL TRUST & RESPECT: To realize a work environment where all employees foster mutual trust & respect and highly regard the work that they perform, all employees must: (1) promote action, creativity, and leadership for all; (2) value the differences, inputs, and talents of each employee; and (3) reward and recognize employees' personal milestones, achievements, and contributions to the team's success.
- SPIRIT & LETTER INTEGRITY: To manifest the highest moral standards in all business/personal interactions, all employees must: (1) adequately and consistently adhere to all ethical business policies, procedures, and practices; (2) deliver on commitments and acknowledge shortcomings instead of hiding them; and (3) operate/behave as an environmentally-conscious, corporate citizen that endorses socially and economically responsible actions.
- DIVERSITY & TEAMWORK: To ensure organizational success, all employees must: (1) take responsibility to work together; (2) share ideas, communicate openly and honestly, and strive for common understanding among all ethnicities and levels of the organization; and (3) advance cross collaboration and communication throughout the entire organization and all affiliates.
- RELENTLESSLY SEEK IMPROVEMENT: To become

responsible for the long-term market competitiveness and success of the organization, all employees must: (1) assume responsibility for improving their processes, products, and themselves through innovative, creative thinking; (2) continually challenge the team and themselves to become better; (3) continuously look for "kaizen" (improvement) opportunities; (4) demonstrate initiative by actively seeking personal development opportunities to achieve full potential; (5) use actual, personal experiences as positive learning opportunities and as the foundation for further growth; and (6) take ownership of their work and be actively engaged in making the organization better for the customer and all diverse talent.

In living these values and keeping with the spirit of Mahatma Gandhi's teachings, the researcher's organization would achieve the vision and ensure the continued development and success of his firm and its team members, while maintaining stable employment, contributing to the community and making the enterprise a great place to work.

Personnel Evaluation

Performance Management -Task Vs. Relations

In the U.S. private sector, while preserving relations with investors, government officials, and all employees, effective CEOs were required to administer specific actions that were essential for swaying all to seek perfection in the fervent completion of tasks. According to Bass (2008), task-oriented leadership "can be a source of expert advice and challenging motivation for subordinates. Misumi conceived of task-oriented leadership behavior as performance leadership —behavior that prompts and motivates the group's achievement of goals" (p. 498). As a continuous improvement leader within both automotive and aerospace manufacturing industries, the researcher characterized himself as a task-oriented leader because he actively concerned himself with all organizational, production goals and the means to achieve those goals through engaging managerial and non-managerial levels to complete specific tasks/roles. To support the researcher's claim, Yukl (1994) proposed five purposes of task-oriented leader behavior:

> *(1) to propose an objective, introduce a procedure, present an agenda, and redirect attention to the task; (2) to stimulate communication, seek specific information, or encourage the introduction of new ideas; (3) to clarify communication, reduce confusion, ask for interpretations, and show how different ideas are related; (4) to summarize accomplishments, to review or ask for reviews; and (5) to test for consensus about objectives, interpretations, evaluations, and readiness for decisions (as cited in Bass, 2008, p. 498).*

Despite the researcher's high regard for task completion, he did not label himself as a *purely task-oriented leader* due to his relational connection with his followers and a resounding compassion for their daily contributions (Bass, 2008).

As task-oriented leadership implied an organizational leader's concern for performance improvement from his/her followers, a relations-oriented leadership style expressed concern for others and attempted "to reduce emotional conflicts, harmonizing relations among others, and regulating participation (Yukl, 1994). Relations-oriented leadership is likely to contribute to the development of followers and to more mature relationships" (Bass. 2008, p.499). The researcher believed that it was important for leaders to foster a supportive environment for followers and this must begin with the establishment of a genuine relationship built on trust and mutual respect. To support the researcher's argument, McGregor (1960) stated that "usually associated with a positive relations orientation are the leader's sense of trust in subordinates, less felt need to control them, and more general rather than close supervision of them" (as cited in Bass, 2008, p.499). At the researcher's firm, a relations-oriented leadership style could be observed during the leader's daily shop floor walks & process observations to better understand and show consideration for the needs of his subordinates. According to Bass (2008), the researcher's daily actions were

> *Linked to relationship behavior: maintaining personal relationships, opening channels of communication, and delegating to give subordinates opportunities to use their potential. It is characterized by involved support, friendship, and mutual trust. It is leadership that is likely to be more democratic and employee-oriented rather than autocratic and production-oriented (p.499).*

Using these insights, the researcher believed that each Fortune 500 CEO leader ought to decisively use a mix of task and relation-orientation leadership to achieve employee engagement, ownership, commitment, and a supportive corporate environment that resembled a family unit.

Performance Assessments & Appraisals

In the researcher's Fortune 500 organization, it was very important to use assessments on both leaders and followers to understand their individual needs and help them to improve their performance. In a traditional sense, an assessment was synonymous with the evaluation of an organization, process, system, situation, possession/object, or person ("What is an Assessment?", n.d.). That said, according to Bass (2008), the "assessment of needs can be initiated in the organization from the top down or from the bottom up" and "training officers differ considerably about the appropriate source of the assessment of their needs of their higher-ups or their subordinates" (Bass, 2008, p. 1069). As previously stated, the purpose/intent of the assessment was to provide CEO leaders with a tool to effectively train and improve employee performance which

> *Depends first on identifying what needs improvement and then demonstrating or helping trainees or students learn how to change their perceptions, cognitions, attitudes, and behavior. Experiences must be provided in which the trainees can exhibit the appropriate leadership. Instructors, observers, and other trainees can give the trainees feedback about the adequacy and effects of their efforts (as cited in Bass, 2008, p. 1069).*

From his managerial experiences, the researcher contended that the success rate of leaders/managers could be improved considerably using assessments and developmental coaching/training.

According to established benchmarks that measured the qualification, merit, or worth of an item, appraisals were impartial examinations and judgements that were administered by a qualified appraiser to assess the value of others ("What is an Appraisal?", n.d.). It should also be noted that some annual appraisals were conducted by employees on themselves to evaluate interpersonal behaviors. For example, Bass (2008) claimed the existence of "seven factors that are involved in interpersonal competence: (1) preferred awareness, (2) actual awareness, (3) submissiveness, (4) reliance on others, (5) favoring group decision making, (6) concern for good human relations, and (7) cooperative relationships with peers" (p. 1019). Typically, a documented leader-led performance appraisal was required by manufacturing sites to rate each subordinate's ability to produce results, measured his/her competency in respective areas such as diversity, foster career & developmental growth, and rewarded behaviors and actions that were consistent with the vision and values of the firm.

In the CEO/President role, leadership facilitated assessments and appraisals to assess individual and organizational needs, promoted developmental learning and provided career growth across all levels of the researcher's Fortune 500 organization. For example, Ellis and Sonnenfeld (1994) listed

> *eight programmatic approaches that firms have used to encourage and support diversity: (1) multicultural workshops; (2) meetings on a monthly basis to confront stereotypes and personal biases; (3) minority support groups, networks, and advisory councils that report directly to senior management; (4) reward systems for training and promotion of minorities; (5) fast-track programs for minorities who demonstrate exceptional talent and potential; (6) mentoring of minorities by senior managers; (7) corporate announcements of appreciation; and (8) commitment to diversity (as cited in Bass, 2008, p. 948).*

Additionally, according to Bass (2008), a "number of studies have shown that direct training in the techniques of leadership can improve trainees' leadership and effectiveness in groups" (p. 1099). Having said all of this, the researcher believed that the transformational leader, while simultaneously striving to understand the dynamics of all cultural differences, both respected and accommodated the employees' needs, strategically assessed the diversity within his workforce, and fairly appraised the effectiveness of each employees' contributions.

Positive Development Culture

In the CEO/President role within Fortune 500 manufacturing environments, the transformational leader fulfilled leadership responsibilities that involved establishing and sharing a clear vision statement, providing developmental opportunities for subordinates, and ethically managing diverse groups to minimize conflicting interests. To meet specific cultural development objectives and requirements, each organizational leader learned to drive the systematic use of assessments and appraisals. This developmental process of social transformation was based on the interactions of complex cultural and environmental factors within each respective manufacturing facility ("What is Development?", n.d.). According to Bass (2008), organizational "training and education programs, both off the job and on the job, have been developed and evaluated to train individuals to be more successful leaders on the job" (p. 1100). In the researcher's opinion, it was the Fortune 500 CEO/President's responsibility to mandate leadership training and employee education requirements to ensure the firm's employees and managers strived for the implementation and sustainment of a positive corporate culture.

The sustainment of a positive corporate culture depended heavily upon the developmental strategic approach taken by the Fortune 500 CEO leader. For example, there were three basic strategies of development: (1) incremental; (2) evolutionary; and (3) grand design. An incremental training strategy involved a gradual but consistent approach in which a previously conceived result was anticipated. An evolutionary training strategy involved a slow but stable approach in which there was no pre-conceived result; however, each subsequent developmental method was a purification of the previous iteration. Lastly, a grand design strategic approach for developing a positive culture involved a total transformation through identifying all critical points of failure and engineering a business development plan that was right 'the first' time ("What is Development Strategy?", n.d.).

Organization Behavior or Culture Theories

Frederick Fiedler's Contingency Theory

In the Frederick Fiedler's (1967) Theory, it was recommended that corporations put managers into situations that were appropriately aligned with the manager's leadership style; therefore, organizations should not strive to change the manager's leadership style because it was too difficult to alter (Palestini, 2011). According to Palestini (2011), the Fiedler's theory suggested that

> *Managers can choose between two styles: task oriented and relationship oriented. Then the nature of leader-member relations, task structure, and position power of the leader influences whether a task-oriented or a relationship-oriented leadership style is more likely to be effective. Leader-member relations refer to the extent to which the group trusts and respects the leader and follows the leader's directions. Task structure describes the degree to which the task is clearly specified and defined or*

> structured, as opposed to ambiguous or unstructured. Position power means the extent to which the leader has official power, that is, the potential or actual ability to influence others in a desired direction owing to the position he or she holds in the organization (p.41).

In the U.S. workforce, the contingency theory was most popular with organizational leaders that believed in the old school of thought that "leaders were born" rather than leaders were developed to be successful.

In the mid-1960s, numerous organizational leadership intellectuals and experts would have agreed with the thought that contingency theory was conceivably "the most powerful current and future trend in the organization field" (Palestini, 2011, p.14). In keeping with his views, Palestini (2011) stated that Fiedler's (1967) contingency theory was a theoretical tool that "facilitates our understanding of the situational flow of events and alternate organizational and individual responses to that flow. Thus, as a conceptual tool, contingency theory does not possess the holistic character of the three major models" – classical organization theory, social systems theory, open system theory (p.14). Having said, Fiedler's theory on contingency

> Dominated much of the research on leadership during the 1970s and 1980s. For Fiedler, the effectiveness of task-oriented and relations-oriented leaders was contingent on the demands imposed by the situation. Leaders were assessed as task oriented or relations oriented according to the way they judged their least preferred coworker. A situation was favorable to the leader if the leader was esteemed by the group; if the task was structured, clear, simple,

> *and easy to solve; and if the leader had legitimacy and power by virtue of his or her position. The task-oriented leader was most likely to be effective in situations that were most favorable or most unfavorable to him or her. The relations-oriented leader was most likely to be effective in situations between the two extremes of favorable and unfavorable (Bass, 2008, p. 62).*

To this, Chemers (1994) added that the leadership would be more successful to the extent that it was adjusted to fit with culture-specific values or universal conduct (Bass, 2008). Specifically, Chemers (1994) suggested

> *An integrated contingency theory of cross-cultural leadership involving three components: (1) projection of a "leaderly" image that instills in followers an acceptance of the leader's influence; (2) motivating relationships based on understanding followers' needs and providing opportunities to meet those needs; and (3) coordinating efforts and followers' capacities to meet those needs (Bass, 2008, p. 981).*

In the researcher's perspective, the contingency theory was successful when the organizational leader's style matched the dominate theme within the workplace's culture; however, some cultural differences remained strong for the smaller ratio of African Americans that worked in predominately White Fortune 500 organizational settings.

Classical Organization Theory

With respect to classical theory, Bass (2008) pontificated that early theorists focused most of their efforts towards identifying principles that correlated with effective management. Regarding the business of running an organizational structure, classical theorists suggested that corporations ought to consist of a hierarchy of authority and a fixed set of rules to address administrative problems within the institution. According to Palestini (2011), as the classical philosophers began to study the problems of:

> *Management erupting in the production centers of society, they shaped notions about organizations that were intended to resolve many of the administrative ills within them. Many of the classical theorists' ideas on work and management were defined as universal scientific principles. If these principles were applied to almost any organizational setting, it was argued, the result would be the efficient use of time, materials, and personnel. The classical theorists believed that an application of the bureaucratic structure and processes or organizational control would promote rational, efficient, and disciplined behavior, making possible the achievement of well-defined goals (p.10-11).*

That said, in organizational life, the classical theory had greatly influenced the study of business and had quickly incorporated itself into the management of all private and public sectors.

Social Systems Theory

According to the classical organization theory, as the organization grew and prospered, the employee also benefitted from the growth and prosperity, but this theory was challenged by organizational leaderships' revelation that employees could assert authority over their production process to some extent. As a response to this discovery, the social systems theory grew to address the growing needs of the skilled employees which began to differ from the needs of the organization. According to Palestini (2011), the social systems theory suggested that "by being considerate, using democratic procedures whenever possible, and maintaining open lines of communication, management and workers could talk over their respective problems and resolve them in a friendly, congenial way" (p.11). As cited in Bass (2008), "for Heifitz (1994), leadership is adaptive work, the activity of mobilizing a social system to face challenges, clarify aspirations, and adapt challenges faced" (p. 17). Having said, according to the researcher, the social systems theory and its approach were designed to reduce conflict between the people and the Fortune 500 corporation.

Open Systems Theory

In classical organization and social systems theory, the perspective of open systems theory was that managing organizations was a complex task for leadership due to the ever-changing conditions in the subsystems of the organization and society – demographic shifts, new laws, values, political climate, vested interests, and traditions. According to Palestini (2011), the open systems theory emerged from the aforementioned and it underscores the relationship of the corporation with "its surrounding environment and thus places a premium on planning and programming for events that cannot be controlled directly. The key to making an open system work effectively and efficiently is its ability to gather, process, and utilize information" (p.14). As cited by Bass (2008), Katz & Kahn (1966) stated that

> *An open-systems point of view implies sensitivity to the larger environment and organization in which leaders and their subordinates are embedded. To convert inputs into outputs, flows of energy and of information must occur in the system. In open systems, the effects of the outputs on the environment are feedback and new inputs. The relations within the system grow and become more intricate with repeated input-output cycles. The cyclical conversion process can be increased in rate and intensity. Leaders or followers can import and introduce more information. Directive leaders do this alone; if followers are included, the process is participative. Energy can be increased by selecting as leaders and followers more highly motivated individuals or by increasing the reinforcements that accrue from outputs (p. 68).*

That said, the classical organizational and social systems theories viewed organizational life as a closed system; however, the open systems theory viewed organizations as a component of interwoven pieces that related with the surrounding environment.

Organizational Leadership Theories

Trait Theory

The trait theory sought to envision which individuals victoriously became leaders and if they would be effective at leading others. Between the years 1920 and 1947, trait theory drew lots of attention by many researchers that were seeking to identify specific qualities of leadership in connection with traits of character and personality (Bass, 2008). According to Bass (2008), it wasn't

> *Until the 1940s, much research about leaders and leadership focused on individual traits. Leaders were seen as different from nonleaders in various attributes and tested personality traits. Two questions were usually posed: (1) What traits distinguish leaders from other people?; (2) What is the extent of the differences? The pure trait theory eventually fell into disfavor. Stogdill's (1948) critique concluded that both person and situation had to be included to explain the emergence of leadership (p. 50).*

Regarding the trait theory, Palestini (2011) further "suggests that we can evaluate leadership and propose ways of leading effectively by considering whether an individual possesses certain personality traits, social traits, and physical characteristics" (p.37). Additionally, one study of senior management positions advocated that "effective leadership requires a broad knowledge of and solid relations within the industry and the company, an excellent reputation, a strong track record, a keen mind, strong interpersonal skills, high integrity, high energy, and a strong drive to lead" (Palestini, 2011, p.38). As noted, this historical theory gained interest to administrators and managers; however, further studies had found that not all effective Fortune 500 leaders possessed Bird's (1940) compiled list of 79 relevant traits that derived from twenty psychologically oriented research studies (Bass, 2008).

Managerial Roles Theory

Using empirical results from multiple studies on role and psychoanalytical theories, Miner (1965) introduced the theory of managerial role motivation (Bass, 2008). Miner's (1965) theory was specifically directed toward "role-taking propensities within the ideal large organization, formalized and rationalized to function bureaucratically. Miner argued that people who "repeatedly associate positive rather than negative emotion" with various managerial role prescriptions are more likely to meet the existing requirements" for success (Bass, 2008, p. 139). As stated by Bass (2008),

> *Six managerial role prescriptions were presented by Miner, along with the required motivation for success as a manager in a hierarchical organization: (1) Managers must behave in ways that do not provoke negative reactions from their superiors. To represent their group upward in the organization and to obtain support for their actions, managers should maintain good relationships with those above them. A generally positive attitude toward those holding positions of authority is required; (2) Since a strong competitive element is built into managerial work, managers must compete for the available rewards, both for themselves and for their groups. If they do not, they may lose ground as functions are relegated to lower their status. Without a willingness to complete, promotion is improbable. To meet this role requirement, managers should be favorably disposed toward engaging in competition; (3) There is a parallel between managerial role requirements and the assertiveness that is traditionally demanded of the masculine role. Both a manager and a father are supposed to take charge, to make decisions, to take such disciplinary action as may be necessary, and to protect others. Even*

women managers will be expected to follow the essentially masculine pattern of behavior as traditionally defined. A desire to meet the requirements of assertive masculinity will generally lead to success in meeting certain role prescriptions of the managerial job; (4) Managers must exercise power over subordinates and direct their behavior in a manner that is consistent with organizational and personal objectives. Managers must tell others what to do, when necessary, and enforce their words through the appropriate use of positive and negative sanctions. The person who finds such directive behavior difficult and emotionally disturbing will have difficulty meeting this managerial role prescription; (5) Managers must stand out from their groups and assume positions of high visibility. They cannot use the actions of their subordinates as a guide for their own behavior as managers. Rather, they must deviate from their immediate groups and do things that will inevitably invite attention, discussion, and perhaps criticism from those who report to them. When the idea of standing out from the group, of behaving in a different manner, and of being highly visible elicits unpleasant feelings, then behavior appropriate to the role will occur less often than is needed; (6) Managers must "get the work out" and keep on top of routine demands. Administrative requirements of this kind are found in all managerial work, although specific activities will vary somewhat from one situation to another. To meet these prescriptions, a manager must at least be willing to deal with routines and ideally gain some satisfaction from doing so (p. 139).

Having said all of this, it is the researcher's opinion that Miner (1965) argued that Fortune 500 organizational structures should consist of leaders that accepted authority, sought upward mobility, and were masculine, competitive, assertive, hard-nosed, and power-brandishing people that focused heavily on details (Bass, 2008).

Additionally, in managerial roles theory, it was observed that manager roles encompass ten role types: 1) leader; 2) figurehead; 3) liaison; three positions that focused entirely on information processing – 4) disseminator; 5) monitor; 6) spokesperson; and four positions involving decision making – 7) disturbance handler; 8) entrepreneur; 9) negotiator; and 10) resource allocator (Palestini, 2011). According to Palestini (2011), "managing individual performance and instructing subordinates are less important for middle managers than for first-line supervisors, and less important for executives than for either lower level of manager" (p.40). The managerial role approach appeared to be like the trait theory viewpoint; however, the roles theory was more consistent with the early situation theory and had demonstrated to be more compelling than the trait theory.

Early Situational Theories

An effective Fortune 500 manager would identify the problem, accurately gather the facts by going to the source, identify the root cause, develop countermeasure activities to prevent reoccurrence, monitor the progress of the improvement, evaluate the successes, and standardize the improvement. According to Palestini (2011), "early situational research suggested that subordinate, supervisor, and task considerations affect the appropriate leadership style in a given situation. The precise aspects of each dimension that influence the most effective leadership style vary" (p.40). Many others had "proposed that personal traits resulting in the emergence or success of a leader would be influenced by the task or goals, the followers' traits, and the organizational context of the situation" (Bass, 2008, p. 62). That said, situational models diverged from the earlier trait models in affirming that there was not one specific way of leading people for all given situations in Fortune 500 organizations.

Theory X And Theory Y

In McGregor's (1960, 1966) Theory X and Theory Y studies, the leader's style of management was based on the individual's suppositions about other people, jointly with appearances of the person, the job to be performed, the corporation, and the environment (Palestini, 2011). As reported by Palestini (2011), a Theory X manager assumed that people "are lazy, extrinsically motivated, and incapable of self-discipline or self-control and that they want security and no responsibility in their jobs. Theory Y managers assume people do not inherently dislike work, are intrinsically motivated, exert self-control, and seek responsibility" (p.40). In accordance with Palestini (2011), Bass (2008) stated

> *McGregor's (1960, 1966) postulation of two types of organizational leadership—Theory X and Theory Y. Theory X assumed that people are passive: they resist organizational needs and attempts to direct and motivate them to fit these needs. Theory Y assumes that people already have motivation and a desire for responsibility: organizational conditions should be arranged to make it possible for people to fulfill their needs with efforts toward achieving organizational objectives (p. 58).*

That said, a Theory X manager would struggle with supporting diverse viewpoints whereas a Theory Y manager, if the leader had all the necessary facts, would use their skillset to effectively manage Fortune 500 employees and situations.

Path-Goal Theory

The path-goal model was a theory that was built on the establishment of a leader's style/behavior that best fit the employees and work environment to achieve business goals. As stated in Bass (2008),

> *Along with House's path-goal theory, Fiedler's contingency theory (1967a) dominated much of the research on leadership during the 1970s and 1980s. For Fiedler, the effectiveness of task-oriented and relations-oriented leaders was contingent on the demands imposed by the situation. Leaders were assessed as task oriented or relations oriented according to the way they judged their least preferred coworker. A situation was favorable to the leader if the leader was esteemed by the group; if the task was structured, clear, simple, and easy to solve; and if the leader had legitimacy and power by virtue of his or her position. The task oriented leader was most likely to be effective in situations that were most favorable or most unfavorable to him or her. The relations oriented leader was most likely to be effective in situations between the two extremes of favorable and unfavorable (p. 62).*

Despite having yielded mixed results, the path-goal theory assisted corporation leadership to select the most effective leadership style due to the requirement that the leader had to first perform a thorough assessment of the conditions before selecting the most harmonious leadership style (Palestini, 2011). As reported by Palestini (2011), the process of

> *Choosing a style requires a quality diagnosis of the situation to decide what leadership behaviors would be most effective in attaining the desired outcomes. The appropriate leadership style is influenced first by subordinates' characteristics, particularly the subordinates' abilities and the likelihood that the leader's behavior will cause subordinates' satisfaction now or in the future; and second by the environment, including the subordinates' tasks, the formal authority system, the primary work group, and organizational culture. According to this theory, the appropriate style for an administrator depends on his or her subordinates' skills, knowledge, and abilities, as well as their attitudes toward the administrator. It also depends on the nature of the activities, the lines of authority in the organization, the integrity of the work group, and the task technology involved. The most desirable leadership style helps the individual achieve satisfaction, meet personal needs, and accomplish goals while complementing the subordinates' abilities and the characteristics of the situation (p.42).*

The path-goal theory could best be thought of as a process in which Fortune 500 leaders selected specific behaviors that were best suited to the employees' needs and the working environment so that they would best guide the employees through their path towards the obtainment of their specific work targets.

That said, the organizational leader would try to control the employees' perceptions of intention and the path to accomplish his/her goals.

Motivation and Needs Theories

Maslow's Hierarchy Of Needs Theory

Maslow (1943, 1954) stated that all individuals were motivated to achieve certain needs and that some needs took precedence over other needs (Mcleod, 2020). Maslow's hierarchy of needs was a motivational theory in psychology consisting of a five-tier model of human needs, often illustrated as hierarchical ranks/levels within a pyramid. Fortune 500 organizational leaders recognized that the huge following of the Maslow's Hierarchy of Needs Theory of motivation mainly stemmed from its obviousness and coherence. According to Maslow's needs theory, "organizations must meet unsatisfied needs. In Maslow's scheme, the lowest unsatisfied need, starting with the basic physiological needs and continuing through safety, belonging and love, esteem, and self-actualization needs, becomes the prepotent or most powerful and significant need" (Palestini, 2011, p.59). This theory contends that humans most basic need was for physical survival, and this would be the first thing that motivated their behavior(s). Once that level was fulfilled the next rank/level up was what motivated them, and so on, until reaching the highest level in Maslow's hierarchy, which was the realization of a person's potential & growth, self-fulfillment, and peak experiences (Mcleod, 2020). Maslow (1943) described this level as the desire to accomplish everything that a person could, to become the most that he/she could be. Additionally, the arrangement/

sequence of needs diverged in different cultures; therefore, it could not be assumed that Maslow's theory would be generalized across all organizational cultures.

Alderfer's Erg Theory

Clayton Paul Alderfer was an American psychologist who further developed Maslow's hierarchy of needs into a theory of his own. Alderfer's ERG (1969) theory suggested that there were three groups of core needs: existence (E), relatedness (R), and growth (G)—hence the acronym ERG. And, these three groups aligned with Maslow's levels of physiological, social, and self-actualization needs, respectively (Al., L., 2020). In Alderfer's ERG Theory, he addressed a disparagement to the Maslow's Hierarchy of Needs Theory by compressing the hierarchy into existence, relatedness, and growth (ERG) needs rather than a five-tiered pyramid of desires (Palestini, 2011). In line with the ERG theory, Palestini (2011) stated that existence comprised both safety and physiological and needs and linked with "Maslow's lower-order needs; relatedness comprises both love and belongingness needs. Growth incorporates both esteem and self-actualization needs. Individual differences in various needs may be associated with differences in an individual's developmental level as well as differences in group experiences" (p.60). Additionally, the ERG theory suggested that unmet needs would motivate people and those individuals usually moved up the hierarchy in satisfying their own needs (such as opportunities for autonomy/growth).

Mcclelland's Needs For Achievement Theory

The McClelland's Needs for Achievement Theory resembled the higher-order needs of affiliation, achievement, and power from Maslow's and Alderfer's theories. In McClelland's theory (or Trichotomy of Needs), the need for achievement was a need to triumph and show "competence or mastery; a person who continuously asks for and masters increasingly difficult tasks demonstrates a need for achievement. Early and recent research linked this need to effective managerial performance in the United States and abroad" (Palestini, 2011, p.61). McClelland's theory also suggested, to some degree, all individuals had these three higher-order needs but only one of these needs tended to motivate each person at any given timeframe (Palestini, 2011). To successfully measure these needs, the projective Thematic Apperception Test (TAT) was administered and scored by a trained professional. As stated by Harrell & Stahl (1981), "although scientists and engineers were found to prefer jobs that provide opportunities to satisfy their need for achievement, successful executives had a higher need for power" in a Fortune 500 organization (as cited by Bass, 2008, p. 158). During the study of the Fortune 500 company, McClelland and Boyatzis (1982) discovered that although a strong need for achievement predicted the success of lower-level managers, the intermediate to high need for power, the lower need for affiliation, and higher scores in activity inhibition predicted the achievement of most other leaders/managers (Bass, 2008).

Frederick Herzberg's Two Factor Theory

In Herzberg's Two-Factor Theory (1959), the behavioral scientist described motivators, characteristics of a job's content including autonomy, responsibility, self-actualization opportunities, and self-esteem, which motivated individuals to put forth extra effort thereby improving performance (Palestini, 2011). According to Palestini (2011), Herzberg also described

> *Hygiene factors, aspects of a job that can meet physiological, security, or social needs, including physical working conditions, salary, company or institutional policies and practices, and benefits, that satisfy the lower-order needs and prevent dissatisfaction. Although hygiene factors per se do not encourage individuals to exert more effort, they must be at an acceptable level before motivators can have a positive effect (p.62).*

According to Herzberg (1959), there were some job factors that resulted in satisfaction (the opposite of "Satisfaction" is "No satisfaction") while there were other job factors that prevented dissatisfaction (the opposite of "Dissatisfaction" is "No Dissatisfaction") (MSG Management Study Guide, 2020). Having said, due to the absence of the acknowledgement of people's differences and the overemphasis on the importance of pleasure, the Herzberg's Two-Factor Theory had undergone much criticism.

William Glasser's Control Theory

In William Glasser's Control Theory (1984), the contemporary psychiatrist suggested that all humans were born with five basic needs: love, survival, power, freedom, and fun (Palestini, 2011). Pursuant to the Glasser Institute (2020), the control theory was

> *Based on the simple premise that every individual only has the power to control themselves and has limited power to control others. Applying Choice Theory allows one to take responsibility for one's own life and at the same time, withdraw from attempting to direct other people's decisions and lives. Individuals are empowered to take responsibility for their choices and support others in taking ownership of their choices. Negative behaviors reduce in frequency and intensity, relationships strengthen and satisfaction in life increases (n.p.).*

In keeping with the Glasser Institute, Palestini (2011) stated that power was the desire to acquire knowledge and "expertise. To Glasser, knowledge is power. Our inalienable right to the pursuit of happiness is our effort to fulfill the need for fun. And the opportunity to make free choices is what Glasser believes satisfies our need for freedom" (p.63). With respect to William Glasser's Control theory, an effective Fortune 500 organization would see that all five of these basic human needs were being satisfied for all employees, including the black professionals/leaders (Palestini, 2011).

Equity Theory Of Motivation

Also known as the Equity Theory of Motivation, Adam's Equity Theory was introduced in 1963 by John Stacey Adams, an organizational behavioral psychologist. As stated in Denis (2018),

> *Equity Theory was based on the idea that individuals were motivated by fairness. In simple terms, equity theory stated that if an individual identified an inequity between themselves and a peer, they would adjust the work they do to make the situation fair in their eyes (n.p.).*

In the Equity Theory (1963), there was an assumption that employees evaluated their attitudes and job performance by "comparing both their contribution to work and the benefits they derive from work to the contributions and benefits of a comparison other, an individual whom the person selects and who, in reality, may be like or unlike the person" (Palestini, 2011, p.64). For example, this theory implied that a black Fortune 500 employee might compare his/her effort and rewards to another black Fortune 500 employee but would compare his/her effort to that of the white Fortune 500 employee and manager/leader/executive too. Nevertheless, the best method/tool to uncover whether equity existed in a specific corporation was to perform an assessment utilizing an Organizational Fairness Questionnaire (Palestini, 2011).

Reinforcement Theory

Reinforcement Theory, also known as Skinner's Reinforcement Theory, was one of the earlier theories that focused on human motivation and was published by American social psychologist, philosopher, and behaviorist Burrhus Frederic Skinner in 1957. Kadlecova (2016) stated that

> The theory is based on the principles of causality and knowledge that a worker's behavior is regulated by the type of reward. The theory does not assess personality, but focuses on behavior and recognizes three basic rules

of consequences:
- Reward for positive behavior reinforces positive behavior
- Punishment for negative behavior weakens negative behavior
- If there is no reward or punishment, behavior is fading (n.p.).

In support of Kadlecova (2016), Palestini (2011) stated that the reinforcement theory "emphasizes the importance of feedback and rewards in motivating behavior through diverse reinforcement techniques, including positive reinforcement, punishment, negative reinforcement, or extinction" (p.65-66).

In Fortune 500 organizations, employee reinforcement was a time-sensitive activity that had to be done in a timely fashion and had to be performed often to maximize the impact. Using formative follow up meetings and coaching techniques, each Fortune 500 employee fully grasped their work requirements, found their own motivation for delivering results, and used the evaluation touchpoints as a time of reflection. For some, the formative process of evaluations, follow-up meetings, and coaching seemed costly; however, human resource development should never be viewed as a cost, since it was a business-critical investment required to refine business practices and achieve professional excellence.

Expectancy Theory Of Motivation

Though Maslow and Herzberg observed the relationship between internal needs and the resulting effort expended to fulfil them, Victor Vroom's expectancy theory (1964) separated performance, effort (which arose from motivation), and outcomes. In the Vroom expectancy motivation theory (2009) article, it was stated that

> *Vroom's expectancy theory assumes that behavior results from conscious choices among alternatives whose purpose it is to maximize pleasure and to minimize pain. Vroom realized that an employee's performance is based on individual factors such as personality, skills, knowledge, experience and abilities. He stated that effort, performance and motivation are linked in a person's motivation. He uses the variables Expectancy, Instrumentality and Valence to account for this (n.p.).*

Additionally, Palestini (2011) articulated that the expectancy theory had strong experimental support, assimilated with "diverse perspectives on motivation, and provides explicit ways to increase employee motivation. Perhaps more than the preceding theories, expectancy theory offers a comprehensive view of motivation that integrates many of the elements of the needs, equity, and reinforcement theories" (p.67). Both authors agreed that, in the expectancy theory, there were three basic components in the model which stated that motivation was a function of: (1) expectancy; (2) valence; and (3) instrumentality.

In keeping with this theory and its application to Fortune 500 black employees, this researcher contended that an African American leader with high expectancy would perceive that if he/she worked harder then he/she would produce (and achieve) more. Regarding lower expectancy, if a Black Fortune 500 employee perceived that if he/she worked harder, then that employee would be ostracized by other colleagues/employees, resulting in a lack of support needed to perform exceptionally well, that employee could be said to have low expectancy (Palestini, 2011). Regarding instrumentality, it was argued that a Fortune 500 employee who perceived that he/she would receive greater pay or benefits if he/she performs well was said to have a high degree of instrumentality (Palestini, 2011). Lastly, concerning valence, Palestini (2011) stated that it referred to

> *A person's perception of the value of specific outcomes, that is, how much the person likes or dislikes receiving these outcomes. An individual with high esteem needs generally will attach a high valence to a new job title or a promotion. When valence is high, motivation is likely to be higher than when valence is less positive or negative (Palestini, 2011, p. 68).*

Having said all of this, the expectancy theory offered a comprehensive diagnostic tool for understanding and quantifying individual's differences in motivation.

Goal Setting Theory

The Edwin Locke goal-setting theory of motivation (1968) stated that goal setting was essentially linked to task performance, and that specific and challenging goals along with appropriate feedback contributed to higher and better task performance. Young (2018) further explained that

> *Locke's primary revelation was around the power of setting specific and measurable goals, rather than keeping outcomes general. With his theory he demonstrated how targets like "increase sales by 20%" or "reach a customer NPS of 50" are much more effective than vague direction such as "complete your work to a higher*

> *standard". This might seem obvious to those of us who have sat down to work out our KPIs, but this really was Locke's brainchild. He gave us the foundation for modern goal setting which had momentous practical implications for managers (n.p.).*

In simple terms, goals indicated and gave direction to Fortune 500 employees about what needed to be done and how much effort was required to complete the task.

In the realm of academic research, there were numerous studies on goals, which varied in three ways: difficulty, specificity, and acceptance, and their relationship to performance. According to Palestini (2011),

> *We can focus on goals and make three assessments. First, we ask whether the individual has goals. Second, we determine whether the individual accepts his or her goals; such acceptance depends on whether the individuals perceive the goals as reasonable, are themselves self-assured, and have previous successes in accomplishing goals. Third and finally, we must assess whether feedback has been provided en route to goal accomplishment (p.71).*

That said, early studies had shown that goal-setting programs increased managerial and nonmanagerial job performance over an extended period in a variety of enterprises (Palestini, 2011).

Upper Echelon Theory

In Hambrick & Mason's (1984) upper echelon theory, their central argument was that executives' personalities, values, and experiences considerably influenced their judgements of the circumstances that they faced and, in proper sequence, affected their actions and choices. In today's U.S. labor markets, upper echelon executives were responsible for making decisions and engaging in business practices that contributed to the overall health, wealth, and prosperity of the employees, shareholders, community, and organization; however, due to the highly homogenous executive level of American Fortune 500 CEOs, their selective perceptions and individual interpretive biases, not all executives were capable of making decisions with positive outcomes. As of 2019, there were only four Black Fortune 500 CEOs which was down from the meager seven executives from less than a decade ago, moreover, not a single Black woman led a Fortune 500 or S&P 500 corporation which affected the organization's recruiting and promotion decisions, diversity actions and initiatives, and hiring choices (Dingle, 2019).

According to Hambrick & Mason (1984), these executive decision makers brought subjective opinions and cognitive beliefs to their attention-directed decisions and his/her beliefs created a filter between the condition/circumstance and their limited perception of the phenomenon. Furthermore,

> *The manager's eventual perception of the situation combines with his/her values to provide the basis for strategic choice. Values are treated here as something that, on the one hand, can affect perceptions (Scott & Mitchell, 1972) but, on the other hand, can directly enter into a strategic choice, because theoretically a decision maker can arrive at a set of perceptions that suggest a certain choice but dis-*

> *card that choice on the basis of values (Hambrick & Mason, 1984, p.195).*

Having said, regarding all efforts to educate respective organizations of the benefits in attracting, recruiting, and retaining diverse talent, these senior-level executive managers mattered most. To this argument, Hambrick (2007) agreed but further argued that when upper echelons researchers "assert that
executives matter, we don't mean that they only matter positively. They matter for good and for ill. They sometimes do smart things and sometimes do dumb things. They sometimes deserve our applause and sometimes deserve our scorn" (p. 341). That said, Fortune 500 CEOs achieved significant performance gains and positively impacted the firm's culture by simply employing and effectively managing the diversity within its organizational structures; however, for an organization to benefit from diversity, mutual understanding and true unification needed to be well-established and openly supported by its leadership team.

Disparate Impact Theory

As an aftereffect of immigration and multiculturalism in the United States, many public and private-sector workplaces were experiencing human rights issues such as racism and discrimination based on disability, age, illness, gender, and religion. One such discriminatory practice was called disparate impact which referred to unintentional discrimination that occurred in workplaces. According to Paetzold & Rholes (2017), disparate impact was a theory of

> *Discrimination that indicates that there is a structural discriminatory practice that pervades the or-*

> *ganization. Individuals affected may be current employees, former employees, applicants, or even would-be applicants. The focus has never been on the individuals, but on the organizational entity itself and the fact that it systematically engages in disparate treatment discrimination (p.116).*

As evidence that disparate impact existed within the organizational structures of the United States' 500 largest corporations by revenue, Walmart topped the Fortune 500 list for the seventh year in a row while being accused of significant discriminatory practices (Youn, 2019).

In the landmark case against Walmart, several plaintiffs claimed that certain promotion and pay and policies and practices purportedly resulted in discriminatory treatment that was consistent across the largest private employer in the world – Walmart. In this case,

> *Commonality was established by social science evidence that suggested that Wal-Mart's corporate culture allowed virtually unfettered decision-making for pay and promotion decisions, thus allowing all women to be potentially subject to sex stereotyping and unconscious bias. The statistical evidence and anecdotal evidence supported the notion that women were potentially treated in an intentionally discriminatory manner, corporate-wide (p.162).*

The establishment of commonality of disparate impact against Walmart further showed that unconscious biases hindered the progress of minorities in Fortune 500 organizations.

In U.S. society, social science research uncovered that implicit preferences for some social groups over others was prevalent, even among people who strongly believed that they were unbiased. According to Paetzold & Rholes (2017),

> *One major topic in implicit cognition research is the evaluation of social groups (e.g., men versus women, white people versus black people, older people versus younger people). Implicit influences on evaluations need not and often do not correspond highly with explicit influences (i.e. evaluations made consciously and deliberately). People may have consciously held attitudes, beliefs, or values that contradict their implicit cognitions. As has been pointed out, many people with egalitarian (i.e., not explicitly prejudicial) views implicitly link the concept of good with white people, young people, thin people, and heterosexual people, but not with their counterparts (p. 148).*

Ironically, individuals that perceived themselves as being objectively fair: (1) normally did not exhibit bias against their own social groups; (2) were more discriminatory once they were made aware of their unconscious biases against other social groups; and (3) had implicit stereotypes and beliefs that had the potential to affect personnel decisions (Paetzold & Rholes, 2017).

Rawls Theory of Justice

In U.S. business environments, justice was loosely defined as impartiality in the protection of human rights and punishments for those individuals that had committed harmful acts and/or mistreatments on other persons ("What is Justice?", n.d.). According to Rebore (2013),

> *Justice regulates how people live their lives as members of a given community. The substance of justice is entitlement, the rights to which individuals and groups of people have a claim. Distributive justice refers to the responsibilities of society to the individual, legal justice refers to the responsibilities of each person to society, and commutative justice refers to the responsibilities that exist between individuals (p. 232).*

While all legal systems aimed to uphold this ideal through fair and proper administration of the law of the land, it was possible to have unjust laws; therefore, all institutions were encouraged to consider John Rawls' (1971) theory of justice that: (1) each person had equal rights and liberties that were accessible to all people; and (2) all economic and social inequalities helped the least-advantaged person to achieve equal opportunities to obtain business responsibilities and positions as everyone else (Rebore, 2013). For justice to be realized in the workplace, there existed an equal distribution of resources and opportunities, morally sound business practices, and ethical leadership that identified talent and ability among diverse workforces.

Critical Race Theory

Closely connected to fields such as history, philosophy, sociology, and law, the Critical Race Theory (CRT) was a theoretical and explanatory approach that explored the presence of race and racism across America through examining the nation's legacy of slavery, the Civil Rights Movement, and recent events. Having said, the critical race theory presented the notion that both career and social ascendency served white, working-class elites, racism was uncharacteristically normal, and only the blatant racist inequalities were focused on in America today (Jackson, 2018); however, the conventional forms of discrimination – economic despair, workplace inequality, and social injustice – faced by minorities most often carried on without any legal recourse (Williams, 2014).

Born out of many legal scholars' frustrations with the dangerously slow progress following Civil Rights in the 1960s, CRT was developed during the mid-1970s and grew into its current form in the 1980s during the height of numerous race-related legal injustices (Jackson, 2018). According to the Purdue Writing Lab (n.d.),

> *Prominent CRT scholars like Kimberlé Crenshaw, Mari Matsuda, and Patricia Williams share an interest in recognizing racism as a quotidian component of American life (manifested in textual sources like literature, film, law, etc). In doing so, they attempt to confront the beliefs and practices that enable racism to persist while also challenging these practices in order to seek liberation from systemic racism. As such, CRT scholarship also emphasizes the importance of finding a way for diverse individuals to share their experiences. However, CRT scholars do not only locate an individual's identity and experience of the world in his or her racial identifications, but also their membership to a specific class, gender, nation, sexual orientation, etc. They read these diverse cultural texts as proof of the institutionalized inequalities racialized groups and individuals experience every day (para.3-4).*

Since the inception of the CRT approach, academics often strived to: (1) explain how victims of systemic racism were affected by injustices by analyzing the works of scholars like Derrick Bell, Richard Delgado, and Alan Freeman; (2) interpreted cultural perceptions of race and racism drawing from work by writers like Fredrick Douglass, Sojourner Truth, Dr. Martin Luther King, Jr., and W.E.B. Du Bois; and (3) clarified how victims effectively addressed acts of discrimination and prejudices by following the advice of legal scholars to shape social constructs that positioned everyone with equal opportunities (Purdue Writing Lab., n.d.).

Skin Tone Labor Market Segmentation

In the United States labor market, there was great concern for the equal distribution of employment opportunities for Blacks that were entering the workforce and/or already in the marketplace. According to Doeringer & Piore (1970),

> *In part, racial employment practices can be understood in terms of a dual labor market. Workers and jobs in the United States can be characterized as operating in one of two sectors of the labor market, a primary sector and a secondary sector. The primary market offers jobs which possess several of the following traits: high wages, good working conditions, employment stability and job security, equity and due process in the administration of work rules, and chances for advancement. The other, or secondary sector, has jobs which, relative to those in the primary sector, are decidedly less*

> *attractive. They tend to involve low wages, poor working conditions, considerable variability in employment, harsh and often arbitrary discipline, and little opportunity to advance. Employers in the secondary sector customarily employ black or other disadvantaged workers (p. 324).*

Further, if Blacks gained employment in the primary sector, they tended to be restricted to the less desirable and least paid positions. That said, any public policy changes to improve equal employment opportunities for Blacks were encouraged to endeavor to change the relative position of those Blacks "already attached to primary type employment situations. Both aspects of the equal opportunity problem require an understanding of the factors which generate the two labor markets, and, in the case of the primary market, which determine movement within it" (Doeringer & Piore, 1970, p. 325). Even if an understanding of the factors surrounding unequal employment opportunities were uncovered, there was a compelling argument that a transition was less likely to occur for Blacks because of the current U.S. discriminatory practices in housing, education, and employment which excluded blacks by monopolizing opportunities based on race to enhance the security and advancement for Whites (Doeringer & Piore, 1970).

In agreement with the Doeringer & Piore (1970) study, other research suggested that Black U.S. workers experienced "colorism", skin tone discrimination, business practices due to their darker complexions which ultimately resulted in the procurement of lower-quality job opportunities. According to Visser (2019),

> *The results of the study offered evidence that work-*

> ers with darker skin tones experience lower levels of job quality than do their lighter skin peers across all racial and ethnic groups. The results also indicated that there was no statistically significant difference in the impact of variations in skin tone within each broad racial/ethnic group, suggesting as Hunter (2008) argues that colorism impacts all racial groups in a similar manner in the US. The analysis further identified a strong geographical element to the impact of colorism as results indicated skin-tone labor market segmentation is experienced more significantly by workers in the southern US than workers in other regions of the nation (p. 55).

Since colorism was mainly concerned with the lightness or darkness of the complexion and questions pertaining to the direction and degree of discrimination imposed within the racial group, it was said to be different than "racism" which had roots in discriminatory practices based on racial categories such as Black or White (Vissor, 2019). Despite the five decades of economic and workplace change since the Doeringer & Piore (1970) study, labor market segmentation continued to create wage disparities across the U.S. workforce resulting in the current distribution of lower quality jobs across most industries to people of color (Vissor, 2019).

Human Capital Theory

In Fortune 500 organizations, human capital theory was concerned with the collective value of the organization's intellectual principle such as knowledge, competencies, and skills; however, this capital was not visible in the firm's financial statements ("What is Human Capital?", n.d.). According to Taylor (1981),

> *Basically, human capital theory states that job skills obtained by workers through formal schooling and on-the-job training increase productivity. Because workers put aside time for training in which earnings otherwise could be made, they expect a return on this investment analogous to that on invested funds. This return is in the form of increased earnings for higher productivity (p. 28).*

For the organization, human capital was a sustainable source of creative innovation that afforded diverse workforces with numerous opportunities to continuously conceive new ideas for strategic change(s). Contrasting from structural capital, human capital was most-often owned by the individuals who had it and could 'walk out the door with it' unless it was documented in a real form or was integrated in the firm's structure and procedures ("What is Human Capital?", n.d.).

In the United States, a gap in earnings, often used interchangeably with the term net income or net profit, existed and had widened between Whites and Blacks due to racial discriminatory business practices ("What are Earnings?", n.d.). According to Taylor (1981),

> *The interplay of social and economic factors complicates the analysis of the black-white earnings gap. For example, discrimination historically has played an important role in keeping black workers out of occupations which provide higher levels of earnings, skills training, and job stability. Racial disparities in education and other spheres that influence the worker's productivity also affect earnings (p. 28).*

That said, only a small fraction of Black men profited from high-paying stable jobs in the U.S. labor market (Taylor, 1981).

Career Development Theory

While career development was a lifelong process of managing an employee's work experience within or between organizations, career development theory (CDT) was concerned with the study of career paths, success rates, and behaviors. Introduced by Frank Parsons, the career development theory derived from four main areas of study – personality, sociology, developmental, and differential psychology – and aspired to reveal the reason why an individual would be a good candidate for a specific career path, provided recommendations on how to successfully realize a promising career ascension, and focused on recognizing frequent career stages where guidance, education, and other actions were necessary (Career Guide, 2019). According to Ollis & Dietrich (1994), Parsons argued that an individual's career choice ought to be based on two factors: (a) an understanding of their own interests, ambitions, abilities, limitations, resources, aptitudes, and (b) an awareness of their labor market. With regard to the second factor, Parsons "labeled this factor "the Industrial Investigation" and devoted six chapters in Choosing a Vocation (1989) to specific areas of labor market exploration"; unfortunately, the chapters offered no cultural factors to assist Blacks in any segment of the population as it focused mainly on White males and devoted one chapter to industries open to White women (p. 312). Having said, many historical CDT models had not adequately considered racial ethnicity of minority groups; therefore, it was encouraged that more theoretical models be constructed to accommodate the many lived experiences of individuals from diverse and ethnic backgrounds in the United States (Williams, 2014).

Structuration Theory

Giddens's (1984) structuration theory began with the realization that culture was taken-for-granted in daily life and ought to be viewed as a social practice (Warf, n.d.). According to Busco (2009),

> *The term structuration refers to the conditions governing the continuity or transformation of structures and social systems, and indicates that structure—the 'codes' for social actions—and agency—the activities of individual members of the systems—exist in a recursive relationship. Thus, while agents draw on structures during their processes of interaction, by performing social activities they reproduce the actions that make these practices possible (p.250).*

Fundamentally, the structuration theory asserted that neither the experience of the person under authority nor the presence of any collective social system created structure; however, when these two realms were incorporated and synthesized, social practices were formed to create the structure which guided human behavior in social settings (Busco, 2009).

Social Cognitive Career Theory

Developed by Robert W. Lent, Steven D. Brown, and Gail Hackett in 1994, the social cognitive career theory (SCCT) contended that employees actively seek a career path that correlated with their individual interests, values, and abilities rather than merely becoming byproducts of their respective environments (Aure, Dui, Jimenez, Daradar, Gutierrez, Blasa, & Sy-Changco, 2019). SCCT was a

> *Relatively new theory that is aimed at explaining three interrelated aspects of career development: (1) how basic academic and career interests develop, (2) how educational and career choices are made, and (3) how academic and career success is obtained. The theory incorporates a variety of concepts (e.g., interests, abilities, values, environmental factors) that appear in earlier career theories and have been found to affect career development (Social Cognitive Career Theory - Career Development – IresearchNet, 2016, para.1).*

Through variable analysis, SCCT made clear that any professional objective to pursue a specific career path came directly from a prospective candidate's judgement of what he/she believed could feasibly be done.

SCCT contained three variables that served as basic architectural framework for the theory. According to Social Cognitive Career Theory (2016),

> *Three intricately linked variables—self-efficacy beliefs, outcome expectations, and goals—serve as the basic building blocks of SCCT. Self-efficacy refers to an individual's personal beliefs about his or her capabilities to perform particular behaviors or courses of action. Unlike global confidence or self-esteem, self-efficacy beliefs are relatively dynamic (i.e., changeable) and are specific to particular activity domains. People vary in their self-efficacy regarding the behaviors required in different occupa-*

tional domains (para. 2).

That said, SCCT assumed people chose to pursue activities that they were excited about and/or likely to become interested in later. Additionally, if they also had necessary skills and environmental supports to pursue these activities, SCCT estimated that employees with strong self-efficacy beliefs would better perform the tasks in assignment (Social Cognitive Career Theory, 2016).

Glass Ceiling

In a phenomenological study of the glass ceiling, Witherspoon (2009) examined the constructs of gender, race, and ethnicity while exploring the perceptions and experiences of 26 sampled minority Federal government senior executive professionals. For the research, Witherspoon (2009) conducted telephone interviews with a variety of men and women of various ethnic groups which included American Indian/Alaskan Natives, Asians, Blacks, Hispanics, and White women (not men). According to Witherspoon (2009), the researcher developed a theoretical framework that "conceptualized multifaceted complexities in the glass ceiling phenomenon. The research is important given current workforce diversity and future workforce trends, which makes it imperative that the face of leadership in the Federal government reflect the face of America" (p.I). Further recommendations by Witherspoon (2009) involved: 1) nurturing the diversity of the high-potential minority employees to further develop their talents and promote a diverse organizational culture; 2) improving leadership support of organizational diversity initiatives and practices; 3) training leadership team to value diversity & inclusion; and 4) mentoring and developing

employees to offer support for career progression of diverse talent. According to Witherspoon (2009), future research was needed to further study "the landmark 1995 Federal Glass Ceiling Commission report, in order to identify improvements in eliminating glass ceiling barriers that were identified in the original report. Findings could enhance sensitivity to diversity issues among
employees and promote diversity in organizations" (p.177). That said, numerous cited researches of the glass ceiling had observed the same phenomena and found a massive under-representation of black male professionals in top management positions (Williams, 2014).

Career Ascension & Upward Mobility

In the Williams (2014) research design, the author presented a qualitative study, using a phenomenological approach, of ten African American (black) male's ascension to the heights of senior level positions of authority in American Fortune 500 corporations. To collect data for the qualitative study, the author used observations, interviews, and documentation review to construct an interview guide. The purpose of the study was to explore the lived experiences of black men's ascension up the corporate ladder and the influences associated with their rise. Dr. Williams (2014) addressed three key research questions: 1) "what are the "lived experiences" of African American males who have ascended to senior levels in Fortune 500 companies?"; 2) "how have these "lived experiences" influenced the career ascension of African American males in Fortune 500 companies beyond the glass ceiling?" and 3) "through these "lived experiences", what challenges have African American males who ascended to senior levels in Fortune 500 companies experienced?" (p. 17). The referenced literary reviews illustrated theoretical concepts preventing black men from rising to the peak of the corporate business level, continuing stereotypes linked with black men's leadership abilities, and the disadvantages facing African Americans in the U.S. labor market. In this study, Dr. Williams (2014) stated that "career development, leadership competency and performance, organizational and social dynamics, personal and professional ideals, performance quality, knowledge and competency, initial perceptions, and organizational politics as themes that impacted the participants' ascension to senior management" (p. V). Dr. Williams (2014) recommended further research involving a larger sample size of African American males, a "phenomenological analysis capturing the lived experiences of African American males in senior-level positions that have line or profit and loss responsibility in Fortune 500 or 1000 companies" (p.160), and career ascension of African American women working in Fortune 500 organizations.

In the Bugg (2009) research, the author presented a "culturally sensitive" qualitative research design to study African American males, working as community college presidents, and their career advancement experiences. To collect data for the qualitative study, the author used questionnaires that were comprised of four elements and focused questions that were administered to five African American male participants that were serving as "president" or retired with the same job classification. The purpose was to explore the structure and essence of black men's career ascension experiences that served as community college presidents and provided insight to assist other black male administrators in obtaining the community college presidency. Dr. Bugg (2009) addressed three key research questions: 1) "how have a select group of African American males experienced their journey to community college presidency?"; 2) "what were the essential qualities and characteristics that enabled them to take advantage of the career advancement opportunities they sought?"; and 3) "what professional and social barriers did they encounter in their career management efforts, and how did they overcome those barriers on their journey to the presidency?" (p.7). The author's literary review was structured with three themes that negatively impacted the African American male administrator's aspirations for the community college presidency: "(a) employment practices in community colleges; (b) the relationship of institutional culture to promotion opportunities in community colleges; and (c) the road to the community college presidency" (Bugg, 2009, p.21).

From the use of interview field data, Dr. Bugg's study (2009) yielded detailed accounts of the five African American male community college presidents' career paths from their experiences. Specifically, Dr. Bugg (2009) suggested that

> *The participants recounted experiencing their journey in four ways: external mobility; internal mobility; positional variety; and emotional journey. These five participants acknowledged being influenced on their journey to the presidency of an American community college and, more specifically, identified three major categories of influences that had an impact on their journey to the presidency: familial, professional, and legislative. The participants identified four qualities they felt essential to their successful journey to an American community college presidency—qualities that they would recommend to other African American males aspiring for a community college presidency: be goal-oriented; be a builder of interpersonal relationships; be technically sound; and be balanced in life. The five participants, also, perceived three broad areas of barriers on their journey to the presidency of an American community college: race as a barrier; perception as a barrier; the assignment as a barrier (p.86).*

Additionally, Dr. Bugg's (2009) study recommended further

comparative qualitative research to better understand any differences between the career advancement barriers of African American males and their Caucasian (majority) counterparts. Also, the author suggested future study concerning hiring practices for African American male talent for expanding the diversification of the available talent pool (p.106).

In the Glenn (2010) study, the researcher further explored professional barriers to black employee's career progression in higher education institutions. Glenn (2010) sampled five black females and five black male senior level employees in the field of higher education. The research consisted of interviews of the sampled participants and six themes characterized the findings: "lack of African American representation in higher education administration, lack of African American mentors, underestimating the importance of diversity, insufficient hiring pools, additional job duties, and racial barriers" (Glenn, 2010, p.I). Even in the realm of collegiate sports, ethnic minorities were confronted with barriers while striving to achieve upward mobility within their profession (Grant, 2008).

Diversity & Inclusion

In the Hamilton (2009) study, the researcher explored the perceptions of black professional administrators and the disparities of positions occupied by African Americans versus Whites at predominately white institutions (PWIs). Using theoretical frameworks such as Bandura's social learning theory (1977), Vroom's (1964) expectancy theory, Cross's nigrescence model (1971), and Helms' Black racial identity model (1990), the researcher addressed several concerns that influenced the views of how African American administrators thought about their PWI employers. Those concerns were cultural identity and race, complexities surrounding career paths, advancement from mid-level management to senior executive positions, and institutional culture (Hamilton, 2009). Humphrey (2007) also recounted personal experiences when the author observed both male and female White colleagues, with similar credentials, being placed in leadership positions more frequently than Blacks. According to Hamilton (2009), understanding black professional administrators' experiences "may assist in fostering an environment that is inclusive and supportive, which in turn may lead to the promotion of more diversity in higher education institutions themselves" (p.xii). While both the Hamilton (2009) and Humphrey (2007) studies observed diversity & inclusion issues impacting blacks' careers, the Ali (207) explored the relationship between career success and mentorship.

African American Mentorship

In the Ali (2007) study, the author presented a single descriptive (empirical inquiry) case study that used a survey and interviews of African American professionals to explore a quantitative relationship between professional mentorship and perceived career success felt by African Americans. The purpose of the study was to: 1) determine a correlation between mentoring and the perception of career success; 2) measure the black professional mentoring experience in terms of demographics, number of mentors, and duration; 3) characterize and assess the mentoring traits that were associated with the perception of career success; 4) obtain additional data on the black mentoring experiences; and 5) further the progression of African American professionals by validating the relationship between mentorship and success. In this study, Dr. Ali (2007) addressed four key research questions to test if there was "a significant positive correlation between mentoring African American professionals and their perceptions of career success among members of the Peoria

Black Chamber of Commerce" (p. 8). The referenced literary review explored theoretical concepts of mentoring and career development that was applicable to African American professionals. In this study, Dr. Ali (2007) stated that the Pearson correlation coefficient "was used to test the research hypotheses and results indicated a significant positive relationship at the .05 level (p< 0.05) between the mentoring of African American professionals and their perceptions of career success among members of the Peoria BCC" (p. I). Dr. Ali (2007) recommended further research on the topic of mentoring, the mentor's voice, and exploration of the phenomenon involving successful African Americans and the absence of mentorship.

In the Carraway (2008) study, the author presented a qualitative study that used two structured interviews of five African American male protégés (ten interviews total) to explore professional mentorship behaviors and perceived career success felt by African Americans. The purpose of the study was to "gain further insight into how culture plays a role in early career cross-cultural mentoring relationships consisting of African American male protégés and the White male mentors functioning in predominately White organizations" (Carraway, 2008, p.23). Dr. Carraway's (2008) research focused on "career development functions that are aimed at helping the protégé advance in the organization" and "psychosocial functions that provide mutual trust, counseling, acceptance, and personal support to the protégé and are essential to forming collegial relationships" (p.23). In this study, Dr. Carraway addressed two key research questions in the study (2008): 1) "How do White male mentors and African American male protégés within formal matched cross-cultural career mentoring relationships characterize the career function of their mentoring experiences?"; and 2) "How do White male mentors and African American male protégés within formal matched cross-cultural career mentoring relationships characterize the psychosocial functions of their mentoring experiences?" (p. 24).

The referenced literary review explored concepts of mentoring and career advancement of African American professionals. In this study, Dr. Carraway (2008) stated

> *A review of extant literature on cross-cultural mentoring reveals that scant attention has been paid to cross-cultural mentoring, but that some of what has been said about cross-gender mentoring may also be said for cross-culture. In this chapter several factors have been identified as influencing mobility and career advancement for persons of color. The literature indicates that factors such as stereotyping, coupled with the dimensions of culture, impact the early-entry socialization process of the individual. In addition, such factors as the organizational culture, the lack of access to social networks, and the lack of access to mentors can prevent qualified Blacks, and other minorities from achieving levels of career advancement comparable to those of their White counterparts (p.61).*

Additionally, the referenced literature suggested the necessity of having a mentor early in the protégés career to achieve career advancement, and that early-entry black professionals, in higher numbers than their white counterparts, reported less valuable career advancing, mentoring relationships.

Dr. Carraway's (2008) study of cross-cultural mentoring relationships, involving white male mentors and black male mentees in predominately white institutions, suggested the presence of social constraints and perceptual barriers that inhibit upward mobility and career advancement of the African American protégés. Further, the author stated that these concealed social constraints and barriers had the potential to damage the protégés reputation as well as the mentor's. Dr. Carraway (2008), also found that

> *African American male protégés paired with White male mentors in a predominately White organization may face two barriers related to networking in the organization. First, the protégé's performance may be perceived by others in the organization as untrustworthy and less than desirable (visibility and performance pressures, exclusion from informal networks and workgroup support, issues of alienation in the organization, etc.). Such perceptions may cast performance threats on the protégé, further inhibiting mobility and advancement in the organization. Second, power associated with group membership may affect the behavioral, perceptual, and psychological processes unique to cross-cultural mentoring relationships that are directly linked to professional development and maintenance of the relationship. More specifically, negative attributions and stereotypes, inaccurate perceptions of competence, and negative work group reactions, combined with increased visibility and performance pressures, may restrict African American males' access to informal network relationships and the outcomes associated with cross-cultural relationships (p. 183).*

To further Dr. Carraway's (2008) study, the author suggested "each of the previously mentioned areas needs a careful and comprehensive examination (developmental functions, interaction patterns, the peculiar set of experiences, organizational circumstances) to address the links among culture, professional development, and opportunity in organizations" (p.187). And, the author recommended further research would strive to acquire more knowledge, awareness, comprehension, and learned action skills relating to diverse individuals than mentors in more compatible/homogenous relationships (Carraway, 2008).

African American Recognition and Retention Rates

In the Allen, Bryant, and Vardaman (2010) scholarly article, the authors presented a guide to understand employee turnover and retention using evidence-based strategy. Allen, Bryant, and Vardaman (2010) focused on: 1) major organizational concern of employer's ability to retain key employees; 2) the "broader implications for organizational competitiveness in an increasingly global landscape, and for how to address social and demographic trends such as an aging and increasingly diverse workforce" (p.48); and 3) the prospect that numerous present day employees endured their organizations for the reason that there were insufficient external opportunities, therefore, the likelihood for extensive pent-up turnover to arise "when labor markets become more favorable for employees. A recent survey reported that 54% of employed adults, including 71% of those between the ages of 18 and 29, are likely to seek new jobs once the economy improves" (p.49). All three authors were respected associate professors in their respective academic institutions. David G. Allen was an Associate Professor and First Tennessee Professor of Management in the Fogelman College of Business and Economics at the University of Memphis, Phillip C. Bryant was an Assistant Professor at Christian Brothers University, Memphis, TN, and James M. Vardaman was an Assistant Professor in the College of Business at Mississippi State University.

The purpose of the study was to "review the research evidence concerning how and why individuals make turnover decisions and what organizations can do about it" (Allen et al.,

2010, p.52). The precedent literature focused on recruitment, selection, socialization, training & development, compensation & rewards, supervision, and engagement as evidence based human resource management strategies for reducing turnover. The method for collecting evidence-based data for systemic strategies included but was not limited to: retention research from the precedent literature; best practices drawn from the experiences of other firms; and benchmarking surveys. Allen et al. (2010) suggested further study on: a) "boundary conditions that specify under what conditions turnover theories hold for what subgroups of employees" (p.62); b) interventions, experimental and/or quasi-experimental designs. "Most turnover studies consist of correlational designs that limit the ability to draw firm conclusions about causality. Future research that manipulates turnover antecedents with appropriate controls for alternative explanations would be valuable for scientists and practitioners" (p.62); and c) "the effectiveness of evidence-based approaches to retention management with alternative approaches could provide important evidence as to whether scholarly research on turnover adds significantly to managerial experience and judgment in retention management" (p.62). That said, in the Allen, Bryant, and Vardaman (2010) scholarly article, the researcher uncovered theories on the impact of rewards & recognition on retention rates and the workplace conditions.

Image & Perception of African American Males

In the Abdulhaqq (2008) study, the author presented a qualitative research design to study senior level African American males, working in American banking corporations, and the factors that led to the under representation of black males in those positions. To collect data for the qualitative study, the author used questionnaires that were comprised of four background questions and six focused questions that were administered to ten African American senior-level banking executives. The purpose was to explore the leadership traits of black men serving as senior-level executives in the banking industry, identify deterring factors that perceptually lead to the under representation of black men in that capacity, and explore influential factors that were believed to assist black men in obtaining those positions. Dr. Abdulhaqq (2008) addressed two key research questions: 1) "what is the perception of the African American senior-level male executive regarding the leadership traits (enablers) or motivating factors the African American senior-level male attributes to his ascension into a senior-level executive position?"; and 2) "what are the leadership traits in the perception of African American male senior level executives that would prohibit African American males from attaining senior-level executive positions in the banking industry?" (p. 55). The author's literary review was exhaustive and resulted in over 500 academic journal sources and 387 references using a variety of library search terms on EBSOhost, ProQuest, and a Google search engine. Dr. Abdulhaqq's findings (2008) suggested that there existed "characteristics that African American males aspiring to reach the senior executive levels in organizations should possess, should not possess, and should strive for and inhibitors that would prevent them from attaining senior level positions in the banking industry" (p.I). Additionally, Dr. Abdulhaqq's (2008) study recommended further study of African American males outside of the banking profession and an examination of those needed leadership traits, comparison of leadership traits needed for African American women working in the banking organizations, and the contrast between diversity centered and non-diversified organizations.

In the Cornileus (2013) research design, the author presented a qualitative study, using interviews, to examine the impact of racism on African American (black) male's careers in corporate America. The study consisted of three parts grounded in the frames of Black masculinity, critical race theory, and career development theory. To collect data for the qualitative study, the author used semi-structured interviews both in individual and focus group settings involving fourteen African American professional men. With a purpose of exploring the lived experiences of racism towards black professional men in corporate America, Dr. Cornelius (2013) addressed four key research questions: 1) "how do African American professional men describe their career development?"; 2) "how has racism shaped the career development of African American professional men?"; 3) "what factors influence the career development of African American professional men?"; and 4) "What strategies do African American professional men employ to negotiate the impact of racism on their career development?" (p.447). The referenced literary reviews illustrated theoretical concepts of the earlier mentioned tripartite frames facing African Americans in the U.S. labor market. In this study, Dr. Cornileus (2013) stated that African American professional men

> *Experience repressive structures due to gendered racism, which impacts their careers in ways that are different from their White male counterparts and African American professional women. The study also identifies facilitative structures African American men employ to negotiate the impact of racism on their career development (p. 444).*

Dr. Cornileus' (2013) study added to the small body of research on racism and career development and recommended further research involving

> *More critical research on the repressive and facilitative structures identified in this study and on generational*

> *differences that may exist between first-generation African American executives and the generations who have entered corporate America since then. Studying generationally diverse executives may help us to understand the salience of race and impact of racism across generations in this increasingly multicultural society (p.458).*

In the Abdulhaqq (2008) and Cornileus' (2013) studies, the researchers uncovered issues impacting the image and perception of black professionals. To address the cultural comfort of this demographic, the researcher referred to the Roberts-Clarke (2004) for additional insights into the blacks' perceptions about their organizations.

Cultural Comfort of African American Males in the U.S. Labor Market

In the Roberts-Clarke (2004) study, the author conducted quantitative research to understand the lived experiences of employees of color and their perceptions about their workplaces. To collect data, Roberts-Clarke developed a questionnaire that was completed by 204 study participants that were recruited at professional conferences and on-line. The study focused on perceptions of corporation's commitment to diversity, cultural comfort, discriminatory practices, social relations, and instrumental relations. According to Roberts-Clarke (2004), product variables included degree of job satisfaction, turnover intentions, retention rates, and opportunities for advancement. Additionally, the study observed perceptions of discrimination in the employees' placed of employment based on the racioethnic identities of the minority participants. To analyze the data, Roberts-Clarke (204) used quantitative procedures which included structural equation models, principal components analyses, and univariate t tests. The researcher found that

> *The cultural comfort of employees of color was predicted by organizations' commitment to diversity and discriminatory practices. Employees of color experienced less cultural comfort where there were more discriminatory practices, and experienced more cultural comfort where there was greater organizational commitment to diversity. Participants' perceptions about opportunities for advancement and retention rates were predicted by their perceptions about the organization's commitment to diversity, discriminatory practices, and cultural comfort. Perceptions about the organizations' commitment to diversity and discriminatory practices mediated by cultural comfort predicted their job satisfaction and intention to remain at their jobs. Additionally, African Americans perceived higher levels of discriminatory practices in the workplace than other employees of color (p.ii).*

In Roberts-Clarke (2004) study, with respect to organizations that were not committed to diversity initiatives, black professionals perceived discrimination within their respective organizations and felt lower cultural comfort.

Underrepresentation of African American Males in the U.S. Labor Market

In the current U.S. labor market, many Blacks encountered obstacles when seeking better employment opportunities despite consistent job growth over the last 9 years (Weller, 2019). According to Weller (2019), Blacks continue to experience

> *Systematically higher unemployment rates, fewer job opportunities, lower pay, poorer benefits, and greater job instability. These persistent differences reflect systematic barriers to quality jobs, such as outright discrimination against African American workers, as well as occupational segregation—whereby African American workers often end up in lower-paid jobs than whites—and segmented labor markets in which Black workers are less likely than white workers to get hired into stable, well-paying jobs. Despite African American workers having increased access to jobs and actually getting more jobs, labor market outcomes—including higher unemployment and fewer good jobs—continue to be worse for African American workers and their families (para. 1).*

The author contended that the U.S. market seek to create new business practices, innovative policies, and visionary approaches towards shrinking the racial wealth gap by ensuring that African Americans had the same access to better employment opportunities as their white counterparts did (Weller, 2019).

Additionally, due to the lack of representation of African Americans in Fortune 500 organizations, there were fewer employment networking opportunities for the minority leaders/managers. As stated by Bass (2008),

> *Revealed wisdom suggests that corporate advancement depends on whom you know as much as what you know. Minority managers are seen to have more difficulty gaining support (Thomas & Alderfer, 1989). Minorities' advancement is handicapped by*

> *their exclusion from social networks (Morrison & Van Glinow, 1990). To study this issue, Ibarra (1995) examined the contacts outside their business unit of 17 minority middle managers (12 black, 3 Hispanic, and 2 Asian American) with a survey and interviews, and compared them with the contacts of 46 white middle managers. Altogether, 20 were women, but sex was statistically controlled when the results were extracted. Compared to white managers, minority managers felt that networking was less important to their advancement. The managers reported more racially mixed networks but fewer intimate ones. Minority managers with high potential balanced same and cross-race contacts rather than being dominated by whites. They had more contacts outside their groups (p. 947).*

Since social networking correlated with corporate advancement opportunities and minorities were observed to have fewer contacts, the researcher believed that the Black employees experienced: (1) fewer close ties which meant less access to information that was shared informally; (2) decreased likelihood of receiving sensitive work-related information regarding job opportunities; (3) fewer resources at work for people of color (POC); (4) exclusion by the White majority; and (4) less support and acceptance by their work group than did White employees.

Disparate Treatment of African American Males in the U.S. Labor Market

In the Agbara (2012) research, the author presented a

study of racism and discriminatory issues that compound the African American male experience in society today. The study references statistical data to strengthen the author's position that a correlation existed between disparate treatment of African American men and the rate of unemployment in that demographic. Additionally, the author stated that corporate officials should explore methods for leveraging culture differences to gain a competitive advantage in the market. The recommendations from this study suggested the formation of diversity workplace committees, open communication channels for black men's voices to be heard, and career development opportunities.

Managerial Progression of African American Males in the United States

In the Bacchus (2005) study, the author presented a deliberate examination of his exploratory research concerning the underrepresentation of Black males serving as corporate executives in Fortune 500 companies. As Bacchus (2005) suggested, "the reasoning behind this phenomenon takes on a multiplicity of factors. Many Black males have grown up in a hostile world" (p.5). According to the author, the purpose of the study was to: 1) uncover the profile of the African-American male executive in the Fortune 500 company; 2) discover the perceived obstructing dynamics that had resulted in the under-representation of African-American male executives and Fortune 500 CEOs in the American labor market; and 3) survey the enabling factors that aided the African-American male executives in attaining their senior positions in the Fortune 500 companies. The study dealt with three research questions that ran parallel to the author's three statements of purpose. In Bacchus' (2005) precedent literature that was presented in four sections,

> *The first section examines an overview of human development – with special emphasis on the development of the Black male. The study includes the theories and processes of William Cross, Albert Bandura, Charles Thomas, and Ralph Turner. This leads to the second section, where the history of Blacks in corporate America is reviewed for a period of the last twenty years relative to upward mobility in senior management, and the theory of survival – Machiavelli's theory (Prezzolini, 1967). The third section examines the motivation for Black males entering corporate America through Hieder's Theory of Attributional Causality. In this section, the researcher examines the conditions or situations that act as obstacles or inhibitors to the Black males entering corporate America's executive management, including the Glass Ceiling. Finally in the fourth section, the mentoring relationship theories and processes are covered (p.18).*

This exploratory study utilized a survey to collect both quantitative and qualitative data from 200 Black male executives in Fortune 500 companies.

The author interpreted the research findings for each research question to uncover the profile of the Black male executive, highlighted the top three inhibitors that prevented the Black males from reaching the upper ranks in corporate America, and motivating factors (goals, skills, etc.) that assisted in the Black male executives attaining senior executive positions in Fortune 500 companies. Bacchus' (2005) study concluded that: (1) "the profile of the Black male executives (the participants) compares favorably to their White counterparts; however, there were a few deviations (Marquis, 2002)" (p.106); (2) the research participants had faced and logged numerous inhibitors for African-American male executives in Fortune 500 companies. "The results showed that there were numerous challenges (many being of a racial nature) and roadblocks for Black males in their struggle to get to the top of corporate America" (p.106); (3) the research participants had noted numerous enablers. "As a matter of fact, all the Black male executives that have achieved the level of CEO (six as of this writing) have noted the extreme necessity of having influential mentors" (p.106); and (4) "literature has shown some important gains in the upper mobility of the Black male, other minorities, and women in corporate America in recent years" (p.107). The findings from the Bacchus (2005) study demonstrated that, despite the black professionals having comparable profiles, many blacks in Fortune 500 companies had been subjected to racial challenges.

Suggestions for further research included gathering all of the current Black male CEOs in the Fortune 500 companies, expanding research to Fortune 1,000 companies, spread out research to include all corporations and industries in America, and interviewing the top twenty highest-ranked Black executives to uncover the "why and how" top executives "explain the difference (in percentages) in inhibitors and enablers for Black males in general and the participants themselves, which might enhance and augment the upward mobility of other minorities and women in corporate America" (Bacchus, 2005, p.110). To address the recommendation for further study, the researcher endeavored to sample more black males for this research.

In the Clarke-Anderson (2004) study, the author presented a quantitative descriptive correlational study, using a Likert-type instrumental scale with survey questions, at a mid-western U.S. energy corporation that employs 8,000 people of diverse racial/ethnic backgrounds, to discover the relationship between self-efficacy and leadership aspirations in a business environment. As stated by Dr. Clarke-Anderson (2004), the purpose of the study was to uncover if there existed a relationship between "self-efficacy (dependent variable) and leadership aspirations (independent variable) in a business setting and if there was a difference among leadership aspirations and self-efficacy of African Americans and other minorities (Hispanic Americans, Asian Americans, and American Indians) compared to Caucasians" (p.49). Findings from this study aided the researcher in understanding the leadership aspirations of multiple ethnic backgrounds.

Dr. Clarke-Anderson (2004) hypothesized that: 1) there existed a correlation involving self-efficacy and aspirations; and 2) there existed a difference between self-efficacy and leadership aspirations amongst diverse ethnic groups to attain leadership positions (p. 51). The referenced literary reviews presented supporting data to "substantiate the hypothesis presented in this study, that is, self-efficacy (dependent variable) and leadership aspirations (independent variable) and the relationship to self-efficacy of African Americans' and other minorities' attainability to leadership positions in organizations compared to Caucasians" (Clarke-Anderson, 2004, p.48). Dr. Clarke-Anderson (2004) amassed an exhaustive literature review to support the hypotheses comparing the leadership aspirations of whites with all remaining ethnic groups.

In this study, Dr. Clarke-Anderson (2004) hoped to provide American organizational business settings with practical learnings from the research's conclusion that

> *Self-efficacy (independent variable) and leadership aspirations (dependent variable) showed no significant relationship ($r = .066$) when the data were aggregated.*

> However, according to this study's findings there was a difference between self-efficacy and leadership aspirations among different ethnic groups (p < 0.05), when the data were disaggregated. When the independent variables ethnicity and self-efficacy are combined the effect on leadership aspirations is different among ethnic groups (p.ii).

Dr. Clarke-Anderson (2004) provided findings from this study that encouraged companies to "assist minorities to gain the necessary skills to obtain leadership positions in a business setting" (p.98). Additionally, this study recommended further research involving: 1) "using more variables: education, typecasting in the workplace, or blue-collar workers verses white-collar workers to determine the relationship between self-efficacy and aspirations of minority groups compared to majority groups to obtain leadership positions in a business setting"; 2) "a study using an organization that is less diverse. In addition, utilizing a school setting might also be appropriate to conduct a study"; 3) "a similar study using a larger population sample could be conducted that includes more than one organization that focuses on blue-collar workers to determine if leadership aspirations differ among racial and ethnic groups" (Clarke-Anderson, 2004, p.99). To expand upon the study, the researcher aimed to use more variable, organizations, and larger sample.

Conclusion

As a leader, the researcher believed that it was important to build a long-lasting legacy of accomplishment for institutions and this began with the establishment of an insightful system of beliefs & values, a mission statement, vision statement, and cultural transformative strategy. Schein (2010) said that "by obtaining self-insight, the organization is presumed to be more able to be effective" (p. 167). Additionally, the researcher believed that it was best to openly communicate organizational direction to establish a culture of open communication and build trust within the team. Palestini (2011) said that management needs to establish a culture that nurtures "honest upward communication as a way of counteracting employees' tendencies to hide potentially damaging information. Such a culture encourages employee participation in decision making, rewards openness, and limits inflexible policies and arbitrary procedures. It also promotes creativity and innovation" (p. 91). In the review of cited studies, the researcher chose to exhaust the literature review by citing various organizational & motivational theories as well as cultural and racial theories.

In this researcher's experience, communication was key in building trust; however, there was another important piece of the puzzle that could not be overlooked –employee support!
Palestini (2011) stated that, when administrators were communicating with their direct and indirect teams, the leadership team knew "they must create a trusting and supportive environment. Creating such a climate has the objective of shifting from evaluation to problem solving and formation in communication. Administrators must avoid making employees feel defensive, that is, threatened by the communication" (p. 94). The organizational leaders adapted to a collaborative problem-solving structure to mitigate the numerous ills associated with racial inequality within Fortune 500 companies.

After new professionals gained experience in their roles and began to contribute to the attainment of the corporation's shared goals and objectives, it was encouraged that the leader seek feedback from the team to evaluate the leadership and cultural relationships. According to Schein (2010), one approach to this evaluation process, best illustrated by Denison (1990), was

> To identify a number of dimensions of culture that are presumed to be relevant to a given organizational outcome such as performance, growth, innovation, or learning. The survey questions are then focused on just the dimensions considered relevant, and if those dimensions cannot conveniently be measured with a survey, the researcher/consultant can supplement with interviews and observations. This approach worries less about creating a typology and more about measuring key dimensions in many organizations and then relating those to performance. For example, Denison's survey measures the following twelve dimensions under four general headings: 1) Mission – Strategic direction and intent, Goals and objectives, Vision; 2) Consistency – Core values, Agreement, Coordination and integration; 3) Involvement – Empowerment, Team orientation, Capability development; and 4) Adaptability – Creating change, Customer focus, Organizational learning (p. 169-170).

That said, all organizational leaders were encouraged to be diligent in their efforts to close the feedback loop with their employees and strive to build a trusting and transparent environment where all members understand the mission and are all involved in the achievement of the shared goals.

CHAPTER III: METHOD OF RESEARCH

Introduction

The purpose of this study was to understand the complexities of the racial inequality of African American professionals in their Fortune 500 workplaces and develop a theoretical model of the constructs that predicted perceptions that employees of color had about their workplace arenas in the following areas: respect & treatment, company effectiveness, the job itself, and teamwork & cooperation. The researcher's study of racial inequality was based on the extent to which African American professionals exhibit negative perceptions of their workplaces resulting in high turnover. Specifically, the researcher asked the following quantitative research questions:

- To what extent are lack of employee recognition, lack of career opportunities, job dissatisfaction, company ineffectiveness, and high job turnover correlated to employees' race in Fortune 500 companies?

- How do differences in the racial composition of teams influence teamwork and cooperation in Fortune 500 companies?

The review of related literature from Chapter 2 provided an overview of the theoretical framework, research problem, and presented references related to what was known about the variables that were associated with the problem. In this manner, the literature review, which concluded with a brief summary of the literature and its implications, systematically led to logical methodology that was appropriate for devising testable hypotheses. Having said, the research tested the following hypotheses:

- *Null Hypothesis 1*: African American professionals do not report more unfair treatment than Caucasian professionals in Fortune 500 companies.

- *Alternative Hypothesis 1*: African American professionals report more unfair treatment than Caucasian professionals in Fortune 500 companies.

- *Null Hypothesis 2*: There is no predictable correlation between unfair treatment and fewer opportunities for career ascension of African American professionals in Fortune 500 companies.

- *Alternative Hypothesis 2*: There is a predictable correlation between unfair treatment and fewer opportunities for career ascension of African American professionals in Fortune 500 companies.

- *Null Hypothesis 3*: There is no predictable correlation between company ineffectiveness and job dissatisfaction for African American professionals in Fortune 500 companies.

- *Alternative Hypothesis 3*: There is a predictable correlation between company ineffectiveness and job dissatisfaction for African American professionals in Fortune 500 companies.

- *Null Hypothesis 4*: There is no predictable correlation between the lack of respect of African American professionals and negative perceptions of the Fortune 500 job itself.

- *Alternative Hypothesis 4*: There is a predictable correlation between the lack of respect of African American professionals and negative perceptions of the Fortune 500 job itself.

- *Null Hypothesis 5*: There is no predictable correlation between the lack of employee recognition and high turnover of African American professionals in Fortune 500 companies.

- *Alternative Hypothesis 5*: There is a predictable correlation between the lack of employee recognition and high turnover of African American professionals in Fortune 500 companies.

- *Null Hypothesis 6*:
  There is no predictable correlation between racial inequality and teamwork & cooperation for African Americans in Fortune 500 companies.
- *Alternative Hypothesis 6*:
  There is a predictable correlation between racial inequality and teamwork & cooperation for African Americans in Fortune 500 companies.

The researcher utilized a descriptive correlational, quantitative research design with a goal of learning about a large population by surveying a sample of that population. With respect to the survey questionnaire distribution and method of collection, the researcher emailed potential adult participants an online survey link using both a social network, LinkedIn, that focused on professional networking and career development and a survey tool, SurveyMonkey, that captured the voices and opinions of the people who mattered most to the study. Using a Likert-style survey on the internet, the researcher administered a stratified random sampling research method to conduct the anonymous data collection without the need of a physical location/dwelling.

Research Design

As reported by Paul D. Leedy and Jeanne Ellis Ormrod (2012), there existed different types of quantitative research studies that were generally categorized as descriptive quantitative research designs. These general designs typically fell under two subcategories which involved identifying the characteristics of an observed phenomenon or explored possible associations between two or more phenomena. In either case, descriptive quantitative research didn't seek to change or modify the situation, nor did it assert causation. It simply described the situation "as it is" within the observation study, correlational research, developmental design, and survey research (p. 184).

In the literature review of research comparisons between Ali (2007) and Clarke-Anderson (2004), this researcher evaluated each study and determined that:
- The quantitative methodological research approach of Ali (2007) was a single descriptive case study to provide a full description of the phenomenon.
- The quantitative methodological research approach of Clarke-Anderson (2004) was a descrip-

tive correlational study to discover the relationship between two or more phenomena.

In this study, the researcher utilized a descriptive correlational, quantitative research design. The goal was to learn about a large population by surveying a sample of that population.

Research Setting and Participants

As stated in Leedy and Ormrod (2012), there were "eight approaches to sampling, which fall into two major categories: probability sampling and nonprobability sampling" (p. 207). From this researcher's review of Ali (2007) and Clarke-Anderson (2004) studies, it was understood that the sample design of:

- Ali (2007) used a probability cluster sampling of participants using pre-established criteria.
- Clarke-Anderson (2004) used a stratified random selection of study participants.

As stated in Brooks (2019),

> *Despite spending millions on corporate diversity efforts, U.S. companies aren't retaining black professionals or promoting them to top positions, causing many of those workers to walk out the doors in frustration, according to a new report. Black people account for about 12% of the U.S. population, but occupy only 3.2% of the senior leadership roles at large companies in the U.S. and just 0.8% of all Fortune 500 CEO positions, according to the analysis by the Center for Talent Innovation, a workplace think tank in New York City. The study was funded by Disney, Pfizer and other major corporate players. Its conclusions were drawn from a survey conducted online and via telephone in June of more than 3,700 people who work in white-collar jobs and have at least a bach-*

elor's degree (n.p.).

In this study, the researcher utilized the same sampling approach used by Clarke-Anderson's study which was a stratified random sampling. There was an advantage to using this sampling method due to the likelihood "of guaranteeing equal representation of each of the identified strata. It is, of course, most appropriate when those strata are roughly equal in size in the overall population as well" (Leedy & Ormrod, 2012, p.211). Again, the researcher planned to use an anonymous, Likert-type online survey to collect the data using a stratified random sampling approach.

Sample Size

In keeping with Leedy and Ormrod (2012), a basic rule of thumb in determining the sample size is: "the larger the sample, the better. But such a generalized rule is not very helpful to a researcher who must make a practical decision about a specific research situation" (p. 215). For this study, the researcher anticipated approximately 400+ individuals participating in the anonymous online survey from the 12% of Blacks living in the United States. The researcher e-mailed potential adult participants an online survey using both a social network, LinkedIn, that focused on professional networking and career development and a survey tool, SurveyMonkey, to capture the voices and opinions of the people who mattered most to the study. None of the participants were compensated as all participation in this research study was voluntary. At any time, the research participants could choose not to participate. And, all sampled participants could refuse to participate or withdraw from the study at any time. Further, if the sampled participants chose not to participate, no part of their data would be used in the research.

Data Collection Methods

Collecting data in descriptive studies invariably involved the procurement and measurement of one or more variables for quantitative research designs. According to Leedy, Paul D., and Jeanne Ellis Ormrod (2012), there existed two distinctions of phenomena – substantial and insubstantial:

> *When studying the nature of substantial phenomena—phenomena that have physical substance, an obvious basis in the physical world—a researcher can often use measurement instruments that are clearly valid for their purpose. Tape measures, balance scales, oscilloscopes, MRI machines—these instruments are indisputably valid for measuring length, weight, electrical waves, and internal body structures, respectively. Some widely accepted measurement techniques also exist for studying insubstantial phenomena —concepts, abilities, and other intangible entities that cannot be pinned down in terms of precise physical qualities (p.191).*

These authors further suggested that many descriptive studies were being conducted on complex variables where there did not exist a "ready to use" measurement instrument. In this study, the researcher e-mailed potential adult participants in an online survey using both a social network, LinkedIn, that focused on professional networking and career development and a survey tool, SurveyMonkey, to capture the voices and opinions of the people who mattered most to the study (see Appendix A). Having said, the researcher constructed and utilized an anonymous Likert-type survey questionnaire that was completed using SurveyMonkey technology by all sampled Black Fortune 500 participants. The data collection timing was originally scheduled for two weeks; however, due to the COVID-19 pandemic in April 2020, the survey data collection period was extended to two months.

Data Analysis Methods

In accordance with Leedy and Ormrod (2012), there were five suggestions for using technology to facilitate questionnaire administration and analyze the collected data: 1) "use e-mail to request participation and obtain participants' responses"; 2) "if you use paper mail delivery rather than e-mail, use a word processing program to personalize your correspondence"; 3) "use a computer database to keep track of who has responded and who has not"; 4) "use a scanner to facilitate data tabulation"; and 5) "when participants are in the same location that you are, administer the questionnaire directly on a computer" (p.201). That said, in the literature review of two Ali (2007) and Clarke-Anderson (2004), the researcher found that

- Ali (2007) analyzed the data of 41 surveys received from responding participants, eliminated one survey, and achieved a return rate of 60% from the web-based survey. The dependent and independent variables were tested and analyzed using the Pearson's Correlation Coefficient and the One-Sample t test.
- In Clarke-Anderson (2004) study, a statistical analysis was used to "test the research questions and hypotheses for this study was conducted through a progression or series of analyses using a common test for correlation that produces a result called r, known as the Pearson Correlation Coefficient" (p.60).

After the literature review of both studies, the researcher implemented the suggested data analysis techniques along with the statistical tests (Statistical Package for Social Sciences).

Additionally, Leedy and Ormrod (2012) argued that "collecting data for study and organizing it for inspection require care and precision, extracting meaning from the data —the interpretation of the data—is all-important" (p.220). In the Ali (2007) study, the Pearson correlation coefficient results showed a noteworthy positive relationship. Additionally, in the Clarke-Anderson (2004) study, the data analysis of the independent and dependent variables showed no significant relationship. As illustrated, both studies used statistical instruments to validate the findings and each acknowledges the probable presence of bias. This researcher collected data for the study using statistical tests in SurveyMonkey and Minitab 19 software.

Bias

As reported by Leedy and Ormrod (2012), in quantitative research "bias is any influence, condition, or set of conditions that singly or in combination distort the data. Data are, in many respects, delicate and sensitive to unintended influences (p.217). Potential biases acknowledged by the researcher included but was not limited to: 1) sampling bias; 2) internet-based questionnaires – "studies involving Internet-based questionnaires are apt to be biased in favor of computer-literate individuals with easy access to the Internet" (Leedy & Ormrod, 2012, p.217); 3) generalizations – "the researcher's generalization may not be accurate. We need to consider how the nonrespondents" could be different from respondents to the online questionnaire (Leedy & Ormrod,

2012, p.217); 4) non-probability sampling; 5) convenience sampling – "people who happen to be readily available for a research project—those who are in the right place at the right time—are almost certainly not a random sample of the overall population" (Leedy & Ormrod, 2012, p.218); and 6) response rate – "potential differences between respondents and nonrespondents—was the source of bias" (Leedy & Ormrod, 2012, p.218). The researcher endeavored to eliminate all aspects of bias in this study.

Methodological Assumptions

Ellis & Levy (2009) stated that methodological assumptions "can be viewed as something the researcher accepts as true without a concrete proof. Essentially, there is no research study without a basic set of assumptions" (p.331). As an African American professional, having worked in a Fortune 500 organization, this researcher acknowledged his deep beliefs regarding racial inequality in Corporate America to which may result in methodological assumptions. Further, the researcher understood that it was imperative for new researchers to grasp a firm understanding of how to accurately "document their assumptions in order to ensure that they are aware of those things taken as givens, rather than trying to hide or smear them from the reader. Explicitly documenting the research assumptions may help reduce misunderstanding and resistance" (Ellis & Levy, 2009, p.331). Furthermore, the researcher's assumptions were that: (1) all participants would participate voluntarily and would respond to questions completely, honestly, and openly; (2) black professionals are employed by Fortune 500 organizations in the United States; (3) ongoing changes in the customer demand, requirements for career development/attrition, and financial impacts would continue during the global COVID-19 pandemic; and (4) the total population and labor markets will continue to diversity.

Trustworthiness

The trustworthiness of research methodology is a concern for some organizational managers due to the belief that what appears to work for one firm may not work for their firm (Degen, 2017). According to Degen (2017), due to this logic, organizational leadership "need to form their own assessment as to which theories are potentially enduring for and applicable to their particular case and so are trustworthy; and which are tinted by particular circumstances or are simply just management fads" (p. 19). Leedy & Ormrod (2012) stated that "not all research data need to be collected through careful, thoughtful sampling procedures. But without such safeguards, the conclusions drawn from the research may not be trustworthy" (p. 214). With respect given to trustworthiness of the applied theories and collected research data, this researcher argued that the questionnaire and sampling procedures were executed with great thought and care for the purpose of collecting trustworthy data for conclusive analysis.

Subject Matter Experts (SMEs)

This descriptive correlational study aimed to seek the assistance of professional researchers to simplify the survey instrument's content/wording, questions, and "reduce bias; improve reliability, and validity of each question" (Williams, 2014, p. 81). For the study, the researcher hired the service of SurveyMonkey, an online survey development cloud-based software company, to both design and score a survey instrument that would minimize bias and maximize the questionnaire return rate. During the study, participants were asked to use the SurveyMonkey online survey software system to complete an internet-based questionnaire called the 2020

Fortune 500 Company Morale Survey (see Appendix C). This survey consisted of 11 questions relating to each participant's demographics, 36 questions that ranged from strongly agree to strongly disagree according to how each statement applied to them, and two questions with comment boxes that afforded the participants the opportunity to describe their personal experience(s). According to this researcher, there were no needed changes or revisions to the survey instrument's wording, content, or questions and the subject matter expert, SurveyMonkey, categorized the survey as "Great" with an estimated completion rate of 75% and a 16-minute estimated time of completion.

Credibility

Drawing meaningful and credible conclusions from this study, the researcher endeavored to answer two fundamental questions, "first, does the study have sufficient controls to ensure that the conclusions drawn are truly warranted by the data? And second, can the results obtained reasonably be used to generalize about the world beyond that specific research context?" (Leedy & Ormrod, 2012, p.101). To defend the validity of the study, the researcher addressed the common validity issues – internal, face, criterion related, construct, content, statistical conclusion, & external – that disrupt the credibility of quantitative/qualitative research designs (Ellis & Levy, 2009). To determine the validity of the measurement instrument, the researcher submitted the questionnaire to Institutional Research Board (IRB) experts and asked that the instrument be scrutinized and to give an informed opinion about its validity for measuring the characteristics in question.

Transferability

The term transferability was used to describe the method of applying the results from this research on the relationship between the imposed unfair treatment, company ineffectiveness, and lack of respect & employee recognition of African American Fortune 500 professionals and the fewer opportunities for advancement, job dissatisfaction, negative perceptions of the job itself, and high turnover rates amongst blacks to other similar situations in similar organizational structures. As stated by Colorado State University (2020),

> *Transferability is a process performed by readers of research. Readers note the specifics of the research situation and compare them to the specifics of an environment or situation with which they are familiar. If there are enough similarities between the two situations, readers may be able to infer that the results of the research would be the same or similar in their own situation. In other words, they "transfer" the results of a study to another context. To do this effectively, readers need to know as much as possible about the original research situation to determine whether it is similar to their own. Therefore, researchers must supply a highly detailed description of their research situation and methods (n.p.).*

Despite transferability being most relevant to qualitative research methods, this researcher suggested that the results of this study could be applied to organizations that are not Fortune 500 industries.

Ethical Considerations

As in all studies, the researcher was made aware of and attended to the ethical considerations related to the well-being of study participants. Mills, G. & Gay, L. (2019) stated that

> *In research, the ends do not justify the means, and researchers must not put the need or desire to carry out a study above the responsibility to maintain the well-being of the study participants. Research studies are built on trust between the researcher and the participants, and researchers have a responsibility to behave in a trustworthy manner, just as they expect participants to behave in the same manner (e.g., by providing responses that can be trusted). The two overriding rules of ethics are that participants should not be harmed in any way—physically, mentally, or socially—and that researchers obtain the participants' informed consent (p. 61).*

These ethical considerations assisted the leader in the overall development of a research methodology that would promote and support the safety and security of the volunteering human subjects and the assets of the researcher in an ethical and legal manner.

Confidentiality

Before the commencement or recruitment of human subjects and data collection, the researcher documented the entire research protocol and submitted the new research project request to the Oakland City University's (OCU) Institutional Review Board (IRB). The purpose of the IRB was to ensure that the research design conformed to state and national laws regarding the ethical treatment of human subjects. After gaining approval for the study (see Appendix D), the researcher began the process of recruiting potential participants and informed them all about how the study would be conducted under the approval of the Oakland City University

IRB, and how their confidentiality and rights would be protected through guidelines set forth in the IRB policy.

One of the requirements of this process was the development of an Informed Consent release. In the Informed Consent (see Appendix B), the participants were: (1) invited to voluntarily participate in the study; (2) provided with the purpose/significance of the study; (3) informed about the participant's tasks, survey timing, and research location; (4) advised of potential benefits (and no know exposure risks) of participating in the study; (5) told how their information would be protected. There were no identifiers within this survey and all submissions were anonymous, so subject privacy was automatically ensured; and (6) given the researcher's contact information for any questions and/or concerns regarding their consent to the study.

Procedures

The researcher e-mailed all potential adult participants an invitation to participate in an online survey using both a social network, LinkedIn, that focuses on professional networking and career development and a survey tool, SurveyMonkey, to capture the voices and opinions of the people who mattered most to the study. Through both LinkedIn and SurveyMonkey, the researcher presented the OCU informed consent form that described the nature of the research project, as well as the nature of one's participation in the study. After being presented with the opportunity to ask the researcher any questions about the research, the participant would voluntarily decide whether to participate in the study or not. By selecting "OK" and "Next" buttons, the participant certified that they had read and understood the OCU informed consent, were over 18 years of age, and had decided to participate in the study. Responses to the anonymous online survey were collected and stored on a password-protected, external hard drive that was locked in a file cabinet for 3 years. Further, to comply with record retention requirements, the researcher planned to: 1) keep password-protected electronic files on the OKC University network (drive) as it was reliable and backed up; 2) store password-protected data directly on his own laptop or PC outside the University network; 3) have a rigorous backup system in case his device crashed, or was lost or stolen; 4) use password-protected, external hard drive and save his data regularly. And, the researcher would have a safe place to keep his hard drive and remember to take it with him when necessary; and 5) maintain all primary & secondary documentation/notes to be organized, stored, and kept track of in a locked filing cabinet for a minimum of three years.

Limitations

According to Simon & Goes (2013), limitations are "matters and occurrences that arise in a study which are out of the researcher's control. They limit the extensity to which a study can go, and sometimes affect the end result and conclusions that can be drawn" (p.1). Additionally, "correlational research may also have limitations with respect to the generality of the findings. Perhaps the study involved a specific group of people, or that the relationship between the variables was only investigated under some situation or circumstance" (Simon & Goes, 2013, p.2). Lastly, questionnaire surveys often "suffer the limitation of forcing respondents into particular response categories, thereby limiting the range of responses. Unlike an interview, where respondents can ask clarifying questions, respondents are usually limited to the text in the survey for direction" (Simon & Goes, 2013, p.2). The researcher aimed to address any limitations of scope, generality of findings from the correlational study, and potential for limiting questionnaire responses during the design of this study.

The researcher acknowledged the viewpoints on the limitations of the scientific method in this quantitative study. According to Mills, G. & Gay, L. (2019), when preparing, administering, and explaining research studies, it was important to understand the limitations, biases, theoretical precedents, and influences of quantitative research such as: (1) the "scientific method cannot answer all questions. For example, applying the scientific method will not resolve the question "Should we legalize euthanasia?" The answers to questions like this one are influenced by personal philosophy, values, and ethics" (p.5); (2) the

> *Application of the scientific method can never capture the full richness of the individuals and the environments under study. Although some applications of the method lead to deeper understanding of the research context than others, no application—and in fact no research approach—provides full comprehension of a site and its inhabitants. No matter how many variables one studies or how long one is immersed in a research context, other variables and aspects of context will remain unexamined. Thus, the scientific method and, indeed, all types of inquiry give us a simplified version of reality; (3) our measuring instruments always have some degree of error. The variables we study are often proxies for the real behavior we seek to examine. For example, even if we use a very precisely constructed multiple-choice test to assess a person's values, we will likely gather information that gives us a picture of that person's beliefs about his or her values. However, we aren't likely to have an adequate picture of how that person acts, which may be the better reflection of the person's real values (p. 5).*

Having said, the researcher recognized that there were influences foundational to the validity of the study and the research was carried out with the cooperation of participants who agreed to voluntarily provide open and honest Likert-style survey data to mitigate potential biases (Mills, G. & Gay, L., 2019).

Delimitations

The delimitations of this research design originated from the defined scope of work, exclusive & inclusive boundaries set during the development of the body of work, and decisions made by the researcher (Simon & Goes, 2013). In short, the delimitations spoke to all things that the study would not do (Ellis & Levy, 2009). To best clarify all delimitations of the study, it was suggested that researcher clearly state the objective within the purpose statement, pronounce all subjects that would be excluded from the study, and affirmed the decision to exclude subjects from the scope of work "based on such criteria as not directly relevant; *too problematic* because...; *not feasible* and the like" (Simon & Goes, 2013, p.3). That said, the researcher utilized a descriptive correlational, quantitative research design with an ultimate goal of learning about a large Fortune 500 population by surveying a sample of the entire adult, professional population which also consisted of Fortune 500 African Americans, People of Color, and Whites.

Summary

In this methodological chapter, the researcher provided enough information for an experienced researcher to reproduce this study. To that end, the methodology chapter described the stratified random sampling approach and descriptive correlational, quantitative research design, role of the researcher, voluntary participant selection criteria, anonymous Likert-type survey data collection procedures, and data analysis plan using statistical tests in SurveyMonkey and Minitab software. Furthermore, the method of research chapter described how reliability and validity of the data were confirmed and how participants were treated ethically. With a substantial methodological framework linked to a solid review of related literature, the reader would be able to verify the trustworthiness and reliability of the findings, conclusions, and implications presented during the interpretation of the study's data.

CHAPTER IV: PRESENTATION AND INTERPRETATION OF DATA

Restatement of the Purpose

The purpose of this study was to understand the complexities of the racial inequality of African American professionals in their Fortune 500 workplaces and develop a theoretical model of the constructs that predicted perceptions that employees of color had about their workplace arenas in the following areas: respect & treatment, company effectiveness, the job itself, and teamwork & cooperation.

Research Questions

The researcher's study of racial inequality was based on the extent to which African American professionals exhibit negative perceptions of their workplaces resulting in high turnover. Specifically, the researcher asked the following quantitative research questions:

- To what extent are lack of employee recognition, lack of career opportunities, job dissatisfaction, company ineffectiveness, and high job turnover correlated to employees' race in Fortune 500 companies?

■ How do differences in the racial composition of teams influence teamwork and cooperation in Fortune 500 companies?

Overview of Participants

A researcher-created questionnaire was utilized to collect study data from volunteering participants on the largest professional network on the internet, LinkedIn. All study procedures took place using an online survey software – SurveyMonkey. The researcher used this online technology to facilitate an internet-based questionnaire and analyzed the collected data. The sample for this quantitative descriptive correctional study consisted of n = 502 with a return rate of 419 participants which was an acceptable return rate of 83.5%, utilizing a stratified random sampling selection process. See Figure 4.1

Q1 **I have read** the informed consent provided by Principal Investigator or Student Researcher, D'uAndre A. Drain, and included as the introduction to this survey. The informed consent to participate in the study titled, African-American Racial Equality in U.S. Labor Market: Negative Perception Theory, is understandable to me. I have been given the opportunity to ask questions and any questions that I may have had have been answered to my satisfaction. If I have additional questions, I have been provided with their contact information. I agree or decline to participate in the research study described above and can obtain a copy of the informed consent by contacting the investigator or researcher.

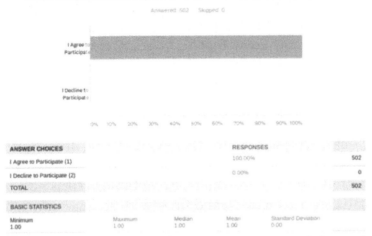

Figure 4.1: Overview of Agreement to participate in the Research Study

Participants' Gender

All research participants were asked to identify their gender for the study. Of the 419 survey respondents, males represented 74.7% (313), females represented 24.58% (103), 0.48% (2) chose not to identify their gender, and 0.24% (1) identified as other. See Figure 4.2.

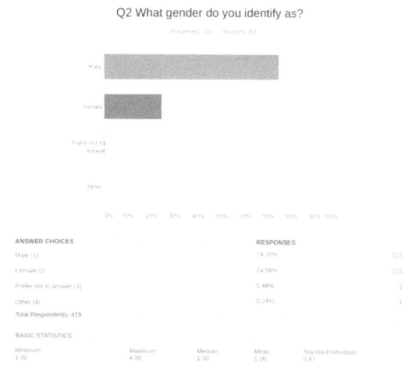

Figure 4.2: Overview of Participants' Gender

Participants' Age Groups

All research participants were requested to state their age for the study. Of the 419 survey respondents, 37.47% (157) responded that they were in the 45 – 54 age group while 34.13% (143) recorded that they were 35 – 44, 15.27% (64) were 55 – 64, 1.91% (8) were 65+, and 0.24% (1) was 18 – 24 years of age. See Figure 4.3.

Figure 4.3: Overview of Participants' Age Group

Participants' Ethnicity

All research participants were asked to describe their ethnic background for the study. Of the 419 survey respondents, 82.58% (346) identified as Black or African American while 13.13% (55) stated White or Caucasian, 2.86% (12) were Hispanic or Latino, 1.91% (8) identified as "another race", 0.95% (4) as Asian or Asian American, and 0.95% (4) were American Indian or Alaska Native. See Figure 4.4.

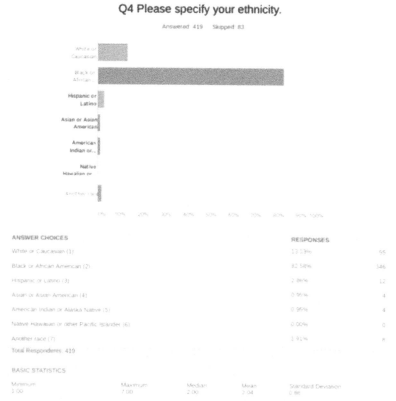

Figure 4.4: Overview of Participants' Ethnic Background

Participants' Birth Country

All research participants were asked to specify their places of birth for the study. Of the 419 survey respondents, 92.6% (388) stated that they were born in North America while 1.19% (5) reported Europe, 1.19% (5) from Africa, 1.19% (5) said Asia, 0.95% (4) claimed Caribbean Islands, 0.95% (4) from Central America, 0.48% (2) recorded South America, 0.24% (1) each reported Australia, Pacific Islander, and "other" respectively. See Figure 4.5.

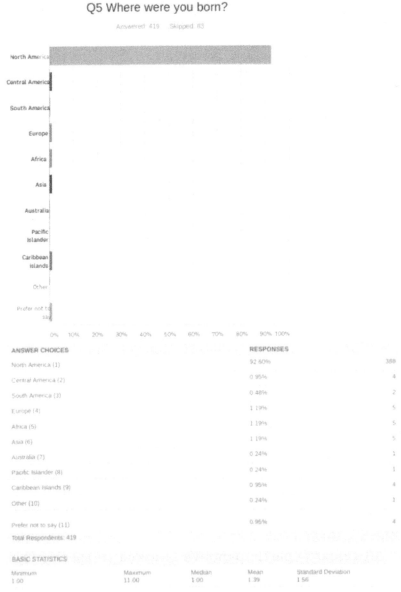

Figure 4.5: Overview of Participants' Country of Birth

Participants' Religious Background

All research participants were asked to record their

religious background for the study. Of the 419 survey respondents, 73.03% (306) expressed that they affiliated with Catholicism/Christianity while 18.85% (79) reported "other", 5.49% (23) preferred not to say, 0.95% (4) claimed Judaism, 0.95% (4) were of Islamic faith, 0.72% (3) practiced Buddhism, and 0.48% said Hinduism. See Figure 4.6.

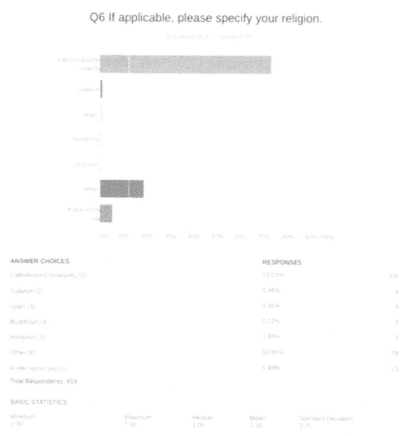

Figure 4.6: Overview of Participants' Religious Affiliation

Participants' Highest Level Of Educational Attainment

All research participants were asked to provide their highest degree or level of education that they completed for this study. Of the 419 survey respondents, 43.2% (181) attained Master's degrees while 38.66% (162) achieved Bachelor's degrees, 7.4% (31) reached Ph.D. or higher, 4.53% (19) reported "other", 4.3% (18) earned high school diplomas, 2.39% (10) completed trade school, 1.19% (5) preferred not to say, and 0.24% (1) completed some high school curriculum. See Figure 4.7.

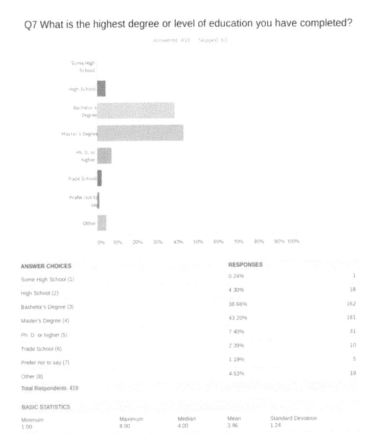

Figure 4.7: Overview of Participants' Highest Educational Attainment

Participants' Country Of Residence

All research participants were asked to note their home location for this study. Of the 419 survey respondents, 96.9% (406) specified North America/Central America as their permanent residence while 0.95% (4) entered Asia, 0.72% (3) said Europe, 0.48% (2) preferred not to say, 0.24% (1) each reported South America, Africa, Australia, and "other" respectively. See Figure 4.8.

Figure 4.8: Overview of Participants' Country of Residence

Participants' Marital Status

All research participants were asked to specify their marital status for this study. Of the 419 survey respondents, 64.44% (270) responded "yes", when asked if they were married, while 34.13% (143) said "no". There were 1.43% (6) respondents that preferred not to classify their marital status. See Figure 4.9.

Figure 4.9: Overview of Participants' Marital Status

Participants' Current Employment Status

All research participants were asked to indicate their current employment status for this study. Of the 419 survey respondents, 84.25% (353) noted that they were employed full-time while 8.11% (34) stated that they were seeking opportunities, 4.53% (19) were retired, 3.10% (13) categorized their employment as "other", 2.63% (11) were employed part-time, and 0.95% (4) preferred not to say. See Figure 4.10.

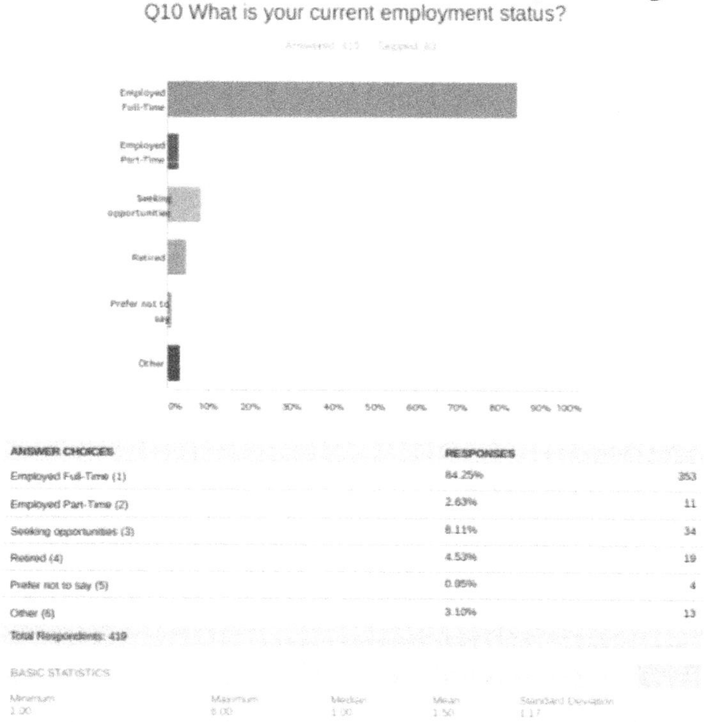

Q10 What is your current employment status?

ANSWER CHOICES	RESPONSES	
Employed Full-Time (1)	84.25%	353
Employed Part-Time (2)	2.63%	11
Seeking opportunities (3)	8.11%	34
Retired (4)	4.53%	19
Prefer not to say (5)	0.95%	4
Other (6)	3.10%	13
Total Respondents: 419		

BASIC STATISTICS

Minimum	Maximum	Median	Mean	Standard Deviation
1.00	6.00	1.00	1.50	1.17

Figure 4.10: Overview of Participants' Current Employment Status

Participants' Fortune 500 Employment

All research participants were asked to assert whether they worked for a Fortune 500 company. Of the 419 survey respondents, 57.52% (241) stated that they did not work for a Fortune 500 company while 42.48% (178) declared that they were Fortune 500 employees. See Figure 4.11.

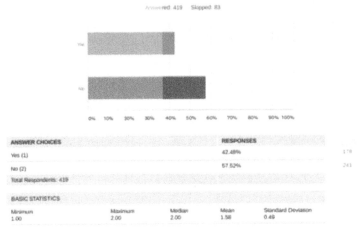

Figure 4.11: Overview of Participants' Fortune 500 Employment

Participants' Job Classification

All research participants were asked to categorize their type of work for the study. Of the 419 survey respondents, 58.47% (245) designated themselves as officials and managers, 12.41% (52) categorized as sales workers, 8.35% (35) were technicians, 6.21% (26) were service workers, 3.1% (13) were skilled craft workers, 2.86% (12) were office and clerical workers, 1.91% (8) were semi-skilled operatives, and 0.48% (2) designated as unskilled laborers. See Figure 4.12.

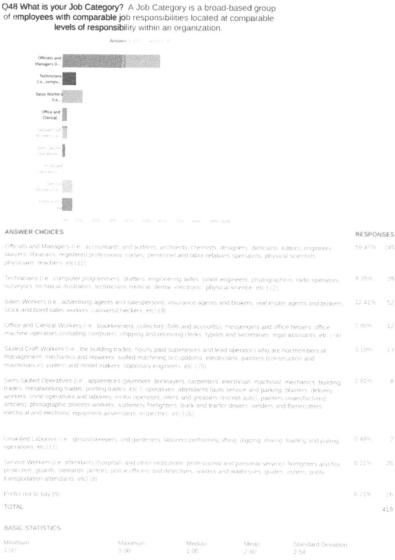

Figure 4.12: Overview of Participants' Job Categories

Participants' Job Length Of Service

All research participants were asked to detail the number of years worked for their organization. Of the 419 survey respondents, 23.15% (97) disclosed that they had been employed for 15+ years while 21% (88) specified their employment as 3 – 5 years, 18.14% (76) said 1 – 2 years, 13.6% (57) for 6 – 9 years, 12.41% (52) for less than a year, and 11.69% (49) reported 10 – 15 years length of service on the job. See Figure 4.13.

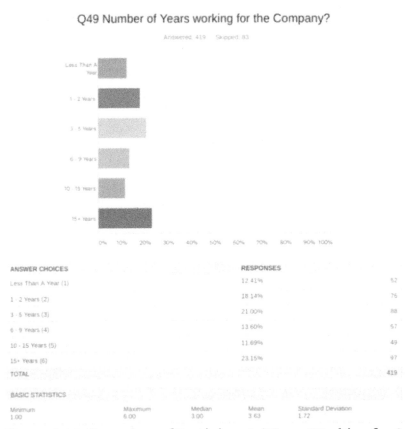

Figure 4.13: Overview of Participants' Years Working for Company

Findings for Each Research Hypothesis

Hypothesis 1

The research tested the following hypotheses: *Alternative Hypothesis 1* – African American professionals report more unfair treatment than Caucasian professionals in Fortune 500 companies, and *Null Hypothesis 1* – African American professionals do not report more unfair treatment than Caucasian professionals in Fortune 500 companies. The findings for respect & treatment in concern reporting were as follows:

From the sample of 419 respondents, the researcher discovered that 33 (19.88%) Whites or Caucasians and 134 (80.72%) Blacks or African Americans reported that they worked for a Fortune 500 company (See Figure 4.14). To bring to light the White and Black survey participants' reporting of unfair treatment, the researcher asked fourteen questions to uncover their perceptions of their individual respect and treatment within their Fortune 500 organizations.

Figure 4.14: Comparative Sample of Whites & Blacks Working

for Fortune 500

Of the 166 respondents, the researcher asked if each subject believed that their organization's management supported diversity in their workplace. When comparing both Whites' and Blacks' perceptions, the researcher discovered a 95% confidence level (p=0.05), significantly higher statistical difference in Whites (54.55%) strongly agreeing that company management supported diversity than Blacks (17.91%). When analyzing the statistical difference in disagreement, the researcher discovered a 95% confidence level (when a = 0.05 then p<0.05, P-value is the probability of making a Type I error. We say that the decision is made at the 95% (1-a) confidence level); therefore, the null hypothesis was rejected due to a significantly higher statistical difference in Blacks (17.91%) disagreeing that company management supported diversity than Whites (3.03%). See Figure 4.15.

Figure 4.15: Whites & Blacks Perception of Company Management and Diversity

Of the 166 respondents, the researcher asked if each subject believed that their company provided a working environment that accepts differences in team member backgrounds, cultures, and lifestyles. When comparing both Whites' and Blacks' perceptions, the researcher discovered a 95% confidence level (p<0.05), significantly higher statistical difference in Whites (48.48%) strongly agreeing that the company provides an environment of acceptance for differences in diversity than Blacks (19.4%). When analyzing the statistical difference in neutrality, the researcher discovered a 95% confidence level (p<0.05), significantly higher statistical difference in Blacks (14.93%) that were neither agreeing or disagreeing that their company supported diverse backgrounds, cultures, and lifestyles than Whites (0%). Null hypothesis was rejected. See Figure 4.16.

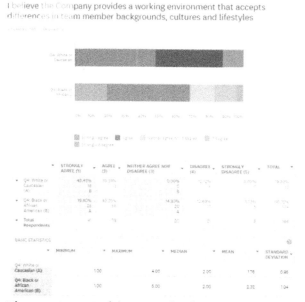

Figure 4.16: Whites & Blacks Perception of Company Acceptance of Differences

Of the 166 respondents, the researcher asked if each

subject believed that their company demonstrated care and concern for the employees. When comparing both Whites' and Blacks' perceptions, the researcher discovered a 95% confidence level (p<0.05), significantly higher statistical difference in Whites (54.55%) strongly agreeing that the company provides care and concern than Blacks (17.91%). Null hypothesis was rejected. See Figure 4.17.

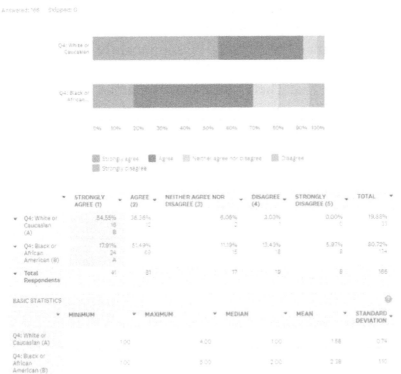

Figure 4.17: Whites & Blacks Perception of Company Care and Concern

Of the 166 respondents, the researcher asked if each subject believed that their company's policies were applied consistently for each employee. When comparing both Whites' and Blacks' perceptions, the researcher discovered a 95% confidence level (p<0.05), significantly higher statistical difference in Whites (36.36%) strongly agreeing that the company was consistent in applying organizational policies than Blacks (11.94%). Null hypothesis was rejected. See Figure 4.18.

Figure 4.18: Whites & Blacks Perception of Company's Policies and Consistency

Of the 166 respondents, the researcher asked if each subject believed that their company's policies were applied consistently to them, as individuals, over the past 12 months. When comparing both Whites' and Blacks' perceptions, the researcher discovered a 95% confidence level (p<0.05), significantly higher statistical difference in Whites (45.45%) strongly agreeing that the company was consistent in personally applying organizational policies than Blacks (16.42%).

Null hypothesis was rejected. See Figure 4.19.

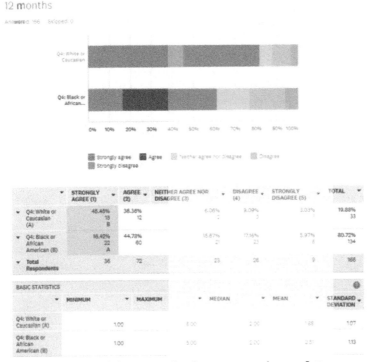

Figure 4.19: Whites & Blacks Perception of Company Policy Application

Of the 166 respondents, if they responded that they believed their company's policies were not consistently applied to them, the researcher asked the participant to state the respective policy(ies). After reviewing each typed survey response, the researcher assigned eight labels/tags to group the responses into the following categories: (1) compliance; (2) equal pay; (3) fairness & consistency of applied policies across all employees; (4) favoritism/nepotism; (5) promotion & growth equal opportunities; (6) rewards & recognition; (7) respect for people; and (8) work life balance. All non-applicable (N/As or Ns) and non-specific responses were left untagged.

NEGATIVE PERCEPTION THEORY

Of the eight tags, Blacks reported more unfair treatment than Caucasian professionals in the following response labels: a) Compliance – 6.1% (B) vs 5.88% (W); b) Fairness & Consistency – 18.29% (B) vs 17.65% (W); c) Favoritism/Nepotism – 9.76% (B) vs 5.88% (W); d) Promotion & Growth Opportunities – 26.83% (B) vs 17.65% (W); and e) Respect for People – 15.85% (B) vs 11.76% (W). In addition to the eight tags, the researcher used SurveyMonkey to create a word cloud to highlight specific words that reoccurred in the typed responses. See Figure 4.20.

Figure 4.20: Which Company Policies were not Applied Consistently over 12 months?

Of the 166 respondents, the researcher asked if each subject believed that they were able to maintain a balance between their company work and personal lives. When comparing both Whites' and Blacks' perceptions, the researcher discovered no statistical difference in Whites' and Blacks' agreeing and/or disagreeing responses regarding their overall work life balance. When analyzing the statistical difference in neutrality, the researcher discovered no statistical difference in Blacks' and Whites' neither agree nor disagree responses. See Figure 4.21.

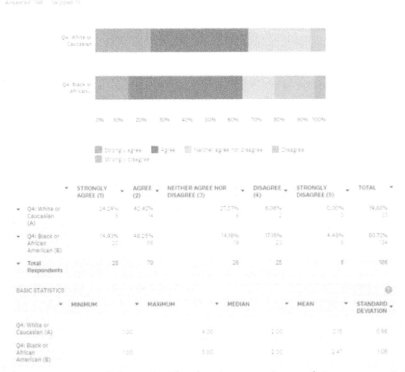

Figure 4.21: Whites & Blacks Perception of Company Work Life Balance

Of the 166 respondents, the researcher asked if each subject believed that their organization adequately addressed complaints of discrimination, harassment, or unethical business conduct in their workplace. When comparing

NEGATIVE PERCEPTION THEORY

both Whites' and Blacks' perceptions, the researcher discovered a 95% confidence level (p<0.05), significantly higher statistical difference in Whites (45.45%) strongly agreeing that company addressed complaints of discrimination, harassment, or unethical business conduct than Blacks (18.66%). When analyzing the statistical difference in disagreement, the researcher discovered a 95% confidence level (p<0.05), significantly higher statistical difference in Blacks (17.91%) disagreeing that company addressed complaints of discrimination, harassment, or unethical business conduct than Whites (0%). When analyzing the statistical difference in neutrality, the researcher discovered a 95% confidence level (p<0.05), significantly higher statistical difference in Blacks (24.63%) that were neither agreeing or disagreeing that their company addressed complaints of discrimination, harassment, or unethical business conduct than Whites (0%). Null hypothesis was rejected. See Figure 4.22.

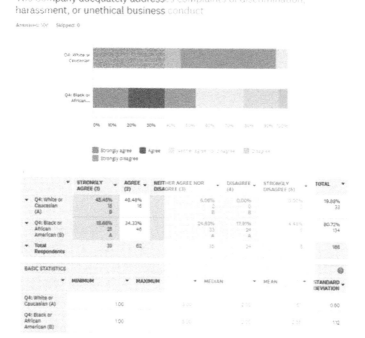

Figure 4.22: Whites & Blacks Perception of Companies Ad-

dressing Complaints

Of the 166 respondents, the researcher asked if their organization took action to prevent discrimination, harassment, or unethical business conduct in their workplace. When comparing both Whites' and Blacks' perceptions, the researcher discovered a 95% confidence level (p<0.05), significantly higher statistical difference in Whites (48.48%) strongly agreeing that company took action to prevent discrimination, harassment, or unethical business conduct than Blacks (20.15%). When analyzing the statistical difference in disagreement, the researcher discovered no statistical difference in Blacks (13.43%) disagreeing that company took action to prevent discrimination, harassment, or unethical business conduct than Whites (6.06%). When analyzing the statistical difference in neutrality, the researcher discovered a 95% confidence level (p<0.05), significantly higher statistical difference in Blacks (20.15%) that were neither agreeing or disagreeing that their company took action to prevent discrimination, harassment, or unethical business conduct than Whites (3.03%).

Null hypothesis was rejected. See Figure 4.23.

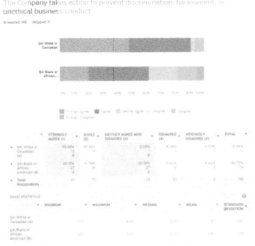

Figure 4.23: Whites & Blacks Perception of Company Taking

Actions

Of the 166 respondents, the researcher asked if their work environment was free from all forms of discrimination or harassment. When comparing both Whites' and Blacks' perceptions, the researcher discovered a 95% confidence level (p<0.05), significantly higher statistical difference in Whites (27.27%) strongly agreeing that their work environment was free from all forms of discrimination or harassment than Blacks (11.19%). When analyzing the statistical difference in disagreement, the researcher discovered a 95% confidence level (p<0.05), significantly higher statistical difference in Blacks (31.34%) disagreeing that their work environment was free from all forms of discrimination or harassment than Whites (12.12%). Null hypothesis was rejected. See Figure 4.24.

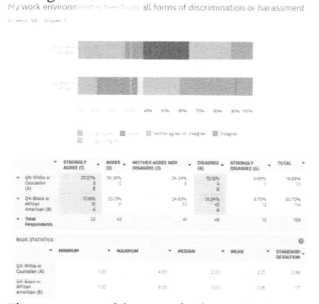

Figure 4.24: Whites & Blacks Perception of Company Work Environments

Of the 166 respondents, the researcher asked if each subject felt comfortable reporting a problem regarding discrimination or harassment in their workplace. When comparing both Whites' and Blacks' perceptions, the researcher discovered a 95% confidence level (p<0.05), significantly higher statistical difference in Whites (51.52%) strongly agreeing that they felt comfortable reporting a problem regarding discrimination or harassment in their workplace than Blacks (25.37%). Null hypothesis was rejected. When analyzing the statistical difference in disagreement, the researcher discovered no statistical difference in Blacks (14.93%) disagreeing that they felt comfortable reporting a problem regarding discrimination or harassment in their workplace than Whites (6.06%). See Figure 4.25.

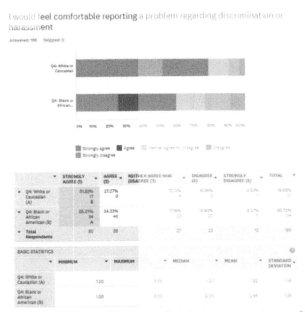

Figure 4.25: Whites & Blacks Perception of Comfort Reporting Discrimination

Of the 166 respondents, the researcher asked if each subject knew what to do if they saw unlawful harassment in their workplace. When comparing both Whites' and Blacks' perceptions, the researcher discovered a 95% confidence

NEGATIVE PERCEPTION THEORY

level (p<0.05), significantly higher statistical difference in Whites (66.67%) strongly agreeing that they knew what to do if they saw unlawful harassment in their workplace than Blacks (43.28%). Null hypothesis was rejected. When analyzing the statistical difference in disagreement, the researcher discovered no statistical difference in Blacks (0.75%) disagreeing that they knew what to do if they saw unlawful harassment in their workplace than Whites (0%). See Figure 4.26.

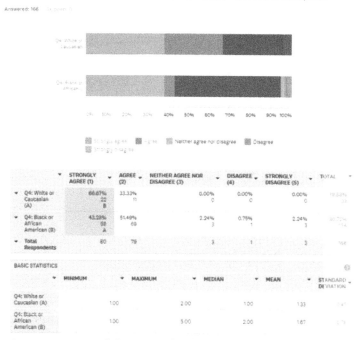

Figure 4.26: Whites & Blacks Perception of Company Unlawful Harassment

Of the 166 respondents, the researcher asked if the hours that they were being asked to work were reasonable, based on their company's business requirements and personal needs. When comparing both Whites' and Blacks' perceptions, the researcher discovered a 95% confidence level (p<0.05), significantly higher statistical difference in Whites

(42.42%) strongly agreeing that the hours that they were being asked to work were reasonable, based on their company's business requirements and personal needs than Blacks (23.13%). Null hypothesis was rejected. When analyzing the statistical difference in disagreement, the researcher discovered no statistical difference in Blacks (2.24%) strongly disagreeing that the hours that they were being asked to work were reasonable, based on their company's business requirements and personal needs than Whites (0%). See Figure 4.27.

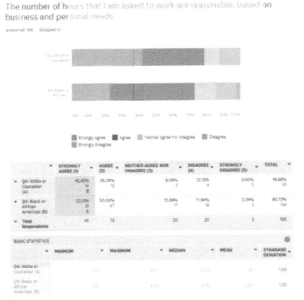

Figure 4.27: Whites & Blacks Perception of Company Balance of Personal Needs

Of the 166 respondents, the researcher directly asked if each subject was treated with respect as an individual. When comparing both Whites' and Blacks' perceptions, the researcher discovered no statistical difference in Whites (42.42%) strongly agreeing that they were treated with respect as an individual than Blacks (25.37%). When analyzing the statistical difference in disagreement, the researcher discovered no statistical difference in Blacks (2.24%) strongly disagreeing that they were treated with respect as an individual than Whites (0%). See Figure 4.28.

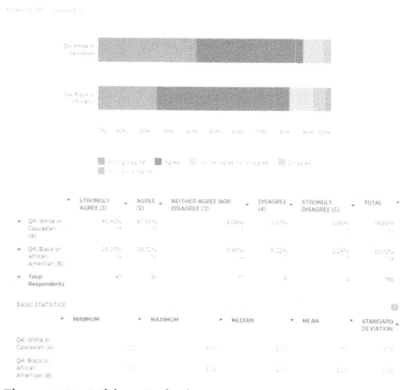

Figure 4.28: Whites & Blacks Perceptions of Individual Treatment with Respect

In summary of the findings for respect & treatment in concern reporting, the research tested *Hypothesis 1* – African American professionals report more unfair treatment than Caucasian professionals in Fortune 500 companies, *Null Hypothesis 1* – African American professionals do not report more unfair treatment than Caucasian professionals in Fortune 500 companies, and the researcher discovered a 95% confidence level (p=0.05) statistical difference in the sample of Black professionals reporting more unfair treatment than the sample of White professionals in Fortune 500 organizations. Using a SurveyMonkey two-sample t-test of fourteen questions, the researcher successfully examined whether the means of two independent groups (Blacks and Whites) were significantly different from one another. The sampled Blacks and Whites perceptions of their individual respect and treatment within their Fortune 500 organizations were found to be statistically different with more unfair treatment for Blacks across multiple variables; therefore, the researcher rejected the null hypothesis #1 due to multiple statistical differences in the mean and standard deviations (i.e., lack of care & concern, less respect for diverse backgrounds, cultures, unfair and inconsistent policy application with favoritism, less promotion and growth opportunities, less addressing and taking actions to prevent discrimination and unethical business conduct, etc.).

Hypothesis 2

The research tested the following hypotheses: *Alternative Hypothesis 2* – There is a predictable correlation between unfair treatment and fewer opportunities for career ascension of African American professionals in Fortune 500 companies, and *Null Hypothesis 2* – There is no predictable correlation between unfair treatment and fewer opportunities for career ascension of African American professionals in Fortune 500 companies. The findings for respect & treatment in career ascension were as follows:

From the sample of 419 respondents, the researcher discovered 134 (80.72%) Blacks or African Americans reported that they worked for a Fortune 500 company (See Figure 4.14). Using statistical correlation analysis to determine whether the values of hypothesis #2 variables were associated with one another, the researcher's findings for the survey participants revealed that the data variables change correspondingly. Specifically, when correlating the 134 Black survey participants' perceptions of career ascension with the company treatment of employees variables, the researcher discovered a 95% confidence interval ($p<0.05$) for the correlation coefficient, which infers that the correlation coefficient is statistically significant, of a positively correlated career ascension with each of the following company actions: (1) *supportive of diversity* – correlation coefficient (r) was 0.501, $p<0.000$, 95% CI 0.363 to 0.618; (2) *acceptance of different backgrounds, cultures, and lifestyles* – r was 0.412, $p<0.000$, 95% CI 0.260 to 0.544; (3) *demonstrates care & concern for employees* – r was 0.599, $p<0.000$, 95% CI 0.478 to 0.698; (4) *policies are applied consistently* – r was 0.537, $p<0.000$, 95% CI 0.404 to 0.647; (5) *policies have been consistently applied to the surveyed participant over the past 12 months* – r was 0.448, $p<0.000$, 95% CI 0.301 to 0.574; (6) *maintains a balance between employees' work and personal lives* – r was 0.244, $p<0.004$, 95% CI 0.078 to 0.397; (7) *addresses complaints of discrimination, harassment, or unethical business conduct* – r was 0.572, $p<0.000$, 95% CI 0.446 to 0.676; (8) *prevents discrimination, harassment, or unethical business conduct* – r was 0.506, $p<0.000$, 95% CI 0.368 to 0.622; and (9) *work environment is free from all forms of discrimination or harassment* – r was 0.406, $p<0.000$, 95% CI 0.253 to 0.538. Null hypothesis was rejected. See Table 4.1.

Correlation: Career Ascension, Supports Diversity, ... ork Environment

Correlations

	Career Ascension	Supports Diversi	Accepts Differen	Care & Concern
Supports Diversi	0.501			
	0.000			
Accepts Differen	0.412	0.707		
	0.000	0.000		
Care & Concern	0.599	0.639	0.646	
	0.000	0.000	0.000	
Consistent Polic	0.537	0.539	0.529	0.719
	0.000	0.000	0.000	0.000
12 Month Inconsi	0.448	0.393	0.335	0.536
	0.000	0.000	0.000	0.000
Work Life Balanc	0.244	0.404	0.298	0.307
	0.004	0.000	0.000	0.000
Addresses Discri	0.572	0.536	0.573	0.525
	0.000	0.000	0.000	0.000
Preventative Act	0.506	0.487	0.611	0.618
	0.000	0.000	0.000	0.000
Discriminatory W	0.406	0.435	0.548	0.560
	0.000	0.000	0.000	0.000

	Consistent Polic	12 Month Inconsi	Work Life Balanc	Addresses Discri
12 Month Inconsi	0.585			
	0.000			
Work Life Balanc	0.442	0.353		
	0.000	0.000		
Addresses Discri	0.545	0.431	0.299	
	0.000	0.000	0.000	
Preventative Act	0.629	0.548	0.336	0.776
	0.000	0.000	0.000	0.000
Discriminatory W	0.658	0.379	0.270	0.633
	0.000	0.000	0.002	0.000

	Preventative Act
Discriminatory W	0.680
	0.000

Cell Contents
  Pearson correlation
  P-Value

Table 4.1: Correlation results between treatment and career ascension of African American professionals in Fortune 500 companies

Hypothesis 3

The research tested the following hypotheses: *Alternative Hypothesis 3* – There is a predictable correlation between company ineffectiveness and job dissatisfaction for African

American professionals in Fortune 500 companies, and *Null Hypothesis 3* – There is no predictable correlation between company ineffectiveness and job dissatisfaction for African American professionals in Fortune 500 companies. The findings for company effectiveness and job satisfaction were as follows:

From the sample of 419 respondents, the researcher discovered 134 (80.72%) Blacks or African Americans reported that they worked for a Fortune 500 company (See Figure 4.14). Using statistical correlation analysis to determine whether the values of hypothesis #3 variables were associated with one another, the researcher's findings for the survey participants revealed that the data variables change correspondingly. Specifically, when correlating the 134 Black survey participants' perceptions of job motivation (satisfaction) with the company effectiveness variables, the researcher discovered a 95% confidence interval ($p<0.05$) for the correlation coefficient, which infers that the correlation coefficient is statistically significant, of a positively correlated motivation (satisfaction) with each of the following productive company actions: (1) *defined business goals and objectives* – r was 0.229, $p<0.008$, 95% CI 0.061 to 0.383; (2) *right strategy and goals* – r was 0.282, $p<0.001$, 95% CI 0.118 to 0.431; (3) *effectively managed and well run* – r was 0.398, $p<0.000$, 95% CI 0.245 to 0.532; (4) *employees gained trust and confidence in the senior management team* – r was 0.449, $p<0.000$, 95% CI 0.302 to 0.575; (5) *developed open and honest communications with employees* – r was 0.455, $p<0.000$, 95% CI 0.310 to 0.580; (6) *provides useful information to employees* – r was 0.478, $p<0.000$, 95% CI 0.335 to 0.599; (7) *socially responsible in its involvement with the community* – r was 0.478, $p<0.000$, 95% CI 0.336 to 0.599; (8) *keeps employees informed about matters that affect them* – r was 0.526, $p<0.000$, 95% CI 0.391 to 0.638; and (9) *instills confidence on having a job as long as the employee performs well* – r was 0.409, $p<0.000$, 95% CI 0.257 to 0.541. Null hypothesis was rejected. See Table 4.2.

Correlation: Motivates Me, Business Objectives, Strategy ... ob Security

Correlations

	Motivates Me	Business Objecti	Strategy & Goals	Effectively Mana
Business Objecti	0.229			
	0.008			
Strategy & Goals	0.282	0.481		
	0.001	0.000		
Effectively Mana	0.398	0.383	0.552	
	0.000	0.000	0.000	
Trust & Confiden	0.449	0.353	0.613	0.742
	0.000	0.000	0.000	0.000
Open & Honest	0.455	0.300	0.403	0.569
	0.000	0.000	0.000	0.000
Useful Info.	0.478	0.410	0.469	0.558
	0.000	0.000	0.000	0.000
Socially Respons	0.478	0.191	0.424	0.500
	0.000	0.027	0.000	0.000
Matters	0.526	0.449	0.536	0.578
	0.000	0.000	0.000	0.000
Job Security	0.409	0.288	0.302	0.559
	0.000	0.001	0.000	0.000

	Trust & Confiden	Open & Honest	Useful Info.	Socially Respons
Open & Honest	0.649			
	0.000			
Useful Info.	0.589	0.595		
	0.000	0.000		
Socially Respons	0.508	0.500	0.417	
	0.000	0.000	0.000	
Matters	0.605	0.652	0.618	0.517
	0.000	0.000	0.000	0.000
Job Security	0.579	0.549	0.474	0.438
	0.000	0.000	0.000	0.000

	Matters
Job Security	0.523
	0.000

Cell Contents
Pearson correlation
P-Value

Table 4.2: Correlation results between company effectiveness and job satisfaction for African American professionals in Fortune 500 companies

Hypothesis 4

The research tested the following hypotheses: *Alternative Hypothesis 4* – There is a predictable correlation between the lack of respect of African American professionals and negative perceptions of the Fortune 500 job itself, and *Null Hypothesis 4* – There is no predictable correlation between the lack of respect of African American professionals and negative perceptions of the Fortune 500 job itself. The findings for employee respect and perception of the job itself were as follows:

From the sample of 419 respondents, the researcher discovered 134 (80.72%) Blacks or African Americans reported that they worked for a Fortune 500 company (See Figure 4.14). Using statistical correlation analysis to determine whether the values of hypothesis #4 variables were associated with one another, the researcher's findings for the survey participants revealed that the data variables change correspondingly. Specifically, when correlating the 134 Black survey participants' perceptions of employee respect with the company job itself variables, the researcher discovered a 95% confidence interval ($p<0.05$) for the correlation coefficient, which infers that the correlation coefficient is statistically significant, of a positively correlated employee respect with each of the following company actions, with the exception of *work importance* – r was 0.079, $p>0.05$: (1) *provides employee with equipment or tools needed to do the job* – r was 0.470, $p<0.000$, 95% CI; (2) *provides adequate training for employee to be able to do the job* – r was 0.389, $p<0.000$, 95% CI; (3) *gives employees opportunities at work to learn and develop* – r was 0.600, $p<0.000$, 95% CI; (4) *ensures understanding of the results expected from the employee in the job* – r was 0.293, $p<0.001$, 95% CI; (5) *provides enough authority to employee to carry out the job effectively* – r was 0.504, $p<0.000$, 95% CI; (6) *recognizes employees when a job is done well* – r was 0.548, $p<0.000$, 95% CI; and (7) *leadership expects employee to use company values and beliefs on a daily basis* – r was 0.286, $p<0.001$, 95% CI. Null hypothesis was rejected.
See Table 4.3.

Correlation: Respect, Work Importance, Equip. ... tion, Values & Beliefs

Correlations

	Respect	Work Importance	Equip. Provision	Adequate Trainin
Work Importance	0.079			
	0.364			
Equip. Provision	0.470	0.345		
	0.000	0.000		
Adequate Trainin	0.389	0.199	0.584	
	0.000	0.021	0.000	
Development Oppo	0.600	0.156	0.533	0.574
	0.000	0.072	0.000	0.000
Job Expectations	0.293	0.547	0.353	0.451
	0.001	0.000	0.000	0.000
Empowered	0.504	0.243	0.414	0.376
	0.000	0.005	0.000	0.000
Recognition	0.548	0.278	0.436	0.428
	0.000	0.001	0.000	0.000
Values & Beliefs	0.286	0.298	0.408	0.325
	0.001	0.000	0.000	0.000

	Development Oppo	Job Expectations	Empowered	Recognition
Job Expectations	0.434			
	0.000			
Empowered	0.331	0.395		
	0.000	0.000		
Recognition	0.553	0.401	0.413	
	0.000	0.000	0.000	
Values & Beliefs	0.376	0.407	0.277	0.442
	0.000	0.000	0.001	0.000

Cell Contents
  Pearson correlation
  P-Value

Table 4.3: Correlation results between respect of African American professionals and perceptions of the Fortune 500 job itself

Hypothesis 5

The research tested the following hypotheses: *Alternative Hypothesis 5* – There is a predictable correlation between the lack of employee recognition and high turnover of African American professionals in Fortune 500 companies, and *Null Hypothesis 5* – There is no predictable correlation between the lack of employee recognition and high turnover of African American professionals in Fortune 500 companies. The findings for employee recognition and retention of African American professionals in Fortune 500 companies were as follows:

From the sample of 419 respondents, the researcher discovered 134 (80.72%) Blacks or African Americans reported that they worked for a Fortune 500 company (See Figure 4.14). Using statistical correlation analysis to determine whether the values of hypothesis #5 variables were associated with one another, the researcher's findings for the survey participants revealed that the data variables change correspondingly. Specifically, when correlating the 134 Black survey participants' perceptions of employee recognition with the African American retention variables, the researcher discovered a 95% confidence interval ($p<0.05$) for the correlation coefficient, which infers that the correlation coefficient is statistically significant, of a positively correlated employee recognition with each of the following company actions: (1) *management supports diversity in the workplace* – r was 0.364, $p<0.000$, 95% CI 0.207 to 0.502; (2) *provides a working environment that accepts differences in team member backgrounds, cultures, and lifestyles* – r was 0.473, $p<0.000$, 95% CI 0.330 to 0.595; (3) *demonstrates care and concern for employee* – r was 0.531, $p<0.000$, 95% CI 0.397 to 0.643; (4) *policies are applied consistently* – r was 0.527, $p<0.000$, 95% CI 0.392 to 0.639; (5) *maintains a balance between employee work and personal life* – r was 0.310, $p<0.000$, 95% CI 0.148 to 0.455; (6) *adequately addresses complaints of discrimination, harassment, or unethical business conduct* – r was 0.427, $p<0.000$, 95% CI 0.278 to 0.557; (7) *takes action to prevent discrimination, harassment, or unethical business conduct* – r was 0.533, $p<0.000$, 95% CI 0.399 to 0.644; (8) *provides work environment that is free from all forms of discrimination or harassment* – r was 0.413, $p<0.000$, 95% CI 0.261 to 0.544; (9) *ensures employee feels comfortable reporting a problem regarding discrimination or harassment* – r was 0.282, $p<0.001$, 95% CI 0.118 to 0.431; (10) *number of hours employee is asked to work are reasonable, based on business and personal needs* – r was 0.383, p<0.000, 95% CI 0.229 to 0.519; (11) *employee is treated with respect as an individual* – r was 0.548, p<0.000, 95% CI 0.417 to 0.657; (12) *company is effectively managed and well run* – r was 0.463, p<0.000, 95% CI 0.318 to 0.586; (13) *senior management builds trust and confidence with the employee* – r was 0.454, p<0.000, 95% CI 0.308 to 0.579; (14) *motivates employee to participate in internal diversity, safety, quality activities, etc.* – r was 0.393, p<0.000, 95% CI 0.239 to 0.527; (15) *is open and honest in communication with/to employee* – r was 0.481, p<0.000, 95% CI 0.340 to 0.602; (16) *instills confidence in having a job at the company as long as the employee performs well* – r was 0.572, p<0.000, 95% CI 0.446 to 0.676; (17) *provides equipment and tools needed for employee to do the job* – r was 0.436, p<0.000, 95% CI 0.288 to 0.564; (18) *adequately trains employee to be able to do the job* – r was 0.428, p<0.000, 95% CI 0.278 to 0.557; and (19) *gives employee the opportunities at work to learn and develop* – r was 0.553, p<0.000, 95% CI 0.424 to 0.661. Null hypothesis was rejected. See Table 4.4.

Correlation: Recognition, Diversity, Cultural Comfort, ... d, Job Growth

Correlations

	Recognition	Diversity	Cultural Comfort	Care & Concern
Diversity	0.364			
	0.000			
Cultural Comfort	0.473	0.707		
	0.000	0.000		
Care & Concern	0.531	0.639	0.646	
	0.000	0.000	0.000	
Policy Consistency	0.527	0.539	0.529	0.719
	0.000	0.000	0.000	0.000
Work/Life Balance	0.310	0.404	0.298	0.307

		0.000	0.000	0.000	0.000
Addresses Complaint		0.427	0.536	0.573	0.525
		0.000	0.000	0.000	0.000
Preventative Act		0.533	0.487	0.611	0.618
		0.000	0.000	0.000	0.000
Discrimination F		0.413	0.435	0.548	0.560
		0.000	0.000	0.000	0.000
Comfort Reporting		0.282	0.358	0.364	0.420
		0.001	0.000	0.000	0.000
Work Hours		0.383	0.400	0.318	0.363
		0.000	0.000	0.000	0.000
Treated w/ Respect		0.548	0.543	0.589	0.646
		0.000	0.000	0.000	0.000
Effectively Managed		0.463	0.464	0.446	0.601
		0.000	0.000	0.000	0.000
Trust Company		0.454	0.527	0.511	0.659
		0.000	0.000	0.000	0.000
Company Motivate		0.393	0.390	0.476	0.461
		0.000	0.000	0.000	0.000
Open & Honest		0.481	0.482	0.588	0.634
		0.000	0.000	0.000	0.000
Job Security		0.572	0.558	0.604	0.608
		0.000	0.000	0.000	0.000
Tools Provided		0.436	0.367	0.362	0.445
		0.000	0.000	0.000	0.000
Training Provide		0.428	0.281	0.320	0.389
		0.000	0.001	0.000	0.000

Job Growth	0.553	0.501	0.412	0.599
	0.000	0.000	0.000	0.000

	Policy Consisten	Work/Life Balanc	Addresses Compla	Preventative Act
Work/Life Balanc	0.442			
	0.000			
Addresses Cmplnt	0.545	0.299		
	0.000	0.000		
Preventative Act	0.629	0.336	0.776	
	0.000	0.000	0.000	
No Discrimination	0.658	0.270	0.633	0.680
	0.000	0.002	0.000	0.000
Comfort Reporting	0.478	0.216	0.504	0.547
	0.000	0.012	0.000	0.000
Work Hours	0.440	0.537	0.295	0.338
	0.000	0.000	0.001	0.000
Treated w/ Respect	0.519	0.368	0.544	0.555
	0.000	0.000	0.000	0.000
Effectively Manage	0.663	0.358	0.550	0.604
	0.000	0.000	0.000	0.000
Trust Company	0.660	0.385	0.637	0.638
	0.000	0.000	0.000	0.000
Company Motivate	0.375	0.162	0.405	0.424
	0.000	0.062	0.000	0.000
Open & Honest	0.664	0.513	0.447	0.564
	0.000	0.000	0.000	0.000
Job Security	0.569	0.243	0.602	0.586
	0.000	0.005	0.000	0.000
Tools Provided	0.465	0.380	0.525	0.494
	0.000	0.000	0.000	0.000
Training Provide	0.340	0.306	0.369	0.356

NEGATIVE PERCEPTION THEORY

		0.000	0.000	0.000	0.000
Job Growth		0.537	0.244	0.572	0.506
		0.000	0.004	0.000	0.000

	Discrimination F	Comfort Reportin	Work Hours	Treated w/ Respe
Comfort Reportin	0.535			
	0.000			
Work Hours	0.265	0.243		
	0.002	0.005		
Treated w/ Respect	0.470	0.394	0.507	
	0.000	0.000	0.000	
Effectively Mana	0.533	0.524	0.373	0.642
	0.000	0.000	0.000	0.000
Trust Company	0.571	0.429	0.321	0.586
	0.000	0.000	0.000	0.000
Company Motivate	0.352	0.336	0.263	0.383
	0.000	0.000	0.002	0.000
Open & Honest	0.539	0.490	0.406	0.619
	0.000	0.000	0.000	0.000
Job Security	0.548	0.526	0.329	0.598
	0.000	0.000	0.000	0.000
Tools Provided	0.389	0.323	0.373	0.470
	0.000	0.000	0.000	0.000
Training Provide	0.283	0.313	0.379	0.389
	0.001	0.000	0.000	0.000
Job Growth	0.406	0.310	0.432	0.600
	0.000	0.000	0.000	0.000

	Effectively Mana	Trust Company	Company Motivate	Open & Honest
Trust Company	0.742			

		0.000			
Company Motivate		0.398	0.449		
		0.000	0.000		
Open & Honest		0.569	0.649	0.455	
		0.000	0.000	0.000	
Job Security		0.559	0.579	0.409	0.549
		0.000	0.000	0.000	0.000
Tools Provided		0.586	0.565	0.369	0.488
		0.000	0.000	0.000	0.000
Training Provide		0.506	0.477	0.335	0.392
		0.000	0.000	0.000	0.000
Job Growth		0.596	0.642	0.531	0.465
		0.000	0.000	0.000	0.000

	Job Security	Tools Provided	Training Provide
Tools Provided	0.414		
	0.000		
Training Provide	0.425	0.584	
	0.000	0.000	
Job Growth	0.560	0.533	0.574
	0.000	0.000	0.000

Cell Contents
   Pearson correlation

   P-Value

Table 4.4: Correlation results between employee recognition and retention of African American professionals in Fortune 500 companies

Hypothesis 6

The research tested the following hypotheses: *Alternative Hypothesis 6* – There is a predictable correlation between racial inequality and teamwork & cooperation for African Americans in Fortune 500 companies, and *Null Hypothesis 6* – There is no predictable correlation between racial inequality and teamwork & cooperation for African Americans in Fortune 500 companies. The findings for employee racial equality and teamwork & cooperation for African American professionals in Fortune 500 companies were as follows:

From the sample of 419 respondents, the researcher discovered 134 (80.72%) Blacks or African Americans reported that they worked for a Fortune 500 company (See Figure 4.14). Using statistical correlation analysis to determine whether the values of hypothesis #6 variables were associated with one another, the researcher's findings for the survey participants revealed that the data variables change correspondingly. Specifically, when correlating the 134 Black survey participants' perceptions of employee racial equality with the teamwork & cooperation for African American variables, the researcher discovered a 95% confidence interval ($p<0.05$) for the correlation coefficient, which infers that the correlation coefficient is statistically significant, of a positively correlated employee recognition with each of the following company actions: (1) *adequately addresses complaints of discrimination, harassment, or unethical business conduct* – r was 0.573, $p<0.000$, 95% CI; (2) *takes action to prevent discrimination, harassment, or unethical business conduct* – r was 0.611, $p<0.000$, 95% CI; (3) *work environment is free from all forms of discrimination or harassment* – r was 0.548, $p<0.000$, 95% CI; (4) *employees feel comfortable reporting a problem regarding discrimination or harassment* – r was 0.364, $p<0.000$, 95% CI; (5) *team shares information and ideas to achieve team results* – r was 0.387, $p<0.000$, 95% CI; (6) *team gets the cooperation it needs from other work groups/teams to achieve business objectives* – r was 0.391, $p<0.000$, 95% CI; and (7) *all people the employee* works with work well as a team – r was 0.356, p<0.000, 95% CI. Null hypothesis was rejected. See Table 4.5.

Correlation: Supports Equality, Addresses Inequality, ... k Well as Team

Correlations

	Supports Equalit	Addresses Inequa	Prevents Inequal	Zero Inequality
Addresses Inequa	0.573			
	0.000			
Prevents Inequal	0.611	0.776		
	0.000	0.000		
Zero Inequality	0.548	0.633	0.680	
	0.000	0.000	0.000	
Comfortable Repo	0.364	0.504	0.547	0.535
	0.000	0.000	0.000	0.000
Team Shares Info	0.387	0.359	0.424	0.376
	0.000	0.000	0.000	0.000
Cooperation from	0.391	0.378	0.477	0.442
	0.000	0.000	0.000	0.000
We Work Well as	0.356	0.471	0.498	0.485
	0.000	0.000	0.000	0.000

	Comfortable Repo	Team Shares Info	Cooperation from
Team Shares Info	0.212		
	0.014		
Cooperation from	0.330	0.616	
	0.000	0.000	
We Work Well as	0.268	0.689	0.522
	0.002	0.000	0.000

Cell Contents
  Pearson correlation
  P-Value

Table 4.5: Correlation results between racial equality and teamwork & cooperation for African Americans in Fortune 500 companies

Findings for Each Research Question

Question 1

The research tested six hypotheses to uncover the extent of lack of employee recognition, lack of career opportunities, job dissatisfaction, company ineffectiveness, and high job turnover correlated to employees' race in Fortune 500 companies. Using Minitab software to perform the statistical analysis of the survey data, the researcher performed the Pearson's correlation coefficient (r) with p-value and confidence intervals of the randomly sampled data pairs to uncover any correlation expressed through changes of the variables.

Schoonjans (2020) explained that

> *If one variable increases when the second one increases, then there is a positive correlation. In this case the correlation coefficient will be closer to 1. For instance the height and age of children are positively correlated.*
> *If one variable decreases when the other variable increases, then there is a negative correlation and the correlation coefficient will be closer to -1.*
> *The P-value is the probability that you would have found the current result if the correlation coefficient were in fact zero (null hypothesis). If this probability is lower than the conventional 5% (P<0.05) the correlation coefficient is called statistically significant.*
> *It is, however, important not to confuse correlation with causation. When two variables are correlated, there may or may not be a causative connection, and this connection may moreover be indirect. Correlation can only be interpreted in terms of causation if the variables under investigation provide a logical (biological) basis for such interpretation (n.p.).*

As graphically shown in Figure 4.29 of hypothesis #5, the number of data pairs for employees' perceptions of recognition were all statistically significant (correlated) to African Americans' turnover variables in Fortune 500 companies.

Figure 4.29: Correlational results for Blacks' turnover and perceptions of their recognition within Fortune 500 organization

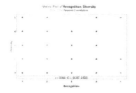

DR. D'UANDRE ANTOINE DRAIN

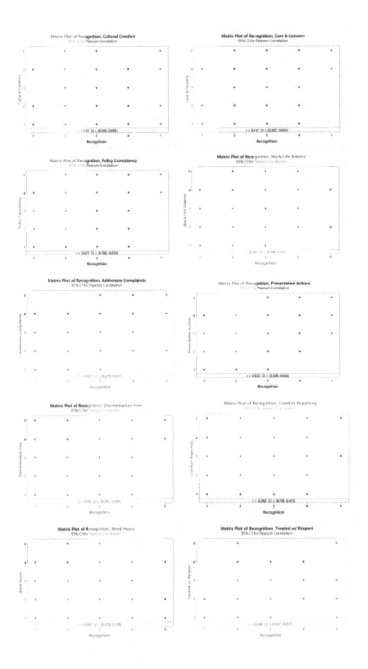

As graphically shown in Figure 4.30 of hypothesis #2, the number of data pairs for employee career opportunities were all statistically significant (correlated) to African Americans' perceptions in Fortune 500 companies.

Figure 4.30: Correlational results for Blacks' variable perceptions of their career ascension within Fortune 500 organization

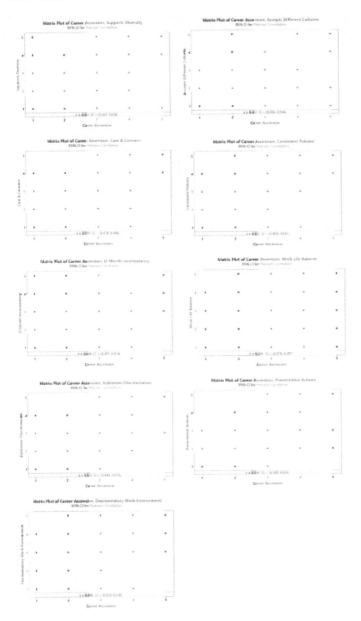

As graphically shown in Figure 4.31 of hypothesis #3, the number of data pairs for employee job satisfaction/motivation were all statistically significant (correlated) to African Americans' perceptions of company effectiveness in Fortune 500 companies.

Figure 4.31: Correlational results for Blacks' variable perceptions of their job satisfaction with company effectiveness within Fortune 500 organization

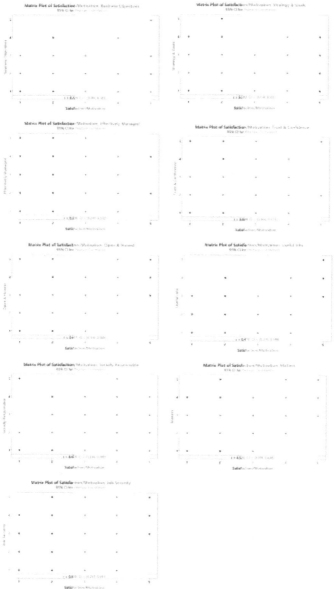

DR. D'UANDRE ANTOINE DRAIN

Question 2

The collected survey data was evaluated using a SurveyMonkey t-test to better understand how differences in the racial composition of teams influenced perceptions of teamwork and cooperation in Fortune 500 companies. The t-test was an effective method for determining whether two numbers were significantly different from one another. There were several types of t-test, and each was calculated using a different formula. For this study, the researcher elected to apply the two sampled t-test for the purpose of examining whether the means of two or more independent groups were significantly different from one another. According to SurveyMonkey (1999),

> We calculate statistical significance using a standard 95% confidence level. When we display an answer option as statistically significant, it means the difference between two groups has less than a 5% probability of occurring by chance or sampling error alone, which is often displayed as $p < 0.05$. To calculate the statistical significance between groups, we use the following formulas (n.p.).

Statistic	Description	Formula
a_1	The proportion of the first group answering a question a certain way multiplied by the sample size of that group.	$a_1 = p_1 * n_1$
b_1	The proportion of the second group answering a question a certain way multiplied by the sample size of that group.	$b_1 = p_2 * n_2$
Pooled Sample Proportion (p)	The combination of the two proportions for both groups.	$p = \dfrac{a_1 + b_1}{n_1 + n_2}$
Standard Error (SE)	A measure of how far your proportion is from the true proportion. A smaller number means the proportion is close to the true proportion, a larger number means the proportion is far away from the true proportion.	$SE = \sqrt{p*(1-p)*\left(\dfrac{1}{n_1}+\dfrac{1}{n_2}\right)}$
Test Statistic (t)	A t-statistic. The number of standard deviations a number is away from the mean.	$t = \dfrac{p_1 - p_2}{SE}$
Statistical Significance	If the absolute value of the test statistic is greater than 1.96 standard deviations of the mean, then it's considered a statistically significant difference.	$|t| > 1.96$

NEGATIVE PERCEPTION THEORY

When comparing the racial composition of teams influenced perceptions (n = 178) of teamwork in Fortune 500 companies, the researcher discovered a 95% confidence level (p<0.05), significantly higher statistical difference in Whites (51.52%) strongly agreeing that their group/team shared more information and ideas to achieve team results than Blacks (23.13%); therefore, the null hypothesis was rejected due to a significantly higher statistical difference in Blacks' and Whites' perceptions on this variable. See Figure 4.32.

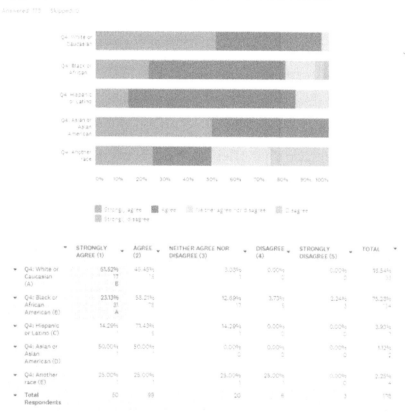

My group shares information and ideas to achieve team results

	STRONGLY AGREE (1)	AGREE (2)	NEITHER AGREE NOR DISAGREE (3)	DISAGREE (4)	STRONGLY DISAGREE (5)	TOTAL
Q4: White or Caucasian (A)	51.52% 17	45.45% 15	3.03% 1	0.00% 0	0.00% 0	18.54% 33
Q4: Black or African American (B)	23.13% 31	58.21% 78	12.69% 17	3.73% 5	2.24% 3	75.28% 134
Q4: Hispanic or Latino (C)	14.29% 1	71.43% 5	14.29% 1	0.00% 0	0.00% 0	3.93% 7
Q4: Asian or Asian American (D)	50.00% 1	50.00% 1	0.00% 0	0.00% 0	0.00% 0	1.12% 2
Q4: Another race (E)	25.00% 1	25.00% 1	25.00% 1	25.00% 1	0.00% 0	2.25% 4
Total Respondents	50	99	20	6	3	178

BASIC STATISTICS	MINIMUM	MAXIMUM	MEDIAN	MEAN	STANDARD DEVIATION
Q4: White or Caucasian (A)	1.00	3.00	1.00	1.50	0.86
Q4: Black or African American (B)	1.00	3.00	2.00	2.04	0.64
Q4: Hispanic or Latino (C)	1.00	3.00	2.00	2.00	0.83
Q4: Asian or Asian American (D)	1.00	2.00	1.50	1.50	0.60
Q4: Another race (E)	1.00	4.00	2.50	2.50	1.12

Figure 4.32: Whites, Blacks, Hispanics, Asians, and Other racial perceptions of teamwork and information sharing in Fortune 500 companies

When comparing the racial composition of teams influenced perceptions (n = 178) of cooperation from other work groups/teams in Fortune 500 companies, the researcher discovered no statistical difference in Whites, Blacks, Hispanics, Asians, or other ethnic participants agreeing, disagreeing, or neutral on their perception that their work group gets the cooperation it needs from other work groups to achieve their business objectives; therefore, the researcher failed to reject the null hypothesis that there was no difference in racial composition of teams influenced perceptions of cooperation from other racial groups/teams. See Figure 4.33.

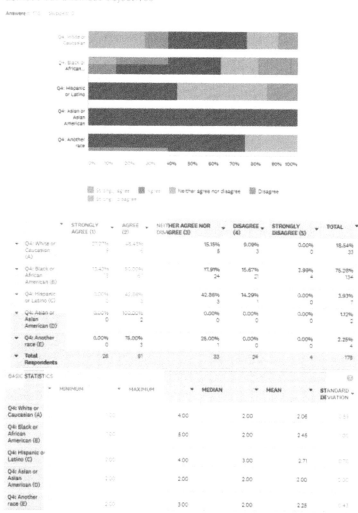

Figure 4.33: Whites, Blacks, Hispanics, Asians, and Other racial perceptions of cooperation from other racial work groups in Fortune 500 companies

When comparing the racial composition of teams influenced perceptions (n = 178) of racial teams working well together in Fortune 500 companies, the researcher discovered no statistical difference in Whites, Blacks, Hispanics, Asians, or other ethnic participants agreeing, disagreeing, or neutral on their perception that the people that they worked with work well together as a team; therefore, the researcher failed to reject the null hypothesis that there was no difference in racial composition of teams influenced perceptions of different people working well together as a team/group. See Figure 4.34.

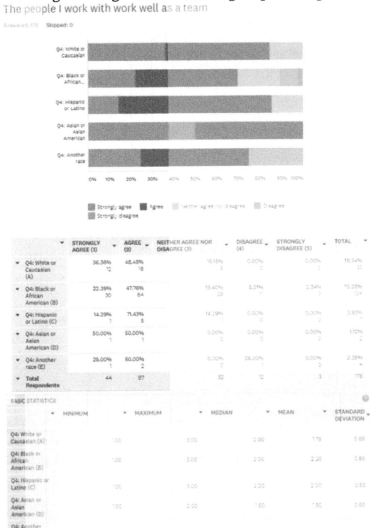

Figure 4.34: Whites, Blacks, Hispanics, Asians, and Other racial perceptions of people working well together as a team in Fortune 500 companies

Theoretical Framework/Connection

The researcher utilized numerous theoretical frameworks to guide this study such as: 1) organizational leadership theory and models; 2) organizational leadership philosophy; 3) cultural diversity, ethics, and fairness; 4) board/employee/constituent relations; 5) visionary leadership; 6) personnel evaluation; 7) four models of organization behavior or culture theories; 8) six models of organizational leadership theories; 9) nine models of motivation and needs theories; 10) upper echelon theory; 11) disparate impact theory; 12) Rawls' Theory of Justice; 13) cultural deficiency theory; 14) critical race theory; 15) labor market segmentation theory; 16) human capital theory; 17) career development theory; 18) structuration theory; and 19) social cognitive career theory. In addition, studies on glass ceiling, career ascension, mentorship, and cultural comfort served as logically structured frameworks outlining fundamental sources that presented barriers associated with racial inequality of African American professionals in Fortune 500 companies.

To better illustrate a direct connection between the survey participants' responses and the theoretical framework, the researcher included two open ended response questions to gather specific feedback regarding company policies that were not applied consistently to the sampled population as well as their observations of the company's values and beliefs they felt needed to be reinforced in their group. According to SurveyMonkey (2020),

> *Open-ended questions ask people to provide answers in their own words and are designed to elicit more information than is possible in a multiple choice or other closed-ended format.*

> *Writing a good open-ended question is a tricky balancing act: It should elicit the respondents to answer with useful information, but also give them the freedom to respond as they choose (n.p.).*

Having said, when voluntarily asked what aspects of their company's values and beliefs they felt needed to be reinforced in their group, the survey participants could elect not to answer and continue with the survey or they were provided with an opportunity to include their criticism/response in the study. There were 76 useful statements to connect the theoretical framework such as:

Respect for People
Practice what they preach
We are a team everyone should be treated fairly and equally
Respect for the individual
Respect for the Individual
Respect for People & Teamwork
Being authentic and valuing differences in thoughts and experiences
More diverse hiring practices and better retention
Implementing actual diversity. See few women and minorities in executive leadership
Diversity
Effective communication Conflict resolution HR personnel

Realistic expectations. The amount of work that's expected to be done in the proper amount of time.
Teamwork
Simplicity
Being fair, honest and transparent.
Respect for people and inclusion of all team members
Hiring and development of the best personnel.
The best or nothing
Commitment to inclusion and promoting diversity of thought and ideas.
Continued diversity reinforcements
Evaluation of internal talent
Commitment to training and development
Taking ownership
The company needs to get back to the old days. This new Company A is a complete lie!
As a group, we must be mindful of project's scope because of the everchanging nature of this business.
OPSEC Training
Respect for People - This is a noted value, but I feel it is selectively applied to those that are in the majority. Social Comfort - I feel that people should be allowed to bring their authentic selves to work without being subjected to uncomfortable situations by whites because of their lack of understanding multi-cultural perspectives. Diversity & Inclusion - These terms are used often but there really is

no value from the minorities' perspectives because there really isn't a "conversation" held about what matters most to others. Instead, there are planned diversity activities that make the whites feel comfortable such as: Chili Cook Offs, Cinco de Mayo Salsa contests, etc. Unfortunately, for the minorities, when we spoke up about issues that impact us, we were perceived as going against the grain or being troublemakers. This had a negative effect on our ability to be promoted and/or receive opportunities for advancement.

Company is great to work for. The culture has a microcosm feel regarding day-to-day I question.
Inclusiveness, Empathy
Fair promotion practices
Communication from all levels
Progress over perfection
Respect for individuals no matter where they are in the company.
Work balance, proper training and quit creating an intimidating environment where leadership pushes the ethical lines. But then says on paper to act ethically.
That contractors are not slaves and don't sluff off grunt work upon them. They are hired because the company has a void of talent or expertise in a particular area.
Appreciation
How we can be honest yet feel safe in our environment
Embracing risk taking & transparency of problems

Accountability for scheduling vacation in advance
Diversity and its importance to the Companies enterprise. Also, more senior management engagement with diversity groups, training and development. The impression is that senior managers participate only because it on their yearly objectives and not that they truly believe in these groups.
The company is very progressive. As of now, I believe that the company's values and beliefs are reinforced.
Integrity, service before self, and being a great customer advocate.
Intensity
Job performance should be based on merit. Company G has a culture of promoting individuals because of "who" you know, rather than "what" you know.
Value customers
Transformation Integrity Knowledge
Respect for people in relation to culture/ethnicity
Accountability
Candor and transparency, prioritization
I do not feel that my company embraces diversity and inclusion. As a person of color, you have to work harder to become notice especially if you are in IT where there is a huge gap and lack of diversity in management roles.
Ethics and embracing diversity and inclusion. Demonstrating respect and being worthy of trust; having a moral compass; fairness in its treatment of employees

Integrity and trust
Diversity
Respect for people
Strong team work ethic and performance
Moral
Diversity training and inclusion
Diversity
Diversity
Opportunity
None in my group. Overall for the site we need to have a more diverse working group and leadership.
Integrity
The care for all employees not just supervisors and up
Promoting a genuinely inclusive and sincere culture at all levels including executive level leaders holding each other accountable for deviations from company values and beliefs
Not applicable at my job level
Transparency
Fairness and cultural awareness
Quality should matter over Production Numbers.
Employee recognition
Diversity and Inclusion, development, respect for ALL people

NEGATIVE PERCEPTION THEORY

Promote diversity candidates
Communication
Acceptance of differences in background.
Open mindedness that all people in the same job role are not a monolithic people.
All of them equally across the board, not just to female and the lasted fad groups.
Being honest and forthcoming with customers i.e., Fees and service

When voluntarily asked if they could state any company policy(ies) that were not consistently applied to him/her over the past 12 months, the survey participants could elect not to answer and continue with the survey or they were provided with an opportunity to include their criticism/response in the study. There were 39 useful statements to connect the theoretical framework such as:

Promotions and opportunities for growth were not applied and given fairly
Equal pay from same job
A few different ones the policy only applies when favoritism is moved out the way
Time in title in order to be promoted. Policy is two years, some only in role 7 months.
Not providing me with a job description
All policies have been applied adequately
Time away from work

Fair and equal consideration.
Career advancement opportunities
I am not sure
Promotion
Equal access to opportunities
Sexual harassment
I just recently started with the company and some of the travel policy changed due to Covid-19
The continued talk about the company being the most diverse is all a lie. The top-heavy positions continue to be white driven and people who have more education and experience who are of color are still mostly on the front lines.
Fair employment performance appraisals (Assistant Managers) - My white counterparts all have higher performance management process (PMP) scores than I do. I, personally, saw the scores listed on my manager's desk as they were documented on a notepad. And, my less tenured counterpart, which I trained and happened to be white, unknowingly left his PMP on our shared desk and I saw that his score had increased to a higher level than mine. At this time, my overall score was lowered by a tenth of a percent with no written explanation offered nor verbalized during the feedback. It also should be noted that my counterpart was friends with my white manager. Discrimination - I applied for a position and my white counterpart had applied for the same position that was in a different segment of the business (requiring relocation). After the HR recruiter and Recruiting Manager expressed interest in me and I shared with my manager, she
(my Manager) decided that she would allow my counterpart

to continue in the hiring process and denied me the opportunity to proceed with the interview process. In the end, I was not allowed to interview despite their interest and my counterpart interviewed and received the job. I, later, voluntarily resigned from the company.

Criteria for promotion, wage increase
Many different ones but basically seems to be a double standard
Promotion and recognition process isn't applied consistently (very subjective in some areas).
Equal pay
Promotional opportunity
Pay increase/raise... Time off
Promoting managers from within of different ethnicities
Promoting from within.
Mobile Equipment Lockout Tagout
The company allowed an Caucasian male employee to say the word Nigger at work several times, with witnesses and he was promoted to Sr. Manager within 6 months and now runs a team. An African American woman was said to have said in a meeting that she did not trust leadership 3 years ago and still cannot move upward into management. No one confronted or asked the young lady is she actually said it and it was a "I heard she said" situation.
Opportunity for advancement: not given the opportunity to apply /be promoted for my position.

Promotional opportunities
Advancement opportunities and promotions
Promotion opportunity
Fair, objective year-end review
Job grade/pay inequality including stock options and bonuses
Diversity in upper management
Using Vacation/Personal time
Retention
Alertness when someone has the Corona virus so we can decide if we want to stay go home to protect ourselves
Complicated but centered around politics.
Medical on the job injury
Equality in monthly coaching.

Summary

In Chapter 4's presentation and interpretation of the instrument data, the research provided a detailed overview of the purpose of the study, research questions, sampled participants' demographics, data collection analysis methods for each hypothesis, survey instrument findings for each research question, and theoretical framework connection to the sampled populations' responses to open ended survey questions.

The sample for this quantitative descriptive correctional study consisted of n = 502 with a return rate of 419

participants which was an acceptable return rate of 83.5%, utilizing a stratified random sampling selection process. Of the 419 survey respondents, males represented 74.7% (313), females represented 24.58% (103), 0.48% (2) chose not to identify their gender, and 0.24% (1) identified as other. Regarding the
419 survey respondents' age groups, the data showed that 37.47% (157) responded that they were in the 45 –54 age group while 34.13% (143) recorded that they were 35 –44, 15.27% (64) were 55 –64, 1.91% (8) were 65+, and 0.24% (1) was 18 –24 years of age. Concerning the 419 survey respondents' ethnic backgrounds, 82.58% (346) identified as Black or African American while 13.13% (55) stated White or Caucasian, 2.86% (12) were Hispanic or Latino, 1.91% (8) identified as "another race", 0.95% (4) as Asian or Asian American, and 0.95% (4) were American Indian or Alaska Native. Pertaining to whether or not the 419 survey respondents worked for a Fortune 500 company, 57.52% (241) stated that they did not work for a Fortune 500 company while 42.48% (178) declared that they were Fortune 500 employees.

The findings from the survey instrument's interpretation of the data for hypothesis #1 concluded that the null hypothesis, which stated that African American professionals did not report more unfair treatment than Caucasian professionals in Fortune 500 companies, was rejected due to a statistically significant difference in Blacks and Whites responses to the fourteen questions used to uncover their perceptions of their individual respect and treatment within their Fortune 500 organizations.

The findings for hypothesis #2 concluded that the null hypothesis, which stated that there was no predictable correlation between unfair treatment and fewer opportunities for career ascension of African American professionals in Fortune 500 companies, was rejected due to the discovery of a 95%

confidence interval ($p<0.05$) for the correlation coefficient, which inferred that the correlation coefficient was statistically significant, of a positively correlated career ascension with each of the following company actions: (1) supportive of diversity; (2) acceptance of different backgrounds, cultures, and lifestyles; (3) demonstrates care & concern for employees; (4) policies are applied consistently; (5) policies have been consistently applied to the surveyed participant over the past 12 months; (6) maintains a balance between employees' work and personal lives; (7) addresses complaints of discrimination, harassment, or unethical business conduct; (8) prevents discrimination, harassment, or unethical business conduct; and (9) work environment is free from all forms of discrimination or harassment.

The findings for hypothesis #3 concluded that the null hypothesis, which stated that there was no predictable correlation between company ineffectiveness and job dissatisfaction for African American professionals in Fortune 500 companies, was rejected due to the discovery of a 95% confidence interval ($p<0.05$) for the correlation coefficient, which inferred that the correlation coefficient was statistically significant, of a positively correlated motivation (satisfaction) with each of the following productive company actions: (1) defined business goals and objectives; (2) right strategy and goals; (3) effectively managed and well run; (4) employees gained trust and confidence in the senior management team; (5) developed open and honest communications with employees; (6) provides useful information to employees; (7) socially responsible in its involvement with the community; (8) keeps employees informed about matters that affect them; and (9) instills confidence on having a job as long as the employee performs well.

The findings for hypothesis #4 concluded that the null hypothesis, which stated that there was no predictable correlation between the lack of respect of African American professionals and negative perceptions of the Fortune 500 job itself, was rejected due to the discovery of a 95% confidence interval ($p<0.05$) for the correlation coefficient, which inferred that the correlation coefficient was statistically significant, of a positively correlated employee respect with each of the following company actions, with the exception of work importance:

(1) provides employee with equipment or tools needed to do the job; (2) provides adequate training for employee to be able to do the job; (3) gives employees opportunities at work to learn and develop; (4) ensures understanding of the results expected from the employee in the job; (5) provides enough authority to employee to carry out the job effectively; (6) recognizes employees when a job is done well; and (7) leadership expects employee to use company values and beliefs on a daily basis.

The findings for hypothesis #5 concluded that the null hypothesis, which stated that there was no predictable correlation between the lack of employee recognition and high turnover of African American professionals in Fortune 500 companies, was rejected due to the discovery of a 95% confidence interval ($p<0.05$) for the correlation coefficient, which inferred that the correlation coefficient was statistically significant, of a positively correlated employee recognition with each of the following company actions: (1) management supports diversity in the workplace; (2) provides a working environment that accepts differences in team member backgrounds, cultures, and lifestyles; (3) demonstrates care and concern for employee; (4) policies are applied consistently; (5) maintains a balance between employee work and personal life; (6) adequately addresses complaints of discrimination, harassment, or unethical business conduct; (7) takes action to prevent discrimination, harassment, or unethical business conduct; (8) provides work environment that is free from all forms of discrimination or harassment; (9) ensures employee feels comfortable reporting a problem regarding discrimination or harassment; (10) number of hours employee is asked to work are reasonable, based on business and personal needs; (11) employee is treated with respect as an individual; (12) company is effectively managed and well run; (13) senior management builds trust and confidence with the employee; (14) motivates employee to participate in internal diversity, safety, quality activities, etc.; (15) is open and honest in communication with/to employee; (16) instills confidence in having a job at the company as long as the employee performs well; (17) provides equipment and tools needed for employee to do the job; (18) adequately trains employee to be able to do the job; and (19) gives employee the opportunities at work to learn and develop.

The findings for hypothesis #6 concluded that the null hypothesis, which stated that there was no predictable correlation between racial inequality and teamwork & cooperation for African Americans in Fortune 500 companies, was rejected due to the discovery of a 95%confidence interval ($p<0.05$) for the correlation coefficient, which inferred that the correlation coefficient was statistically significant, of a positively correlated employee recognition with each of the following company actions: (1) adequately addresses complaints of discrimination, harassment, or unethical business conduct; (2) takes action to prevent discrimination, harassment, or unethical business conduct; (3) work environment is free from all forms of discrimination or harassment; (4) employees feel comfortable reporting a problem regarding discrimination or harassment; (5) team shares information and ideas to achieve team results; (6) team gets the cooperation it needs from other work groups/teams to achieve business objectives; and (7) all people the employee works with work well as a team.

In conjunction with statistically testing the six rejected

null hypotheses, a detailed analysis was provided to analyze two specific research questions in this study. For the first research question, the data analyses were conducted to uncover the extent of lack of employee recognition, lack of career opportunities, job dissatisfaction, company ineffectiveness, and high job turnover correlated to employees' race in Fortune 500 companies. Using Minitab software to perform the statistical analysis of the survey data, the researcher performed the Pearson's correlation coefficient (r) with p-value and confidence intervals of the randomly sampled data pairs to uncover any correlation expressed through changes of the variables. As discovered in hypothesis #5, the number of data pairs for employees' perceptions of recognition were all statistically significant (correlated) to African Americans' turnover variables in Fortune 500 companies. Also, as exposed in hypothesis #2, the number of data pairs for employee career opportunities were all statistically significant (correlated) to African Americans' perceptions in Fortune 500 companies. Lastly, as unveiled in hypothesis #3, the number of data pairs for employee job satisfaction/motivation were all statistically significant (correlated) to African Americans' perceptions of company effectiveness in Fortune 500 companies.

For the second research question, the collected survey data was evaluated using a SurveyMonkey t-test to better understand how differences in the racial composition of teams influenced perceptions of teamwork and cooperation in Fortune 500 companies. When comparing the racial composition of teams influenced perceptions (n = 178) of teamwork in Fortune 500 companies, the researcher discovered a 95% confidence level ($p<0.05$), significantly higher statistical difference in Whites (51.52%) strongly agreeing that their group/team shared more information and ideas to achieve team results than Blacks (23.13%); therefore, the null hypothesis was rejected due to a significantly higher statistical difference in Blacks' and Whites' perceptions on this variable.

Also, when comparing the racial composition of teams influenced perceptions of cooperation from other work groups/teams in Fortune 500 companies, the researcher discovered no statistical difference in Whites, Blacks, Hispanics, Asians, or other ethnic participants agreeing, disagreeing, or being neutral on their perceptions that their work group gets the cooperation it needs from other work groups to achieve their business objectives; therefore, the researcher failed to reject the null hypothesis that there was no difference in racial composition of teams influenced perceptions of cooperation from other racial groups/teams. Lastly, when comparing the racial composition of teams influenced perceptions of racial teams working well together in Fortune 500 companies, the researcher discovered no statistical difference in Whites, Blacks, Hispanics, Asians, or other ethnic participants agreeing, disagreeing, or being neutral on their perception that the people they worked with work well together as a team; therefore, the researcher failed to reject the null hypothesis that there was no difference in racial composition of teams influenced perceptions of different people working well together as a team/group.

The sampled populations' responses to two open ended survey questions provided direct connection to the study's theoretical framework for African American professionals working in Fortune 500 companies. For the first question, when voluntarily asked what aspects of their company's values and beliefs they felt needed to be reinforced in their group, the survey participants provided 76 useful criticisms/responses/statements to connect the theoretical framework to the study. As for the second question, when voluntarily asked if they could state any company policies that were not consistently applied to them over the past 12 months, the survey participants answered with 39 useful criticisms/responses/statements to connect the theoretical framework with the study.

CHAPTER FIVE: DISCUSSION, CONCLUSIONS, AND RECOMMENDATIONS

Introduction

The researcher's study of racial inequality was based on the extent to which African American professionals exhibited negative perceptions of their Fortune 500 workplaces in the following areas: respect & treatment, company effectiveness, the job itself, and teamwork & cooperation. The researcher asked the following quantitative research questions: (1) To what extent are lack of employee recognition, lack of career opportunities, job dissatisfaction, company ineffectiveness, and high job turnover correlated to employees' race in Fortune 500 companies?; and (2) How do differences in the racial composition of teams influence teamwork and cooperation in Fortune 500 companies? The research tested the following hypotheses:

- *Null Hypothesis 1*: African American professionals

do not report more unfair treatment than Caucasian professionals in Fortune 500 companies.

- *Alternative Hypothesis 1*: African American professionals report more unfair treatment than Caucasian professionals in Fortune 500 companies.

- *Null Hypothesis 2*: There is no predictable correlation between unfair treatment and fewer opportunities for career ascension of African American professionals in Fortune 500 companies.

- *Alternative Hypothesis 2*: There is a predictable correlation between unfair treatment and fewer opportunities for career ascension of African American professionals in Fortune 500 companies.

- *Null Hypothesis 3*: There is no predictable correlation between company ineffectiveness and job dissatisfaction for African American professionals in Fortune 500 companies.

- *Alternative Hypothesis 3*: There is a predictable correlation between company ineffectiveness and job dissatisfaction for African American professionals in Fortune 500 companies.

- *Null Hypothesis 4*: There is no predictable correlation between the lack of respect of African American professionals and negative perceptions of the Fortune 500 job itself.

- *Alternative Hypothesis 4*: There is a predictable correlation between the lack of respect of African American professionals and negative perceptions of the Fortune 500 job itself.

- *Null Hypothesis 5*: There is no predictable correlation between the lack of employee recognition and high turnover of African American professionals in Fortune 500 companies.

- *Alternative Hypothesis 5*: There is a predictable correlation between the lack of employee recognition and high turnover of African American professionals in Fortune 500 companies.

- *Null Hypothesis 6*:
  There is no predictable correlation between racial inequality and teamwork & cooperation for African Americans in Fortune 500 companies.
- *Alternative Hypothesis 6*:
  There is a predictable correlation between racial inequality and teamwork & cooperation for African Americans in Fortune 500 companies.

Summary of Findings

Hypothesis 1

The study discovered a 95% confidence level ($p=0.05$) statistical difference in the sample of Black professionals reporting more unfair treatment than the sample of White professionals in Fortune 500 organizations. Using a two-sample t-test of fourteen questions, the researcher successfully examined whether the means of two independent groups (Blacks and Whites) were significantly different from one another. The sampled Blacks and Whites perceptions of their individual respect and treatment within their Fortune 500 organizations were found to be statistically different with more unfair treatment for Blacksacross multiple variables; therefore, the researcher rejected the null hypothesis #1 due to multiple statistical differences in the mean and standard deviations.

Hypothesis 2

When correlating the 134 Black survey participants' perceptions of career ascension with the company treatment of employees variables, the study discovered a 95% confidence interval ($p<0.05$) for the correlation coefficient, which infers that the correlation coefficient is statistically significant, of a positively correlated career ascension with each of the following company actions: (1) supportive of diversity; (2) acceptance of different backgrounds, cultures, and lifestyles; (3) demonstrates care & concern for employees; (4) policies are applied consistently; (5) policies have been consistently applied to the surveyed participant over the past 12 months; (6) maintains a balance between employees' work and personal lives; (7) addresses complaints of discrimination, harassment, or unethical business conduct; (8) prevents discrimination, harassment, or unethical business conduct; and (9) work environment is free from all forms of discrimination or harassment. Null hypothesis was rejected.

Hypothesis 3

When correlating the 134 Black survey participants' perceptions of job motivation (satisfaction) with the company effectiveness variables, the study discovered a 95% confidence interval ($p<0.05$) for the correlation coefficient, which infers that the correlation coefficient is statistically significant, of a positively correlated motivation/satisfaction with

each of the following productive company actions: (1) defined business goals and objectives; (2) right strategy and goals; (3) effectively managed and well run; (4) employees gained trust and confidence in the senior management team; (5) developed open and honest communications with employees; (6) provides useful information to employees; (7) socially responsible in its involvement with the community; (8) keeps employees informed about matters that affect them; and (9) instills confidence on having a job as long as the employee performs well.
Null hypothesis was rejected.

Hypothesis 4

When correlating the 134 Black survey participants' perceptions of employee respect with the company job itself variables, the researcher discovered a 95% confidence interval ($p<0.05$) for the correlation coefficient, which infers that the correlation coefficient is statistically significant, of a positively correlated employee respect with each of the following company actions, with the exception of work importance: (1) provides employee with equipment or tools needed to do the job; (2) provides adequate training for employee to be able to do the job; (3) gives employees opportunities at work to learn and develop; (4) ensures understanding of the results expected from the employee in the job; (5) provides enough authority to employee to carry out the job effectively; (6) recognizes employees when a job is done well; and (7) leadership expects employee to use company values and beliefs on a daily basis. Null hypothesis was rejected.

Hypothesis 5

When correlating the 134 Black survey participants' perceptions of employee recognition with the African American retention variables, the researcher discovered a 95%

confidence interval ($p<0.05$) for the correlation coefficient, which infers that the correlation coefficient is statistically significant, of a positively correlated employee recognition with each of the following company actions: (1) management supports diversity in the workplace; (2) provides a working environment that accepts differences in team member backgrounds, cultures, and lifestyles; (3) demonstrates care and concern for employee; (4) policies are applied consistently; (5) maintains a balance between employee work and personal life; (6) adequately addresses complaints of discrimination, harassment, or unethical business conduct; (7) takes action to prevent discrimination, harassment, or unethical business conduct; (8) provides work environment that is free from all forms of discrimination or harassment; (9) ensures employee feels comfortable reporting a problem regarding discrimination or harassment; (10) number of hours employee is asked to work are reasonable, based on business and personal needs;(11) employee is treated with respect as an individual; (12) company is effectively managed and well run; (13) senior management builds trust and confidence with the employee; (14) motivates employee to participate in internal diversity, safety, quality activities, etc.; (15) is open and honest in communication with/to employee; (16) instills confidence in having a job at the company as long as the employee performs well; (17) provides equipment and tools needed for employee to do the job; (18) adequately trains employee to be able to do the job; and (19) gives employee the opportunities at work to learn and develop. Null hypothesis was rejected.

Hypothesis 6

When correlating the 134 Black survey participants' perceptions of employee racial equality with the teamwork

& cooperation for African American variables, the researcher discovered a 95%confidence interval (p<0.05) for the correlation coefficient, which infers that the correlation coefficient is statistically significant, of a positively correlated employee recognition with each of the following company actions: (1) adequately addresses complaints of discrimination, harassment, or unethical business conduct; (2) takes action to prevent discrimination, harassment, or unethical business conduct; (3) work environment is free from all forms of discrimination or harassment; (4) employees feel comfortable reporting a problem regarding discrimination or harassment; (5) team shares information and ideas to achieve team results; (6) team gets the cooperation it needs from other work groups/teams to achieve business objectives; and (7) all people the employee works with work well as a team. Null hypothesis was rejected.

Research Question 1

The research tested six hypotheses to uncover the extent of lack of employee recognition, lack of career opportunities, job dissatisfaction, company ineffectiveness, and high job turnover correlated to employees' race in Fortune 500 companies. Several important findings emerged from this study: (1) the number of data pairs for employees' perceptions of recognition were all statistically significant (correlated) to African Americans' turnover variables in Fortune 500 companies; (2) the number of data pairs for employee career opportunities were all statistically significant (correlated) to African Americans' perceptions in Fortune 500 companies; and (3) the number of data pairs for employee job satisfaction/motivation were all statistically significant (correlated) to African Americans' perceptions of company effectiveness in Fortune 500 companies.

Research Question 2

When comparing the racial composition of teams influenced perceptions of teamwork in Fortune 500 companies, the researcher discovered a 95% confidence level ($p<0.05$), significantly higher statistical difference in Whites strongly agreeing that their group/team shared more information and ideas to achieve team results than Blacks; therefore, the null hypothesis was rejected due to a significantly higher statistical difference in Blacks' and Whites' perceptions on this variable.

As for cooperation from other work groups/teams in Fortune 500 companies, the researcher discovered no statistical difference in Whites, Blacks, Hispanics, Asians, or other ethnic participants agreeing, disagreeing, or neutral on their perception that their work group gets the cooperation it needs from other work groups to achieve their business objectives; therefore, the researcher failed to reject the null hypothesis that there was no difference in racial composition of teams influenced perceptions of cooperation from other racial groups/teams.

Lastly, regarding racial teams working well together in Fortune 500 companies, the researcher discovered no statistical difference in Whites, Blacks, Hispanics, Asians, or other ethnic participants agreeing, disagreeing, or neutral on their perception that the people that they worked with work well together as a team; therefore, the researcher failed to reject the null hypothesis that there was no difference in racial composition of teams influenced perceptions of different people working well together as a team/group.

Discussion

Implications Of Findings

In this study, the researcher aimed to highlight the experiences and the negative perception of racial discrimination of African American professionals in their Fortune 500 workplaces which impacts their annual performance reviews, job opportunities, raises, bonuses, and retention. Additionally, the researcher interpreted employment and civil rights laws that were intended to address discriminatory issues in today's corporate workplace. The results of this study supported the original six hypotheses. The results can be generalized to all Fortune 500 organizations; however, the results were mostly consistent with research of the organizations that were centralized and/or decentralized within the United States of America concerning the perceptions of Whites, Blacks, Hispanics, Asians, or other ethnic professionals.

In today's business environment, if all stakeholders desire to meet and/or exceed their organizational goals, it is important for organizational leaders to understand their firm's mission statement, the process of human resource development, and the art of strategic planning. Palestini (2011) stated that

> *Strategic planning is a process by which an organization identifies objectives and unfolds strategies for achieving them. Although it can be built into existing structures, it is common practice to create a task force composed of representatives from all levels of the organization that is responsible for planning and making decisions. The process must look forward to the future. It must start with*

> *a statement of mission, which should be brief but adequate enough to clearly express the organization's commitment to selective academic, social, and career outlines for students, faculty, staff, and other stakeholders. The mission statement should be the basis for planning and decision making in an institution." (p. 136).*

Further, to remain competitive in the everchanging U.S. market and ensure growth for the business and all stakeholders, an inclusive and fair succession plan for human resource, talent development must be strategically woven into the firm's mission, vision, and annual competencies.

Succession Planning – Hiring & Performance Management

The overall purpose of a succession plan involves the development of leaders to ensure that a sufficient number of skilled, decision makers are placed into key leadership positions. A key component of constructing a succession plan involves the establishment of clear, measurable goals. Establishing these goals early in the process will enable the leader to strategically align all actions with the firm's mission statement. This action plan requires comprehensive strategic planning on the part of the administration with clear actions for all stakeholders. Palestini (2011) noted that:

> *It is essential that the relationship between strategic organizational planning and human and material resources planning be understood. Human resource directors must be concerned with meshing human resources planning with strategic educational planning. The financial directors of the institution must do likewise. Strategic planning is setting management organ-*

izational objectives and developing comprehensive plans to support those objectives. It involves deciding on the priority of the organization, its process, and its interrelationship with human and material resources" (p. 137).

Furthermore, if a corporation does not have a leadership development program or a strategic promotion process, there will be a lack of diverse talent available to confront problems and make difficult decisions for the firm. According to Palestini (2011), "career-ladder plans focus on recruitment, retention, and performance incentives to enhance the attractiveness of" being employed within the institution (p.73). Fortunately, the researcher's corporation has a human resource hiring strategy and fair performance management process to grow a diverse workforce. That said, there must be touchpoints, recalibrations, and reflections to ensure that the succession plan achieves the future needs of the firm.

Applications Of Findings

In the researcher's opinion, the Drain Negative Perception Theory (NPT) appeared to be a solid, statistically proven theoretical model that can contribute to organizational leadership by helping Fortune 500 corporations better understand the relationship between the imposed unfair treatment, company ineffectiveness, and lack of respect & employee recognition of African American Fortune 500 professionals and the fewer opportunities for advancement, job dissatisfaction, negative perceptions of the job itself, and high turnover rates amongst blacks. Drain's NPT (2020) states that African American Fortune 500 professional employees have negative perceptions of their organizations when they feel, recognize, and/or identify any racial composition of workplace teams, management, and/or the company that demonstrates a lack of the following variables: (1) team/group sharing information to achieve results; (2) management supporting diversity; (3) care & concern for employees; (4) fair & consistent application of company policies; (5) work/life balance; (6) company adequately addressing complaints of discrimination; (7) company taking preventative actions to prohibit discrimination/harassment; (8) work environment that is free from all forms of discrimination or harassment; (9) comfort reporting problems; (10) respect as an individual; (11) career development growth opportunities; (12) company effectiveness & motivation; (12) work/tooling/training provisions; (13) open & honest communication; and (14) job security.

Theoretical Framework – Negative Perception Theory

Numerous theoretical frameworks were used in this study to guide the researcher in contributing new information to existing literature pertaining to racial inequality, such as: 1) organizational leadership theory and models; 2) organizational leadership philosophy; 3) cultural diversity, ethics, and fairness; 4) board/employee/constituent relations; 5) visionary leadership; 6) personnel evaluation; 7) four models of organization behavior or culture theories; 8) six models of organizational leadership theories; 9) nine models of motivation and needs theories; 10) upper echelon theory; 11) disparate impact theory; 12) Rawls' Theory of Justice; 13) cultural deficiency theory; 14) critical race theory; 15) labor market segmentation theory; 16) human capital theory; 17) career development theory; 18) structuration theory; and 19) social cognitive career theory. In addition to these literary reviews, this research also focused on studies like glass ceiling, career ascension, mentorship, and cultural comfort to serve as logically structured frameworks outlining fundamental sources that presented barriers associated with racial inequality of African American professionals in Fortune 500 companies.

During this study, the research participants were asked what aspects of their company's values and beliefs they felt needed to be reinforced in their group. The survey participants voluntarily chose to answer the specific question and included their typed criticism/response in the Chapter 4 results. There were 76 useful statements to connect the Drain NPT theoretical framework with previous results obtained by other researchers in other studies. Concerning African American professional, these typed responses illustrated agreement with a practical need for improvement, within their Fortune 500 organizations, in the following areas: (1) trustworthy culture of respect for people; (2) fair business practices; (3) environment of teamwork; (4) authentic employee recognition & appreciation; (5) diverse candidate hiring; (6) progressive retention rates for POC; (7) formation of diversity affinity groups/councils with consistent leadership participation; (8) implementation, promotion, and participative reinforcement of diversity groups' initiatives with empathy; (9) minorities in executive leadership; (10) effective, honest, and transparent communication with integrity; (11) progressive open mindedness and realistic VABEs; (12) acceptance and inclusivity of all ethnic backgrounds, non-monolithic people; (13) transparency and prioritization of human resource development and job training; (14) fair performance evaluation of Black talent; (15) transparency of racial issues/problems with engagement & ownership from executive leadership; (16) social comfort and job protection; (17) ethical and safe business environment; (18) equal opportunities for all skin tones; and (19) care and concern for all organizational employee levels.

Additionally, the research participants were asked if they could state any company policies that were not consistently applied to him/her over the past 12 months. The survey participants voluntarily chose to answer the specific question and included their typed criticism/response in the Chapter 4 results. There were 39 useful statements to connect the Drain NPT theoretical framework with previous results obtained by other researchers in other studies. Concerning African American professional, these typed responses illustrated agreement with a practical need for improvement, within their Fortune 500 organizations, in the following areas: (1) fair and consistent promotion opportunities for upward mobility; (2) equal pay for same job; (3) fair and equal interpersonal considerations; (4) equal access to opportunities despite skin tone and/or politics; (5) fair and consistent performance appraisals with minimal subjectivity; (5) discriminatory business practice elimination; (6) transparent criteria for career ascension and wage increases; and (7) consistent and equal instruction/advice given to POCs in the capacity of a coach/mentor.

Recommendations for Future Research

While further research is needed, regarding the causation of racial inequalities throughout the United States, the correlational results of negative perceptions of African Americans professionals' Fortune 500 workplaces regarding respect & treatment, company effectiveness, the job itself, and teamwork & cooperation warrant that executive leaders should be cognizant of their internal employee demographics. As concluded in this study, there was a positive correlation relationship between the variables in which both variables moved in the same direction. Therefore, it can be concluded that one variable increased as the other variable increases, or one variable decreased while the other decreases. With respect to this study's findings, one can clearly see that all respective Fortune 500 organizations must raise their awareness of their in-house: (a) diversity & inclusion mission/vision statements, business practices, and interpersonal needs; (b) multi-faceted cultures of VABEs; (c) methods for career development and personal growth plans; (d) behaviors/standards for strategic succession planning; (e) board, employee, and constituent human relations; (f) judicial equal opportunity labor laws to address disparate treatment and impact for protected groups; and (g) Black employee fundamental, motivational needs and comforts to break down the barriers associated with racial inequality in their workplaces. Not only is it important that Fortune 500 organizational leaders grasp a full understanding of the positive correlational results from this study, it is equally important that the firms take swift, fair, and consistent actions towards improving employee perceptions on the aforementioned variables if they chose to gain a competitive advantage over competitors and fully take advantage of the diversity of thought and resources in these United States.

Fortune 500 firms need to create work environments that campaign for diversity in the business structure. After the recent resurgence of police brutality of African Americans such as the homicidal death of George Floyd, a great number of Fortune 500 organizations implemented internal individual partnerships involving POCs and majorities coming together in informal business settings to engage in dialogue to better appreciate the different cultural backgrounds of racial and ethnic groups. Further, to enhance organizational diversity across all levels, Fortune 500 organizations should consider establishing activities with continual diversity & inclusion educational training to strengthen positive employee interaction between both minorities and majority work groups. It is the researcher's opinion that all accountable workplace diversity campaigns must: (1) ensure equable opportunities for all POCs; (2) involve cross-functional working groups to increase diverse employee interactions; (3) focus on assigning diverse managerial mentors to minorities to improve social comfort, decrease identity/skin tone related issues, and increase the firm's understanding of the authentic minority perspectives on leadership goals, wants, and needs and the insurmountable barriers they face to obtain leadership positions in comparison to their White Fortune 500 counterparts. After the diversity campaign has been implemented for a predetermined period of time, the campaign effectiveness shall be studied to uncover the effectiveness of the strategic action plan on the perception of African American racial equality in the U.S. labor market.

Conclusion

Since the establishment of the Title VII of the Civil Rights Act of 1964, many years had come and gone signaling the passing of enough time to revolutionize the façade of the American workplace; however, the voyage in the direction of workplace equality for black professionals is far from over. In fact, due to ongoing racial equality issues in the business world, it was imperative that companies' "managers and supervisors understand the law. Employers who are on top of these issues are doing yearly training with managers and employees" (Lytle, 2014, p.31). Human Resource departments in varying industries were encouraged to push for additional diversity and fairness in the workforce simply because it was in the best interest of the organization. Some asked why it was so important to strive for diversity in corporate America, but most of the U.S. population understood that "the purpose is so we can thrive as companies and as a country because we are taking advantage of this diversity of thought" (Lytle, 2014, p.31). As the Pew Research Center (2016) had demonstrated, the perception of how blacks were treated in the United States was an issue that could not be ignored.

In alarming numbers, Blacks in the United States had reported racial inequality in their workplaces. Despite the barriers placed upon them, black people persisted in their efforts for the attainment of career ascension, leadership development, mentorship, professional relationships, and cultural comfort in the workplace. The focal point of this study was to discover the lived experiences of current African American professionals regarding their perceptions of their Fortune 500 employer and its impact on the organization's retention rates. Furthermore, this research was instrumental in providing facts confirming Fortune 500 racial equality issues and the lack of career ascension, leadership development, mentorship, professional relationships, and cultural comfort of black professionals in the workplace.

This study might help organizations to develop new programs to retain employees of color. Additionally, the study might offer unique insights about respect and treatment of all professionals employed in American, Fortune 500 workplaces. Lastly, the findings from this study might provide corporations with a real-world understanding of potential obstacles that African American professionals face in the realm of advancing to leadership positions.

REFERENCES

Abdulhaqq, H. M. (2008). Leadership traits of African American senior level male executives in banking: A case study (Doctoral dissertation, University of Phoenix). Retrieved from http://search.proquest.com/docview/304333875?accountid=34899

Agbara, S. N. (2012). Barriers faced by African American men in Corporate America (Doctoral dissertation, The College of St. Scholastica). Retrieved from http://search.proquest.com/docview/1112069904?accountid=34899. (1112069904)

Al., L. (2020). Introduction to Business. Retrieved June 13, 2020, from https://courses.lumenlearning.com/wm-introductiontobusiness/chapter/alderfers-erg-theory/

Ali, R. (2007). The relationship between mentoring African American professionals and their perceptions of career success: A case study (Doctoral dissertation, Capella University). Retrieved from http://search.proquest.com/docview/304721168?accountid=34899. (304721168)

Allen, D. G., Bryant, P. C., & Vardaman, J. M. (2010). Retaining Talent: Replacing Misconceptions With Evidence-Based Strategies. Academy Of Management Perspectives, 24(2), 48-64. doi:10.5465/AMP.2010.51827775

Anumeha Chaturvedi. (August 18, 2012 Saturday). Hay Group unveils employee effectiveness model. The Economic Times. Retrieved from Nexis Uni.

Aure, P. A. H., Dui, R. P., Jimenez, S. V., Daradar, D. D., Gutierrez, A. N. A., Blasa, A. C., & Sy-Changco, J. (2019). Understanding Social Entrepreneurial Intention through Social Cognitive Career Theory: A Partial Least Squares Structural Equation Modelling Approach. Organizations & Markets in Emerging Economies, 10(1), 92–110. https://doi-org.ocproxy.palni.edu/10.15388/omee.2019.10.00005

Bacchus, N. J. (2005). The underrepresentation of Black male executives and CEOs in Fortune 500 corporations (Doctoral dissertation, Capella University). Retrieved from http://search.proquest.com/docview/305356630?accountid=34899

Bass, Bernard. (2008). The Bass Handbook of Leadership: Theory, Research & Managerial Application. 4th edition. New York: Free Press Publishing. ISBN: 9780743215527.

Blum, G. S., Rauthmann, J. F., Göllner, R., Lischetzke, T., & Schmitt, M. (2018). The Nonlinear Interaction of Person and Situation (NIPS) Model: Theory and Empirical Evidence. European Journal of Personality, 32(3), 286–305. https://doi.org/10.1002/per.2138

Brooks, K. (2019, December 10). Why so many black business professionals are missing from the C-suite. Retrieved July 06, 2020, from https://www.cbsnews.com/news/black-professionals-hold-only-3-percent-of-executive-jobs-1-percent-of-ceo-jobs-at-fortune-500-firms-new-report-says/

Bugg, E. A. (2009). Knocking on the doors of opportunity: A phenomenological study of how African American males have experienced their journey to the community college presidency (Doctoral dissertation, Colorado State University). Retrieved from http://search.proquest.com/docview/757375729?accountid=35812

Busco, C. (2009). Giddens' structuration theory and its implications for management accounting research. Journal of Management & Governance, 13(3), 249–260. https://doi-org.ocproxy.palni.edu/10.1007/s10997-008-9081-6

Business Law with UCC Applications, 14th Edition (Paul A. Sukys & Gordan W. Brown, 2017) McGraw-Hill Education, 2 Penn Plaza, New York, NY 10121 ISBN 978-0-07-773373-5

Career Guide. (2019, October 7). Retrieved February 7, 2020, from https://www.indeed.com/career-advice/career-development/career-development-theory

Carraway, V. L. (2008). African American male protégés and their mentoring relationships with white male mentors in majority culture organizations (Doctoral dissertation, University of Phoenix). Retrieved from http://search.proquest.com/docview/613812908?accountid=34899

Casuga, J. j. (2016). Tossing Formal, Annual Reviews May Affect Workplace Litigation. HR Focus, 93(3), 4-7.

Clarke-Anderson, P. (2004). Minorities attainability to leadership positions in business settings: A study of self-efficacy and leadership aspirations (Doctoral dissertation). Retrieved from http://search.proquest.com/docview/305047329?accountid=35812

Clawson, James G. (2012). Level Three Leadership: Getting Below the Surface. 5thedition.Pearson Education, Inc, New Jersey.ISBN-13: 9780132556415.

Colorado State University. (2020). Writing@CSU. Retrieved June 22, 2020, from https://writing.colostate.edu/guides/page.cfm?pageid=1374

Cone, D. S. (2008). Perceiver race /ethnicity, attributions of anger, and perceptions of black and white men at work (Order No. 3305352). Available from ProQuest Dissertations & Theses Global. (304817577). Retrieved from https://search-proquest-com.ocproxy.palni.edu/docview/304817577?accountid=41267

Cornileus, T. (2013). "I'm a Black Man and I'm Doing this Job Very Well": How African American Professional Men Negotiate the Impact of Racism on Their Career Development. Journal of African American Studies, 17(4), 444–460. https://doi-org.ocproxy.palni.edu/10.1007/s12111-012-9225-2

Creswell, J. W. (2014). Research design: Qualitative, Quantitative, and Mixed methods Approaches (4th ed.). Los Angeles: Sage. ISBN 978-1-4522-2609-5

Creswell, J. W. (2009). Research design: Qualitative, Quantitative, and Mixed methods Approaches (4th ed.). Los Angeles: Sage. ISBN 978-1-4522-2610-1

Cuyler, A. C. (2007). The career paths of non-European-American executive opera administrators in the United States (Doctoral dissertation, Florida State University). Retrieved from http://search.proquest.com/docview/304873077?accountid=34899

Degen, R. J. (2017). Wisdom, Uncertainty, and Ambiguity in Management Decisions Based on Experiences and the Trustworthiness of Research Methods to Substantiate Them. Revista Ibero-Americana de Estratégia (RIAE), 16(4), 6–22. https://doi-org.ocproxy.palni.edu/10.5585/riae.v16i4.2596

Denis. (2018, May 16). The Equity Theory of Motivation - How to Keep your team Motivated. Retrieved June 14, 2020, from https://expertprogramanagement.com/2017/06/equity-theory/

Dingle, D. T. (2019, October 16). There are Only 4 Black CEOs at Fortune 500 Companies. Here's How the ELC is Changing That. Retrieved January 23, 2020, from https://www.blackenterprise.com/elc-increase-number-black-ceos-nation-largest-public-companies/

Doeringer, P. B., & Piore, M. J. (1970). Equal Employment Opportunity in Boston. Industrial Relations, 9(3), 324–339. https://doi-org.ocproxy.palni.edu/10.1111/j.1468-232X.1970.tb00516.x

Dotson, G. A. (2008). No employee left behind: The lived workplace experiences of inclusion/exclusion of African American engineering professionals within the semiconductor industry. (Doctoral dissertation, Capella University). ProQuest Dissertations and Theses, 306. Retrieved from http://search.proquest.com/docview/304829603?accountid=34899. (304829603)

Ellis, T., & Levy, Y. (2009). Towards a guide for novice researchers on research methodology: Review and proposed methods. Issues in Informing Science and Information Technology, 6, 323-337. Retrieved from http://iisit.org/Vol6/IISITv6p323-337Ellis663.pdf

Equal Employment Opportunity Commission. (2009). United States Government Manual, 372. Retrieved from http://search.ebscohost.com.ocproxy.palni.edu/login.aspx?direct=true&db=f5h&AN=48155714&site=ehost-live

Ferguson, E. D. (2011). What Adlerians Consider Important for Communication and Decision-Making in the Workplace: Mutual Respect and Democratic Leadership Style. Journal of Individual Psychology, 67(4), 432–437. Retrieved from http://search.ebscohost.com.ocproxy.palni.edu/login.aspx?direct=true&db=aph&AN=75045208&site-

=ehost-live

Gafney, W. (2017). A reflection on the Black Lives Matter movement and its impact on my scholarship. Journal of Biblical Literature, 136(1), 204–207. https://doi-org.ocproxy.palni.edu/10.15699/jbl.1361.2017.1363

Gibbs, T. S. (2008). From retention to detention: A phenomenological study of the African American engineer experience (Doctoral dissertation, Walden University). Retrieved from http://search.proquest.com/docview/304379389?accountid=34899

Glasser Institute. (2020). What Is Choice Theory? Retrieved June 14, 2020, from https://wglasser.com/what-is-choice-theory/

Glenn, S. (2010). A qualitative ethnographic study of African American leadership in higher education administration (Doctoral dissertation, University of Phoenix). Retrieved from http://search.proquest.com/docview/193939445?accountid=34899

Grant, G. A. (2008). Structural barriers to upward mobility: An examination of the influence of organizational culture on career advancement opportunities for ethnic minorities in college sport (Doctoral dissertation, Penn State University). Retrieved from http://search.proquest.com/docview/304609632?accountid=34899

Greenhaus, J. H., Parasuraman, S., & Wormley, W. M. (1990). EFFECTS OF RACE ON ORGANIZATIONAL EXPERIENCE, JOB PERFORMANCE EVALUATIONS, AND CAREER OUTCOMES. Academy Of Management Journal, 33(1), 64-86. doi:10.2307/256352

HAMBRICK, D. C. (2007). Upper Echelons Theory: An Update. Academy of Management Review, 32(2), 334–343.

https://doi-org.ocproxy.palni.edu/10.5465/ AMR.2007.24345254

Hambrick, D. C., & Mason, P. A. (1984). Upper Echelons: The Organization as a Reflection of Its Top Managers. Academy of Management Review, 9(2), 193–206. https://doi-org.ocproxy.palni.edu/10.5465/AMR.1984.4277628

Hamilton, C. Y. (2009). The perceptions of African American administrators regarding their work experiences at predominantly white institutions of higher education (Doctoral dissertation, University of North Florida). Retrieved from http://search.proquest.com/docview/305161046?accountid=34899

HENSON, C. (2015). IN DEFENSE OF MCDONNELL DOUGLAS: THE DOMINATION OF TITLE VII BY THE AT-WILL EMPLOYMENT DOCTRINE. St. John's Law Review, 89(2/3), 551-596.

Horowitz, J., Brown, A., & Cox, K. (2020, May 30). Views on Race in America 2019. Retrieved June 04, 2020, from https://www.pewsocialtrends.org/2019/04/09/race-in-america-2019/

Humphrey, D. L. (2007). Career development of African American male high school principals (Doctoral dissertation, The University of Georgia., Athens, Georgia)

Jackson, W. S. (2018). Law is Politics: Why Critical Legal Studies, Critical Race Theory, and Other Critical Legal Disciplines Must Reunite. Journal of the Utah Academy of Sciences, Arts & Letters, 95, 281–296. Retrieved from http://search.ebscohost.com.ocproxy.palni.edu/login.aspx?direct=true&db=ssf&AN=136351616&site-=ehost-live

Kadlecova, B. (2016, August 25). Skinner's Reinforcement Theory. Retrieved June 14, 2020, from https://managementmania.com/en/skinners-reinforcement-theory

Kathman, J. M. (1982). Black Life in Corporate America (Book). Library Journal, 107(14), 1456.

Krishnamoorthy, R. (2015). GE's Culture Challenge After Welch and Immelt. Harvard Business Review. Retrieved from

https://hbr.org/2015/01/ges-culture-challenge-after-welch-and-immelt

Katz, J. H., & Miller, F. A. (2017). Leveraging Differences and Inclusion Pays Off. OD Practitioner, 49(1), 56–61. Retrieved from http://search.ebscohost.com.ocproxy.palni.edu/login.aspx?direct=true&db=bth&AN=121529809&site=ehost-live

Leedy, Paul D., and Jeanne Ellis Ormrod. (2012). Practical Research: Planning and Design. 10th ed. Pearson. ISBN: 9780132693240.

Locke, E. A. 1976. The nature and causes of job satisfaction. In M. D. Dunnette (Ed.), Handbook of industrial and organizational psychology: 1297–1343. Chicago, IL: Rand McNally.

Longenecker, C. O., & Neubert, M. (2000). Barriers and Gateways to Management Cooperation and Teamwork. Business Horizons, 43(5), 37. Retrieved from http://search.ebscohost.com.ocproxy.palni.edu/login.aspx?direct=true&db=bth&AN=3588975&site=ehost-live

Lythreatis, S. S. lythreatis@bristol. ac. u., Mostafa, A. M. S. A. mostafa@wbs. ac. u., & Wang, X. X. wang@bristol. ac. u. (2019). Participative Leadership and Organizational Identification in SMEs in the MENA Region: Testing the Roles of CSR Perceptions and Pride in Membership. Journal of Business Ethics, 156(3), 635–650. https://doi-org.ocproxy.palni.edu/10.1007/s10551-017-3557-8

Lytle, T. (2014). 50 Years of Progress. (cover story). HR Magazine, 59(6), 26.

Mann, David (2015). Creating a Lean Culture: Tools to Sustain Lean Conversions. 3rd Ed. Boca Raton, FL: CRC Press, 2015. ISBN 978-1-4822-4325-3.

McClellan, P. A. (2006). Wearing the mantle: Spirited black male servant leaders reflecting on their leadership journey (Doctoral dissertation, Bowling Green State University). Retrieved from http://rave.ohiolink.edu/etdc/view?acc_num=bgsu1143220325

Mcleod, S. (2020, March 20). Maslow's Hierarchy of Needs. Retrieved June 14, 2020, from https://www.simplypsychology.org/maslow.html

Melton, S. D. (2008). Career framework: A study of black men in corporate executive positions in "Fortune" 1000 companies (Doctoral dissertation, Capella University). Retrieved from http://search.proquest.com/docview/304814745?accountid=35812

Mills, G. E., & Gay, L. R. (2019). Educational research: Competencies for analysis and applications. NY, NY: Pearson.

Momah, S. (2011). The effect of transformational leadership: A phenomenological study of African American leadership concerns (Doctoral dissertation). Retrieved from http://search.proquest.com/docview/873970487?accountid=35812

Monczka, R., et al (2011). Purchasing and Supply Chain Management. 5th edition. Mason, OH: Thomson South-Western. (ISBN-13: 978-0538476423)

MSG Management Study Guide. (2020). Retrieved June 14, 2020, from https://managementstudyguide.com/herzbergs-theory-motivation.htm

Nwaebube, O. C. (2009). Minority representation in the

North Carolina government workforce: An empirical qualitative analysis (Doctoral dissertation, Walden University). Retrieved from http://search.proquest.com/docview/305076788?accountid=35812

Ollis, H., & Dietrich, E. (1994). Parsons' Contribution to Career Information. Journal of Career Development (Springer Science & Business Media B.V.), 20(4), 311–320. https://doi-org.ocproxy.palni.edu/10.1007/BF02106304

On Views of Race and Inequality, Blacks and Whites Are Worlds Apart. (2019, December 31). Retrieved January 19, 2020, from https://www.pewsocialtrends.org/2016/06/27/on-views-of-race-and-inequality-blacks-and-whites-are-worlds-apart/

Oswell, M. L. (2005). A phenomenological inquiry: Managers' perceptions on African American males capacity to lead (Doctoral dissertation). Retrieved from http://search.proquest.com/docview/305361549?accountid=34899

PAETZOLD, R. L., & RHOLES, W. S. (2017). Wal-Mart V. Dukes: Justice Scalia and Systemic Disparate Treatment Theory. Employee Rights & Employment Policy Journal, 21(1), 115–162. Retrieved from http://search.ebscohost.com.ocproxy.palni.edu/login.aspx?direct=true&db=bth&AN=125220764&site=ehost-live

Palestini, Robert (2011). Educational Administration: Leading with Mind and Heart. 3rd Ed. Lanham, MD: Scarecrow Press, 2011. ISBN 978161048397.

Pew Research Center. (2020, May 30). On Views of Race and Inequality, Blacks and Whites Are Worlds Apart. Retrieved June 04, 2020, from https://www.pewsocialtrends.org/2016/06/27/on-views-of-race-and-inequality-blacks-and-whites-are-worlds-apart/

Pew Research Center. (2016, June 21). Black and white Americans differ widely in views on race and race relations. Retrieved June 04, 2020, from https://www.pewsocialtrends.org/2016/06/27/2-views-of-race-relations/st_2016-06-27_race-inequality-ch2-01/

Pew Research Center. (2019, April 03). A majority of U.S. adults say Trump has made race relations worse. Retrieved June 04, 2020, from https://www.pewsocialtrends.org/2019/04/09/race-in-america-2019/psdt_04-09-19_race-00-07/

Pew Research Center. (2019, April 03). Most say it's now more common for people to express racist or racially insensitive views. Retrieved June 04, 2020, from https://www.pewsocialtrends.org/2019/04/09/race-in-america-2019/psdt_04-09-19_race-00-08/

Pew Research Center. (2019, April 03). Blacks are far more likely than whites to say discrimination is a major obstacle for black people. Retrieved June 04, 2020, from https://www.pewsocialtrends.org/2019/04/09/race-in-america-2019/psdt_04-09-19_race-00-04/

Pew Research Center. (2019, April 03). Whites and blacks differ widely in views of how blacks are treated. Retrieved June 04, 2020, from https://www.pewsocialtrends.org/2019/04/09/race-in-america-2019/psdt_04-09-19_race-00-03/

Purdue Writing Lab. (n.d.). Critical Race Theory // Purdue Writing Lab. Retrieved January 24, 2020, from https://owl.purdue.edu/owl/subject_specific_writing/writing_in_literature/literary_theory_and_schools_of_criticism/critical_race_theory.html

Rebore, Ronald W. (2013). The Ethics of Educational Leadership. Allyn & Bacon Educational Leadership)2nd Edition. Upper Saddle River, NJ: Merrill-Prentice Hall. ISBN 9780132907101

Roberts-Clarke, I. (2004). Organizational climate for diversity, cultural comfort, and professional relationships: Predicting perceptions of the workplace among employees of color (Order No. 3135899). Available from ProQuest Dissertations & Theses Global. (305154559). Retrieved from https://search-proquest-com.ocproxy.palni.edu/docview/305154559?accountid=41267

Schafer, D. F. (2005). Leadership role expectations and relationships of principals and pastors in catholic parochial elementary schools: Part 2. Catholic Education: A Journal of Inquiry and Practice, 9(2) Retrieved from https://search-proquest-com.ocproxy.palni.edu/docview/1690503742?accountid=41267

Schein, E.H. (2010). Organizational Culture and Leadership (4th Ed.). Jossey-Bass. San Francisco, CA. ISBN 978-0-470-19060-9.

Schoonjans, F. (2020, May 24). Correlation coefficient. Retrieved June 30, 2020, from https://www.medcalc.org/manual/correlation.php

Simon, M.K, & Goes, J. (2013). Scope, limitations, and delimitations. Retrieved from http://dissertationrecipes.com/wpcontent/uploads/2011/04/limitationscopedelimitation1.pdf

Smith, A. D. (2016). Exploring the retention and career persistence factors of african american women in information technology: A multiple case study (Order No. 10308540). Available from ProQuest Dissertations & Theses Global. (1867063093). Retrieved from https://search-proquest-com.ocproxy.palni.edu/docview/1867063093?accountid=41267

Smith, E. R. (2008). The Rooney rule: Affirmative action policy and institutional discrimination in the national football league (Doctoral dissertation, University of

Miami). Retrieved from http://search.proquest.com/docview/304571081?accountid=35812

Smith, M. L. (2010). Black male leaders' paths to success in counseling: A qualitative study (Doctoral dissertation, Antioch University, New England). ProQuest Dissertations and Theses, 155. Retrieved from http://search.proquest.com/docview/305239836?accountid=34899. (305239836)

Social Cognitive Career Theory - Career Development - IResearchNet. (2016, December 10). Retrieved February 9, 2020, from http://career.iresearchnet.com/career-development/social-cognitive-career-theory/

Solomon, A., & Steyn, R. (2017). Leadership style and leadership effectiveness: Does cultural intelligence moderate the relationship? Acta Commercii, 17(1), 1–13. https://doi-org.ocproxy.palni.edu/10.4102/ac.v17i1.453

Stepler, R. (2016, June 27). 5 key takeaways about views of race and inequality in America. Retrieved January 19, 2020, from https://www.pewresearch.org/fact-tank/2016/06/27/key-takeaways-race-and-inequality/

SurveyMonkey. (2020). What are open-ended questions? Retrieved July 04, 2020, from https://www.surveymonkey.com/mp/open-ended-questions-get-more-context-to-enrich-your-data/

SurveyMonkey. (1999). Statistical Significance. Retrieved July 03, 2020, from https://help.surveymonkey.com/articles/en_US/kb/Significant-Differences

Taylor, D. E. (1981). Education, on-the-job training, and the black-white earnings gap. Monthly Labor Review, 104(4), 28. Retrieved from http://search.ebscohost.com.ocproxy.palni.edu/login.aspx?direct=true&db=bth&AN=6003213&site=ehost-live

Taylor, J. E. (2004). The new frontier for black men: A shifting view of senior leaders in organizations (Doctoral dissertation, University of Georgia). Retrieved from http://search.proquest.com/docview/305045282?accountid=34899

Taylor, T. M. (2011). The ascendancy of African-American males to the superintendency in the Commonwealth of Virginia: An interpretative phenomenological study (Doctoral dissertation). Retrieved from http://search.proquest.com/docview/867096402?accountid=34899

The Black and White in America: Views on Race and Inequality, Worlds Apart. (2017). Journal of Pan African Studies, 10(3), 397–406. Retrieved from http://search.ebscohost.com.ocproxy.palni.edu/login.aspx?direct=true&db=ssf&AN=124181802&site=ehost-live

The Journal of Blacks in Higher Education. (2009). More Than 4.5 Million African Americans Now Hold a Four-Year College Degree. Retrieved June 05, 2020, from http://www.jbhe.com/news_views/64_degrees.html

The Journal of Blacks in Higher Education (2006). The Solid Progress of African Americans in Degree Attainments. Retrieved from http://www.jbhe.com/features/52_degree-attainments.html

Thomas D.A., & Wetlaufer, S. (1997). A question on color: a debate on race in the US workplace. Harvard Business Review, 75(5), 118-132

Thomas, D.A., & Ely, R.J. (1996). Making differences matter: A new paradigm for managing diversity. Harvard Business Review, 74(5), 79-90

Triana, M. C., Jayasinghe, M., & Pieper, J. R. (2015). Perceived workplace racial discrimination and its correlates: A meta-analysis. Journal Of Organizational Behavior, 36(4), 491-513. doi:10.1002/job.1988

U.S. Equal Employment Opportunity Commission. (2020). Title VII of the Civil Rights Act of 1964. Retrieved June 05, 2020, from https://www.eeoc.gov/statutes/title-vii-civil-rights-act-1964

Vann, V. D. (2011). A study of female entrepreneurs seeking capital for start-up business (Doctoral dissertation). Retrieved from http://search.proquest.com/docview/918696608?accountid=34899

VISSER, M. A. (2019). The Color Gradient of Economic Opportunity: Implications of Skin Tone Labor Market Segmentation for Puerto Ricans in the United States. Centro Journal, 31(3), 47–71. Retrieved from http://search.ebscohost.com.ocproxy.palni.edu/login.aspx?direct=true&db=fua&AN=140298790&site=ehost-live

Vroom expectancy motivation theory: Employee motivation theories: YourCoach Gent. (2009). Retrieved June 14, 2020, from https://www.yourcoach.be/en/employee-motivation-theories/vroom-expectancy-motivation-theory.php

Warf, B. (n.d.). Structuration Theory. Retrieved February 9, 2020, from https://www.sciencedirect.com/topics/computer-science/structuration-theory

Watkins, R. T. (2011). Career ascension of African American males in the aeronautics industry (Doctoral dissertation, Argosy University, Atlanta). Retrieved from http://search.proquest.com/docview/911023911?accountid=34899

Weller, C. E. (2019, December 5). African Americans Face Systematic Obstacles to Getting Good Jobs. Retrieved February 14, 2020, from https://www.americanprogress.org/issues/economy/reports/2019/12/05/478150/african-americans-face-systematic-obstacles-getting-good-jobs/

What are earnings? definition and meaning. (n.d.). Retrieved January 28, 2020, from http://www.businessdictionary.com/definition/earnings.html

What is an appraisal? definition and meaning. (n.d.). Retrieved September 21, 2019, from http://www.businessdictionary.com/definition/charismatic-leadership.html

What is an assessment? definition and meaning. (n.d.). Retrieved September 21, 2019, from http://www.businessdictionary.com/definition/ethical-behavior.html

What is code of conduct? definition and meaning. (n.d.). Retrieved September 21, 2019, from http://www.businessdictionary.com/definition/code-of-conduct.html

What is a code of ethics? definition and meaning. (n.d.). Retrieved September 21, 2019, from http://www.businessdictionary.com/definition/code-of-ethics.html

What is culture? definition and meaning. (n.d.). Retrieved September 21, 2019, from http://www.businessdictionary.com/definition/culture.html

What is democratic leadership? definition and meaning. (n.d.). Retrieved September 21, 2019, from http://www.businessdictionary.com/definition/democratic-leadership.html

What is development? definition and meaning. (n.d.). Retrieved September 21, 2019, from http://www.businessdictionary.com/definition/organizational-goals.html

What is development strategy? definition and meaning. (n.d.). Retrieved September 21, 2019, from http://www.

businessdictionary.com/definition/development-strategy.html

What is directive leadership? definition and meaning. (n.d.). Retrieved September 21, 2019, from http://www.businessdictionary.com/definition/directive-leadership.html

What is diversity? definition and meaning. (n.d.). Retrieved September 21, 2019, from http://www.businessdictionary.com/definition/diversity.html

What is diversity management? definition and meaning. (n.d.). Retrieved September 21, 2019, from http://www.businessdictionary.com/definition/diversity-management.html

What is human capital? definition and meaning. (n.d.). Retrieved January 28, 2020, from http://www.businessdictionary.com/definition/human-capital.html

What is justice? definition and meaning. (n.d.). Retrieved September 21, 2019, from http://www.businessdictionary.com/definition/justice.html

What is a Leadership? definition and meaning. (n.d.). Retrieved September 21, 2019, from http://www.businessdictionary.com/definition/leadership.html

What is organizational culture? definition and meaning. (n.d.). Retrieved February 14, 2020, from http://www.businessdictionary.com/definition/organizational-culture.html

What is participative leadership? definition and meaning. (n.d.). Retrieved September 21, 2019, from http://www.businessdictionary.com/definition/participative-leadership.html

What is personal power? definition and meaning. (n.d.). Retrieved September 21, 2019, from http://www.businessdictionary.com/definition/personal-power.html

What is position power? definition and meaning. (n.d.). Retrieved September 21, 2019, from http://www.businessdictionary.com/definition/position-power.html

What is power? definition and meaning. (n.d.). Retrieved September 21, 2019, from http://www.businessdictionary.com/definition/power.html

What is Situational Leadership? definition and meaning. (n.d.). Retrieved September 21, 2019, from http://www.businessdictionary.com/definition/situational-leadership.html

What is a stakeholder? definition and meaning. (n.d.). Retrieved September 21, 2019, from http://www.businessdictionary.com/definition/stakeholder.html

What is a vision statement? definition and meaning. (n.d.). Retrieved September 21, 2019, from http://www.businessdictionary.com/definition/vision-statement.html

Wilde, R., & Messina, P. (2019). Leadership and Influence. Public Management (00333611), 101(4), 26–29. Retrieved from http://search.ebscohost.com.ocproxy.palni.edu/login.aspx?direct=true&db=crh&AN=136403392&site=ehost-live

Williams, H. G., Jr. (2014). Exploring the career ascension of senior-level african american males in fortune 500 companies: A phenomenological study (Order No. 10582943). Available from ProQuest Dissertations & Theses Global. (1878915520). Retrieved from https://search-proquest-com.ocproxy.palni.edu/docview/1878915520?accountid=41267

Witherspoon, D. A. (2009). Burden of leadership: Re-envisioning the glass ceiling based on constructs of race, gender, and ethnicity (Doctoral dissertation, University of Nevada). Retrieved from http://search.proquest.com/docview/305126024?accountid=34899

Wolfe, B.L. (2010). When being black isn't enough: Experiences and persistence strategies of six African American administrators at a PWI (Order No. 3446190, Doctoral dissertation, Auburn University). ProQuest Dissertations and Theses, 198. Retrieved from http://search.proquest.com/docview/856339867?accountid=34899. (856339867).

Wolliston, D. L. (2007). African American decision makers in healthcare: Exploring the impact of mentoring on professional advancement (Doctoral dissertation). Retrieved from http://search.proquest.com/docview/599426552?accountid=34899

Wright, E. S. (2017). Dialogic Development in the Situational Leadership Style. Performance Improvement, 56(9), 27–31. https://doi-org.ocproxy.palni.edu/10.1002/pfi.21733

Youn, S. (2019, May 16). Amazon cracks top 5 in Fortune's top 500 largest companies as Walmart keeps top spot. Retrieved January 23, 2020, from https://abcnews.go.com/Business/walmart-tops-fortunes-list-500-largest-us-corporations/story?id=62852829

Young, J. (2018, December 14). Locke's Goal Setting Theory - What Are the 5 Key Principles? Retrieved June 14, 2020, from https://peakon.com/us/blog/future-work/edwin-locke-goal-setting-theory/

APPENDIX A

Participant E-mail for Anonymous Online Survey

March 4th, 2020

Participant:

You are invited to participate in a research study; African-American Racial Equality in U.S. Labor Market: Negative Perception Theory. The purpose of this study is to examine the complexities of the racial inequality of African American professionals in their Fortune 500 workplaces and develop a theoretical model of the constructs that predicts perceptions that employees of color have about their workplace arenas in the following areas: respect & treatment, company effectiveness, the job itself, and teamwork & cooperation.

A 14-minute anonymous online survey, consisting of demographic questions and Likert scale questions related to workplace perception, will be distributed to African-American professionals working in Fortune 500 organizations during a period of two-weeks.
There are no identifiers within this survey and all submissions are anonymous.

The data obtained from this study will be used to discover the lived experiences of current African American professionals regarding their perceptions of their Fortune 500 employer and its impact on the organization's retention rates. The survey results will be collated and analyzed to determine any relationships between employment experiences and perceptions among African Americans working for a Fortune 500 company.

Voluntary participation: Your participation in this research study is voluntary; you may choose not to participate. You can refuse to participate or withdrawal at any time. If you choose not to participate, no part of your data will be used in the research.

Consent: You are voluntarily deciding whether or not to participate in this study. Your willingness to activate the "OK" and "Next" buttons certifies that you have decided to participate having read and understood the information provided.
If you have questions about the study or the procedures, you may contact the researcher by email at drainduandre@myoak.ocu.edu. Thank you for your participation in my research.

Sincerely,

D'uAndre A. Drain, MSSM

APPENDIX B

Consent to Act as a Research Subject
OAKLAND CITY UNIVERSITY
Consent Form for Research Participation

ABOUT THIS RESEARCH

Study Title: African American Racial Equality in U.S. Labor Market: Negative Perception Theory

Faculty Sponsor: Kevin Smith

Student Researcher: D'uAndre A. Drain

IRB Study Number: FY20-056

I am a student at Oakland City University, in the School of Education. I am planning to conduct a research study, which I invite you to take part in. This form has important information about the reason for doing this study, what we will ask you to do if you decide to be in this study, and the way we would like to use information about you if you choose to be in the study.

TAKING PART IN THIS STUDY IS VOLUNTARY

Your participation in this study is voluntary. You may choose not to take part in the study or may choose to leave the study at any time. If you decide not to participate or leave the study later, it will not result in any penalty or loss of benefits to which you are otherwise entitled and will not affect your relationship with OCU.

Any significant new findings developed during the course of the research that may relate to your willingness to continue participating will be shared.

WHY IS THIS STUDY BEING DONE?

The purpose of this study is to: Understand the complexities of the racial inequality of African American professionals in their Fortune 500 workplaces and develop a theoretical model of the constructs that predicts perceptions that employees of color have about their workplace arenas in the following areas: respect & treatment, company effectiveness, the job itself, and teamwork & cooperation.

You were selected as a possible participant because: the study aspires to learn about a large population of African Americans by surveying a sample of that population.

The study is being conducted by Oakland City University.

HOW MANY PARTICIPANTS WILL TAKE PART?

At this time, we anticipate approximately 400+ individuals participating in this study.

WHAT WILL I DO IF I PARTICIPATE IN THIS STUDY?

You will be asked to use an online survey software system to complete an internet-based questionnaire called the 2020 Fortune 500 Company Morale Survey. This survey consists of 11 questions relating to your demographics and 34 questions that you will answer ranging from strongly agree to strongly disagree according to how each statement applies to you. There are also two questions with comment boxes that afford you the opportunity to describe your personal experience(s).

Study time: The estimated time for study participation is approximately 14 minutes.

Study location: All study procedures will take place using an online survey software – SurveyMonkey.

WHAT ARE THE POSSIBLE RISKS OR DISCOMFORTS ASSOCIATED WITH PARTICIPATING?

There are no known physical, psychological, or exposure risks to any human research participants in the study. All activities are similar to normal survey questionnaire procedures. The research study intends to treat all participants in a courteous and respectful manner.

As with all research, there is a chance that confidentiality of the information we collect from you could be breached – we will take steps to minimize this risk, as discussed in more detail below in this form.

WHAT ARE THE POTENTIAL BENEFITS OF PARTICIPATING IN THE STUDY?

You are not likely to have any direct benefit from being in this research study. This study is designed to learn more about respect and treatment of all professionals employed in American, Fortune 500 workplaces. Additionally, the participants might benefit from uncovering a topic of personal interest in the research. Further, the participants may feel a sense of satisfaction about contributing, in a small way, to the advancements in human society's collective knowledge about the world. To end, the study results may be used to help other people in the future.

HOW WILL MY INFORMATION BE PROTECTED?

Responses to an anonymous online survey will be collected and stored on a password-protected, external hard drive that will be locked in a file cabinet for 3 years. No identifiable data (name, IP address, or voice recording) will be collected.

Organizations that may inspect and/or copy your research records for quality assurance and data analysis include groups such as the study investigator and his/her research associates, the OCU Institutional Review Board or its designees, Dr. Kevin Smith, and (as allowed by law) state or federal agencies.

THE USE OF INFORMATION IN FUTURE STUDIES

We may share the data we collect from you for use in future research studies or with other researchers – if we share the data that we collect about you, we will remove any information that could identify you before we share it.

If we think that you intend to harm yourself or others, we will notify the appropriate people with this information.

FINANCIAL INFORMATION

Participation in this study will involve no cost to you. You will not be paid for participating in this study.

WHAT ARE MY RIGHTS AS A RESEARCH PARTICIPANT?

Participation in this study is voluntary. You do not have to answer any question you do not want to answer. If at any time and for any reason, you would prefer not to participate in this study, please feel free not to. If at any time you would like to stop participating, please tell me. We can take a break, stop and continue at a later date, or stop altogether. You may withdraw from this study at any time, and you will not be penalized in any way for deciding to stop participation.

If you decide to withdraw from this study, any information collected from the participant will not be used if the participant decides to withdraw before finishing the study.

WHO SHOULD I CONTACT IF I HAVE QUESTIONS OR CONCERNS ABOUT THIS STUDY?

If you have questions, you are free to ask them now. If you have questions later, you may contact the researcher(s) at:
D'uAndre A. Drain, drainduandre@myocu.oak.edu.

If you have any questions about your rights as a participant in this research or believe you have suffered a research-related injury, please contact the following office at OCU immediately:

Institutional Review Board
Oakland City University
138 N. Lucretia Street
Oakland City, IN 47660
Phone: (812) 749-1431
Email: irb@oak.edu

CONSENT

I have read this form and the research study has been explained to me. I have been given the opportunity to ask questions and my questions have been answered. If I have additional questions, I have been told whom to contact. I agree to participate in the research study described above and will receive a copy of this consent form.

_____

Participant's Printed Name

_____
_____

Participant's Signature

Date

_____

Printed Name of Person Obtaining Consent

_____
_____

Signature of Person Obtaining Consent

DR. D'UANDRE ANTOINE DRAIN

Date

IF YOU ARE SEEKING WAIVER OF DOCUMENTED (SIGNED) CONSENT, DELETE THE LINES ABOVE FOR THE PARTICIPANT'S NAME AND DATED SIGNATURE and substitute instead the wording "If you agree to participate, please say so [indicate by acknowledging consent by clicking the Next bottom]."

APPENDIX C

2020 Fortune 500 Company Morale Survey

2020 Fortune 500 Company Morale Survey

Informed Consent

* 1. I have read the informed consent provided by Principal Investigator or Student Researcher, D'uAndre A. Drain, and included as the introduction to this survey. The informed consent to participate in the study titled, African-American Racial Equality in U.S. Labor Market: Negative Perception Theory, is understandable to me. I have been given the opportunity to ask questions and any questions that I may have had have been answered to my satisfaction. If I have additional questions, I have been provided with their contact information. I agree or decline to participate in the research study described above and can obtain a copy of the informed consent by contacting the investigator or researcher.

- I Agree to Participate
- I Decline to Participate

Survey Questions

* 2. What gender do you identify as?
- Male
- Female
- Prefer not to answer
- Other

* 3. What is your age?
- Under 18
- 18-24
- 25-34
- 35-44
- 45-54
- 55-64
- 65+

* 4. Please specify your ethnicity.
- White or Caucasian
- Black or African American
- Hispanic or Latino
- Asian or Asian American
- American Indian or Alaska Native
- Native Hawaiian or other Pacific Islander
- Another race

* 5. Where were you born?
- North America
- Central America
- South America
- Europe
- Africa
- Asia
- Australia
- Pacific Islander
- Caribbean Islands
- Other
- Prefer not to say

* 6. If applicable, please specify your religion.
    - [ ] Catholicism/Christianity
    - [ ] Judaism
    - [ ] Islam
    - [ ] Buddhism
    - [ ] Hinduism
    - [ ] Other
    - [ ] Prefer not to say

* 7. What is the highest degree or level of education you have completed?
    - [ ] Some High School
    - [ ] High School
    - [ ] Bachelor's Degree
    - [ ] Master's Degree
    - [ ] Ph.D. or higher
    - [ ] Trade School
    - [ ] Prefer not to say
    - [ ] Other

* 8. Where is your home located?
    - [ ] North America/Central America
    - [ ] South America
    - [ ] Europe
    - [ ] Africa
    - [ ] Asia
    - [ ] Australia
    - [ ] Caribbean Islands
    - [ ] Pacific Islands
    - [ ] Other
    - [ ] Prefer not to say

* 9. Are you married?
    - [ ] Yes
    - [ ] No
    - [ ] Prefer not to say

* 10. What is your current employment status?
    - [ ] Employed Full-Time
    - [ ] Employed Part-Time
    - [ ] Seeking opportunities
    - [ ] Retired
    - [ ] Prefer not to say
    - [ ] Other

* 11. Do you work for a 'Fortune 500' company?
The Fortune 500 is Fortune magazine's yearly list of 500 of the largest US companies ranked by total revenues for their respective fiscal years. ... To be a Fortune 500 company is widely considered to be a mark of prestige.

- [ ] Yes
- [ ] No

* 12. I believe Company management supports diversity in the workplace

○ Strongly agree
○ Agree
○ Neither agree nor disagree
○ Disagree
○ Strongly disagree

* 13. I believe the Company provides a working environment that accepts differences in team member backgrounds, cultures and lifestyles

○ Strongly agree
○ Agree
○ Neither agree nor disagree
○ Disagree
○ Strongly disagree

* 14. The Company demonstrates care and concern for its team members

○ Strongly agree
○ Agree
○ Neither agree nor disagree
○ Disagree
○ Strongly disagree

* 15. The Company's policies are applied consistently

○ Strongly agree
○ Agree
○ Neither agree nor disagree
○ Disagree
○ Strongly disagree

* 16. The Company's policies have been consistently applied to me over the past 12 months

○ Strongly agree
○ Agree
○ Neither agree nor disagree
○ Disagree
○ Strongly disagree

17. If a Company policy(ies) was not applied consistently to you over the past 12 months, which policy(ies) was it?

* 18. In my Company, team members are able to maintain a balance between their work and personal lives

○ Strongly agree
○ Agree
○ Neither agree nor disagree
○ Disagree
○ Strongly disagree

* 19. The Company adequately addresses complaints of discrimination, harassment, or unethical business conduct

○ Strongly agree
○ Agree
○ Neither agree nor disagree
○ Disagree
○ Strongly disagree

* 20. The Company takes action to prevent discrimination, harassment, or unethical business conduct
   - ○ Strongly agree
   - ○ Agree
   - ○ Neither agree nor disagree
   - ○ Disagree
   - ○ Strongly disagree

* 21. My work environment is free from all forms of discrimination or harassment
   - ○ Strongly agree
   - ○ Agree
   - ○ Neither agree nor disagree
   - ○ Disagree
   - ○ Strongly disagree

* 22. I would feel comfortable reporting a problem regarding discrimination or harassment
   - ○ Strongly agree
   - ○ Agree
   - ○ Neither agree nor disagree
   - ○ Disagree
   - ○ Strongly disagree

* 23. I would know what to do if I saw unlawful harassment in the workplace
   - ○ Strongly agree
   - ○ Agree
   - ○ Neither agree nor disagree
   - ○ Disagree
   - ○ Strongly disagree

* 24. The number of hours that I am asked to work are reasonable, based on business and personal needs
   - ○ Strongly agree
   - ○ Agree
   - ○ Neither agree nor disagree
   - ○ Disagree
   - ○ Strongly disagree

* 25. I am treated with respect as an individual
   - ○ Strongly agree
   - ○ Agree
   - ○ Neither agree nor disagree
   - ○ Disagree
   - ○ Strongly disagree

* 26. I understand the Company's business goals and objectives
   - ○ Strongly agree
   - ○ Agree
   - ○ Neither agree nor disagree
   - ○ Disagree
   - ○ Strongly disagree

* 27. I believe that the Company's strategy and goals are the right ones for the company at this time
   - ○ Strongly agree
   - ○ Agree
   - ○ Neither agree nor disagree
   - ○ Disagree
   - ○ Strongly disagree

* 28. All in all, my company is effectively managed and well-run
   - ○ Strongly agree
   - ○ Agree
   - ○ Neither agree nor disagree
   - ○ Disagree
   - ○ Strongly disagree

* 29. I have trust and confidence in the Company's senior management team (organizational equivalent to Plant Manager, General Manager or Director and above)

○ Strongly agree　　　　　　　○ Disagree
○ Agree　　　　　　　　　　　○ Strongly disagree
○ Neither agree nor disagree

* 30. The Company motivates me to participate in internal Company activities (e.g., diversity activities, safety activities, quality activities, etc.)

○ Strongly agree　　　　　　　○ Disagree
○ Agree　　　　　　　　　　　○ Strongly disagree
○ Neither agree nor disagree

* 31. The Company is open and honest in communications to team members

○ Strongly agree　　　　　　　○ Disagree
○ Agree　　　　　　　　　　　○ Strongly disagree
○ Neither agree nor disagree

* 32. The Company information that I receive is useful

○ Strongly agree　　　　　　　○ Disagree
○ Agree　　　　　　　　　　　○ Strongly disagree
○ Neither agree nor disagree

* 33. I believe the Company is socially responsible in its involvement with the community

○ Strongly agree　　　　　　　○ Disagree
○ Agree　　　　　　　　　　　○ Strongly disagree
○ Neither agree nor disagree

* 34. Rate your Company on keeping you informed about matters that affect you

○ Strongly agree　　　　　　　○ Disagree
○ Agree　　　　　　　　　　　○ Strongly disagree
○ Neither agree nor disagree

* 35. I am confident on having a job at my Company as long as I perform well

○ Strongly agree　　　　　　　○ Disagree
○ Agree　　　　　　　　　　　○ Strongly disagree
○ Neither agree nor disagree

* 36. I feel that my work is important and contributes to the Company's success

○ Strongly agree　　　　　　　○ Disagree
○ Agree　　　　　　　　　　　○ Strongly disagree
○ Neither agree nor disagree

* 37. I am provided with the equipment or tools I need to do my job

○ Strongly agree　　　　　　　○ Disagree
○ Agree　　　　　　　　　　　○ Strongly disagree
○ Neither agree nor disagree

* 38. I have received adequate training to be able to do my job

   ○ Strongly agree   ○ Disagree
   ○ Agree   ○ Strongly disagree
   ○ Neither agree nor disagree

* 39. I am given the opportunities at work to learn and develop

   ○ Strongly agree   ○ Disagree
   ○ Agree   ○ Strongly disagree
   ○ Neither agree nor disagree

* 40. I understand the results expected of me in my job

   ○ Strongly agree   ○ Disagree
   ○ Agree   ○ Strongly disagree
   ○ Neither agree nor disagree

* 41. I have enough authority to carry out my job effectively

   ○ Strongly agree   ○ Disagree
   ○ Agree   ○ Strongly disagree
   ○ Neither agree nor disagree

* 42. I receive recognition when I do a good job

   ○ Strongly agree   ○ Disagree
   ○ Agree   ○ Strongly disagree
   ○ Neither agree nor disagree

* 43. I am expected by my leadership to use the Company's values and beliefs on a daily basis

   ○ Strongly agree   ○ Disagree
   ○ Agree   ○ Strongly disagree
   ○ Neither agree nor disagree

44. What aspects of the Company's values and beliefs do you feel need to be reinforced in your group?

* 45. My group shares information and ideas to achieve team results

   ○ Strongly agree   ○ Disagree
   ○ Agree   ○ Strongly disagree
   ○ Neither agree nor disagree

* 46. My work group gets the cooperation it needs from other work groups to achieve our business objectives

   ○ Strongly agree   ○ Disagree
   ○ Agree   ○ Strongly disagree
   ○ Neither agree nor disagree

* 47. The people I work with work well as a team

   ○ Strongly agree   ○ Disagree
   ○ Agree   ○ Strongly disagree
   ○ Neither agree nor disagree

* 48. What is your Job Category? A Job Category is a broad-based group of employees with comparable job responsibilities located at comparable levels of responsibility within an organization.

- ○ Officials and Managers (i.e., accountants and auditors, architects, chemists, designers, dieticians, editors, engineers, lawyers, librarians, registered professional nurses, personnel and labor relations specialists, physical scientists, physicians, teachers, etc)

- ○ Technicians (i.e., computer programmers, drafters, engineering aides, junior engineers, photographers, radio operators, surveyors, technical illustrators, technicians medical, dental, electronic, physical science, etc.)

- ○ Sales Workers (i.e., advertising agents and salespersons, insurance agents and brokers, real estate agents and brokers, stock and bond sales workers, cashiers/checkers, etc)

- ○ Office and Clerical Workers (i.e., bookkeepers, collectors (bills and accounts), messengers and office helpers, office machine operators (including computer), shipping and receiving clerks, typists and secretaries, legal assistants, etc.)

- ○ Skilled Craft Workers (i.e., the building trades, hourly paid supervisors and lead operators who are not members of management, mechanics and repairers, skilled machining occupations, electricians, painters (construction and maintenance), pattern and model makers, stationary engineers, etc.)

- ○ Semi-Skilled Operatives (i.e., apprentices (plumbers, bricklayers, carpenters, electrician, machinist, mechanics, building trades, metalworking trades, printing trades, etc.), operatives, attendants (auto service and parking, blasters, delivery workers, mine operatives and laborers, motor operators, oilers and greasers (except auto), painters (manufactured articles), photographic process workers, stationery firefighters, truck and tractor drivers, welders and flamecutters, electrical and electronic equipment assemblers, inspectors, etc.)

- ○ Unskilled Laborers (i.e., groundskeepers and gardeners, laborers performing lifting, digging, mixing, loading and pulling operations, etc)

- ○ Service Workers (i.e. attendants (hospitals and other institutions, professional and personal service), firefighters and fire protection, guards, stewards, janitors, police officers and detectives, waiters and waitresses, guides, ushers, public transportation attendants, etc)

- ○ Prefer not to say

* 49. Number of Years working for the Company?

- ○ Less Than A Year
- ○ 1 - 2 Years
- ○ 3 - 5 Years
- ○ 6 - 9 Years
- ○ 10 - 15 Years
- ○ 15- Years

APPENDIX D

Research Proposal Approval Form

NEW RESEARCH PROJECT REQUEST
EXEMPT AND LIMITED CATEGORY

RESEARCH PROJECT

Project Title:	African-American Racial Equality in U.S. Labor Market: Negative Perception Theory		
Funding Source(s): [If unfunded, so indicate]	Unfunded	OCU IRB Number: FY20-056	FY20-056

PRINCIPAL INVESTIGATOR [OCU Faculty, staff, or associated parties only.]

Name (Last, First):		Phone:	
OCU E-mail:		Department:	

CO-INVESTIGATOR [OCU Faculty/staff are co-leading the research project.]

Name (Last, First):		Phone:	
OCU E-mail:		Department:	

STUDENT RESEARCHER [OCU student information if the research is a student-initiated study.]

Name (Last, First):	Drain, D'uAndre A.	Phone:	956-313-3018
OCU E-mail:	drainduandre@myocu.oak.edu	Department (in which the student is studying):	Doctoral Student School of Education (SOE)

FACULTY SPONSOR(S) [Student-initiated studies require an OCU faculty sponsor.]

Name (Last, First):	Smith, Kevin	Phone:	812-202-2655
OCU E-mail:	ksmith@oak.com	Department:	School of Education (SOE)

OTHER OCU INVESTIGATORS [List any other OCU personnel engaged in human subjects research on this project. Duplicate rows as needed.]

Name (Last, First):		Phone:	
E-mail:		Department:	
Role in this project:			

OTHER NON-OCU INVESTIGATORS [List any non-OCU personnel engaged in human subjects research on this project and choose A or B for each. Duplicate rows as needed.]

Name (Last, First):		Phone:	
E-mail:		Institution:	
Role in this project:			
☐	A	Home institution has an IRB and IRB approval/exemption has been obtained, or will be obtained prior to beginning research; OR	
☒	B	Researcher is unaffiliated, or home institution does NOT have an IRB, or requesting OCU IRB review on their behalf, and human subjects training certificate is attached (required).	

EXEMPTION CATEGORY

Refer to the attached list of Exemption Categories to complete the following statement: I claim this research to be exempt from review by the Human Subjects Institutional Review Board under the following category(ies):

☐1	☐2i	☐3i(A)	☐4i	☐5	☐6	☐7	☐8i
	☒2ii	☐3i(B)	☐4ii				
	☒2iii	☐3i(C)	☐4iii				
			☐4iv				

RESEARCH INFORMATION

Please respond to each of the following by marking a checkbox.

	✓ Eligible	Not Eligible	
1.	☒No	☐Yes	Does this research involve interaction with prisoners except for research aimed at involving a broader subject population that only incidentally includes prisoners? (If yes, this research does not qualify for an exemption. Please submit a full protocol.)
2.	☒Yes	☐No	Investigators agree to adhere to ethical principles in the Belmont Report.
3.	☒Yes	☐No	Is human subjects training complete for all investigators required to complete it?
4.	☐Yes (only under Cat. 3) ☒No		Does the research involve deception or incomplete disclosure (only eligible under category 3 and only if subjects are notified that they will be unaware of or misled regarding the nature or purpose of the research in advance)?
5.	☒Yes ☐Does not involve interaction / intervention	☐No	Researchers will obtain agreement (consent) of subjects (or their parents if minors) for research that involves interaction or intervention with subjects (not required at exempt level for research involving passive observation or secondary data).
6.	☐Yes ☒No		Will protected health information (PHI) be accessed from a covered entity for this research? (If yes, the IRB will request more information upon review.)
7.	☐Yes ☒No ☐N/A		If the research includes surveys, interviews, or questionnaires, do they seek information about possibly illegal activities or highly personal aspects of the subjects' behavior, experiences, or attitudes that may be painful or very embarrassing to reveal? (This might include sexual attitudes or practices; the use of alcohol or drugs; information that if released could reasonably be damaging to an individual's financial standing, employability, or reputation within the community; or information pertaining to an individual's psychological well-being or mental health.)

DR. D'UANDRE ANTOINE DRAIN

SUBJECTS

Specify the population(s) that will be included in the research. Check all that apply.

☒ Adults	☐ Children	☐ Students
☐ Adults unable to consent for themselves	☐ Non-English Speakers	☐ Prisoners
☐ Other (Specify):		

CONFLICT OF INTEREST

Please affirm that you have read "Disclosure of Investigators' Financial Interests" on the last page AND that one of the following is true:

☒ I affirm	No engaged personnel have a significant financial interest; OR
☐ I affirm	The following personnel have a significant financial of interest (An IRB representative will contact them for more information):

RESEARCH DESCRIPTION [Utilize as much space as needed to thoroughly describe the research. Please do not alter or edit any of the questions or delete them from the form.]

1. Describe your research, including enough information to justify how your study satisfies the criteria for the exemption category or categories you indicated. Where will this study be conducted? How much time will be required of the subjects? If using questionnaires, how will they be distributed and collected? NOTE: "Anonymous" means that no identifying information such as name, address, phone number, email, IP address, voice recordings, etc. can be linked to study data, even by the researcher. Data is not collected anonymously if there is a code linking it to identifiable information, or if subjects will be photographed, audio, or video recorded.

    ❖ PURPOSE: The purpose of this study will be to understand the complexities of the racial inequality of African American professionals in their Fortune 500 workplaces and develop a theoretical model of the constructs that predicts perceptions that employees of color have about their workplace arenas in the following areas: respect & treatment, company effectiveness, the job itself, and teamwork & cooperation.
    ❖ RESEARCH DESIGN: The researcher will utilize a descriptive correlational, quantitative research design. The ultimate goal is to learn about a large population by surveying a sample of that population.
    ❖ QUESTIONNAIRE DISTRIBUTION & COLLECTION: The researcher will e-mail potential adult participants in an online survey using both a social network, LinkedIn, that focuses on professional networking and career development and a survey tool, SurveyMonkey, to capture the voices and opinions of the people who matter most to the study.
    ❖ LOCATION & SAMPLING: The researcher plans to use an anonymous, Likert-type online survey to collect the data. Using a stratified random sampling approach. Exception Categories: 2ii & 2iii
    ❖ QUESTIONNAIRE TIMING: The researcher projects an estimated completion time of 14 minutes to complete the survey.

2. State the potential risks - for example, physical, psychological, financial, social, legal or other - connected with the proposed procedures. Discuss in detail the risks and benefits of the proposed research on the human subjects. Provide an explanation of how the risks are reasonable in relationship to the anticipated benefits. Describe procedures for protecting against, or minimizing, potential risks. Assess their likely effectiveness.

    ❖ POTENTIAL RISK: There are no known physical, psychological, or exposure risks to any research participants in the study. All activities are similar to normal survey procedures. There will be no costs

incurred as a result in the participation in this study. The researcher will treat all participants in a courteous and respectful manner.
- ❖ POTENTIAL BENEFIT: The study might offer unique insights about respect and treatment of all professionals employed in American, Fortune 500 workplaces. Additionally, the participants might benefit from uncovering a topic of personal interest in the research. Lastly, the researcher acknowledges that the participants may feel a sense of satisfaction about contributing, in a small way, to the advancements in human society's collective knowledge about the world.

PRIVACY & CONFIDENTIALITY [Utilize as much space as needed to thoroughly describe the research. Please do not alter or edit any of the questions or delete them from the form.]

1. What kind of data is being collected? Is any of the data that is being collected, data that may identify those participating in the study? What kind of identifiable data is being collected (e.g. name, IP address, voice recording)?

    - ❖ DATA COLLECTED: Responses to an anonymous online survey will be collected and stored on a password-protected, external hard drive that will be locked in a file cabinet for 3 years. No identifiable data (name, IP address, or voice recording) will be collected.

2. Explain where the study data is being stored including identifying data and/or code key(s) to identifiers will be stored, how the data and/or key(s) will be protected, and who will have access to the identifiers/ key. Explain when/if identifiers/code key will be destroyed. State where de-identified/anonymous data will be stored. Explain how long the data will be stored and available to OCU upon request by the IRB (minimum of three-year storage is expected).

    - ❖ The researcher intends to: 1) keep password-protected electronic files on the OKC University network (drive) as it is reliable and backed up; 2) store password-protected data directly on his own laptop or PC outside the University network; 3) have a rigorous backup system in case his device crashes, or is lost or stolen; 4) use password-protected, external hard drive and save his data regularly. And, the researcher will have a safe place to keep his hard drive and remember to take it with him when necessary; and 5) all primary & secondary documentation/notes will be organized, stored, and kept track of in a locked filing cabinet for a minimum of three years.

3. Explain risks that may exist to the study subjects in the event that identifiable study data were inadvertently disclosed:

    - ❖ Identifiable data (name, IP address, etc.) will not be collected.

4. How will subject privacy be protected during recruitment, consent, study procedures, etc.:

    - ❖ Under no circumstances will the identities of potential participants be shared. Furthermore, the survey itself is anonymous, so subject privacy is automatically ensured.

INFORMED CONSENT [Utilize as much space as needed to thoroughly describe the consent efforts associated with the research.]

1. Describe consent procedures and address each subject group separately, if multiple:

    - ❖ Through LinkedIn and SurveyMonkey, the researcher will present the OCU informed consent form that describes the nature of the research project, as well as the nature of one's participation in the study. After being presented with the opportunity to ask the researcher any questions about the research, the participant can voluntarily decide whether to participate in the study or not. By selecting "OK" and "Next" buttons, the participant certifies that they have read and understood the OCU informed consent, are over 18 years of age, and have decided to participate in the study.

DR. D'UANDRE ANTOINE DRAIN

2. Check all that apply:
   ☒ Consent will be obtained electronically (Attach a copy of the electronic consent being used.)
   ☐ Consent will be obtained verbally (Attach the script being used to obtain consent.)
   ☐ Consent will be obtained in writing (on paper) (Attach a copy of the written consent form being used.)
   ☐ Consent will NOT be obtained (NOT eligible for Exempted Review. Please submit a full protocol form.)

3. Please check each box to affirm that subjects are told the following in the consent form (required):
   ☐ That researchers are collecting identifiable information about them.
   ☐ What risks are reasonably anticipated if this information were inadvertently disclosed.
   ☐ When identifiable information will be destroyed or that it will be retained indefinitely.
   ☐ How identifiable information will be protected by researchers (e.g. encryption).

ATTACHMENTS

1. Provide a list of attachments that is being made to the request. Include such as certificate(s) of IRB training, full surveys, interview questions, tests, other data collection instruments, and/or consent documents
   - ✓ Participant email for anonymous online survey
   - ✓ Survey
   - ✓ OCU Consent Form for Research Participation
   - ✓ IRB Training certificate

SIGNATURES

The undersigned accept(s) responsibility for the study, including adherence to federal, state and OCU policies regarding the rights and welfare of human participants participating in this study. In the case of student researchers, the faculty sponsor(s) and the student share responsibility for adherence to policies.

_____
Signature of Principal Investigator (if applicable)   Date

_____
Signature of Co-Investigator (if applicable)   Date

_____
Signature of Student Researcher (if applicable)   3-2-20
                                                  Date

_____
Signature of Faculty Sponsor   3-2-2020
(required for student research studies)   Date

INSTITUTIONAL RESEARCH BOARD APPROVAL

The project described above has been approved by the OCU Institutional Review Board.

_____
IRB Representative / Administrator   03/31/2020
                                                  Date

APPENDIX E

Request to Conduct Research Approval Letter

ENTER TO LEARN   GO FORTH TO SERVE

March 31, 2020

Mr. D'uAndre Drain
c/o School of Education
Oakland City University
138 N. Lucretia Street
Oakland City, IN 47660

RE: Request to Conduct Research

Dear Mr. Drain:

Your request to conduct research described in your application dated March 2, 2020, is approved. Participation by organizations, teachers, and students remains voluntary.

Please let me know if there is any assistance that I can provide as you progress with your research efforts.

Sincerely,

Paul R. Bowdre, Ed.D.
Assistant Provost for Assessment and Institutional Effectiveness
Assessment Professor of Criminal Justice

Title of Research   African-American Racial Equality in U.S. Labor Market Negative Perception Theory
OCU IRB Number: FY20-056

DR. D'UANDRE ANTOINE DRAIN

Table of Contents

Cover
Front Cover
Title Information
Abstract
Dedication
Epigraph
Acknowledgements
Contents
List of Figures
Black and white Americans differ widely in views on race and race relations
A majority of U.S. adults say Trump has made race relations worse
Most say it's now more common for people to express racist or racially insensitive views
Blacks are far more likely than whites to say discrimination is a major obstacle for Black people
Whites and Blacks differ widely in views of how Blacks are treated
Over the past 20 years, the number of African Americans earning Master's degrees has more than tripled
Overview of Agreement to participate in the Research Study
Overview of Participants Gender
Overview of Participants' Age Group
Overview of Participants' Ethnic Background
Overview of Participants' Country of Birth
Overview of Participants' Religious Affiliation
Overview of Participants' Highest Educational Attainment
Overview of Participants' Country of Residence
Overview of Participants' Marital Status
Overview of Participants' Current Employment Status
Overview of Participants' Fortune 500 Employment
Overview of Participants' Job Categories
Overview of Participants' Years Working for Company
Comparative Sample of Whites & Blacks Working for Fortune 500
Whites & Blacks Perception of Company Management and

Diversity
Whites & Blacks Perception of Company Acceptance of Differences
Whites & Blacks Perception of Company Care and Concern
Whites & Blacks Perception of Company's Policies and Consistency
Whites & Blacks Perception of Company Policy Application
Which Company Policies were not Applied Consistently over 12 months?
Whites & Blacks Perception of Company Work Life Balance
Whites & Blacks Perception of Company Addressing Complaints
Whites & Blacks Perception of Company Taking Actions
Whites & Blacks Perception of Company Work Environments
Whites & Blacks Perception of Comfort Reporting Discrimination
Whites & Blacks Perception of Company Unlawful Harassment
Whites & Blacks Perception of Company Balance of Personal Needs
Whites & Blacks Perceptions of Individual Treatment with Respect
Correlational Results for Blacks' turnover and perceptions of their recognition within Fortune 500 organizations
Correlational results for Blacks' variable perceptions of their career ascension within Fortune 500 organizations
Correlational results for Blacks' variable perceptions of their job satisfaction with company effectiveness within Fortune 500 organizations
Whites, Blacks, Hispanics, Asians, and Other racial perceptions of teamwork and information sharing in Fortune 500 companies
Whites, Blacks, Hispanics, Asians, and Other racial perceptions of cooperation from other racial work groups in Fortune 500 companies
Whites, Blacks, Hispanics, Asians, and Other racial perceptions of people working well together as a team in Fortune 500 companies

List of Tables
Correlation results between treatment and career ascension of African American professionals in Fortune 500 companies
Correlation results between company effectiveness and job satisfaction for African American professionals in Fortune 500 companies
Correlation results between respect of African American professionals and Perceptions of the Fortune 500 job itself
Correlation results between employee recognition and retention of African American professionals in Fortune 500 companies
Correlation results between racial equality and teamwork & cooperation for African Americans in Fortune 500 companies
Chapter 1: Introduction
Racial Equality
Annual Formal Performance Reviews
Perceived Workplace Discrimination
Effects of Race on Experience, Job Performance Evaluations & Outcomes
Employment at Will
Civil Rights Laws
Title VII of the Civil Rights Act of 1964
56 Years of Progress
Statement of the Problem and Subproblems
Purpose of the Study
Research Questions & Hypotheses
Definition of Terms
Significance of the Study
Overview of the Study
Chapter 2: Review of Literature
Literature Review
Historical Overview
Theoretical Framework
Organizational Leadership Theory and Models
What is Leadership?
Characteristics Attributed to Effective Leadership
Leadership Theories & Researcher's Experience
Charismatic / Transformative Leadership
Servant Leadership Theory

Personal-Situational Leadership Theory
Leadership Traits & Researcher's Experience
Interpersonal & Socioemotional Traits
Emotional Intelligence & Control
Organizational Leadership Philosophy
Autocratic & Democratic Leadership Styles
Directive & Participative Leadership Styles
Consideration vs. Initiation
Cultural Diversity, Ethics, and Fairness
Diversity Management / Conflict of Values
Diversity & Pluralism in Leadership
Justice
Discourse Ethics
Board / Employee / Constituent Relations
Personal vs. Positional Power
Leaders Sharing Power
Ethics & Codes of Conduct
Interests of Stakeholders
Centralized & Decentralized Organizational Structure
Human Resource Management
Visionary Leadership
Vision Statement
Corporate Values
Personnel Evaluation
Performance Management - Task vs. Relations
Performance Assessments & Appraisals
Positive Development Culture
Organizational Behavior or Culture Theories
Frederick Fiedler's Contingency Theory
Classical Organization Theory
Social Systems Theory
Open Systems Theory
Organizational Leadership Theories
Trait Theory
Managerial Roles Theory
Early Situational Theories
Theory X and Theory Y
Path-Goal Theory
Motivation and Needs Theories
Maslow's Hierarchy of Needs Theory
Alderfer's ERG Theory

McClelland's Needs for Achievement Theory
Frederick Herzberg's Two Factor Theory
William Glasser's Control Theory
Equity Theory of Motivation
Reinforcement Theory
Expectancy Theory of Motivation
Goal Setting Theory
Upper Echelon Theory
Disparate Impact Theory
Rawls Theory of Justice
Critical Race Theory
Skin Tone Labor Market Segmentation
Human Capital Theory
Career Development Theory
Structuration Theory
Social Cognitive Career Theory
Glass Ceiling Phenomena
Career Ascension & Upward Mobility
Diversity & Inclusion
African American Mentorship
African American Recognition and Retention Rates
Image & Perception of African American Males
Cultural Comfort of African American Males in the U.S. Labor Market
Underrepresentation of African American Males in the U.S. Labor Market
Disparate Treatment of African American Males in the U.S. Labor Market
Managerial Progression of African American Males in the United States
Conclusion
Chapter 3: Method of Research
Introduction
Research Design
Research Setting and Participants
Sample Size
Data Collection Methods
Data Analysis Methods
Bias
Methodological Assumptions
Trustworthiness

Subject Matter Experts (SMEs)
Credibility
Transferability
Ethical Considerations
Confidentiality
Procedures
Limitations
Delimitations
Summary
Chapter 4: Presentation and Interpretation of Data
Restatement of the Purpose
Research Questions
Overview of Participants
Findings for Each Research Hypothesis
Hypothesis #1
Hypothesis #2
Hypothesis #3
Hypothesis #4
Hypothesis #5
Hypothesis #6
Findings for Each Research Question
Question #1
Question #2
Theoretical Framework / Connection
Summary
Chapter 5: Discussion, Conclusions, and Recommendations
Introduction
Summary of Findings
Hypothesis #1
Hypothesis #2
Hypothesis #3
Hypothesis #4
Hypothesis #5
Hypothesis #6
Research Question #1
Research Question #2
Discussion
Implications of Findings
Succession Planning
Applications of Findings

Theoretical Framework - Negative Perception Theory
Recommendations for Future Research
Conclusion
References
Appendices
Participant E-mail for Anonymous Online Survey
Consent to Act as a Research Subject
2020 Fortune 500 Company Morale Survey
Research Proposal Approval Form
Request to Conduct Research Approval Letter

Made in the USA
Coppell, TX
05 February 2022